BROO

THE REMARKABLE STORY OF THE
FREE BLACK COMMUNITIES
THAT SHAPED A BOROUGH

 A WASHINGTON MEWS BOOK

KLYNITES

PRITHI KANAKAMEDALA

NEW YORK UNIVERSITY PRESS NEW YORK

WASHINGTON MEWS BOOKS

An Imprint of

NEW YORK UNIVERSITY PRESS

New York

www.nyupress.org

Library of Congress Cataloging-in-Publication Data

Names: Kanakamedala, Prithi, author.

Title: Brooklynites : free Black communities in the nineteenth century / Prithi Kanakamedala.

Other titles: Free Black communities in the nineteenth century

Description: New York : New York University Press, [2024] | Includes bibliographical references and index.

Identifiers: LCCN 2023053496 (print) | LCCN 2023053497 (ebook) | ISBN 9781479833092 (hardback) | ISBN 9781479833122 (ebook) | ISBN 9781479833139 (ebook other)

Subjects: LCSH: Brooklyn (New York, N.Y.)—History—19th century. | African American neighborhoods—New York (State)—New York—19th century. | Croger family. | Hodges family. | Wilson family. | Gloucester family. | African American families—New York (State)—New York—19th century. | African Americans—New York (State)—New York—19th century. | Freed persons—New York (State)—New York—19th century. | New York (N.Y.)—Race relations—History.

Classification: LCC F129.B7 K36 2024 (print) | LCC F129.B7 (ebook) | DDC 974.7/2300496073—dc23/eng/20240315

LC record available at https://lccn.loc.gov/2023053496

LC ebook record available at https://lccn.loc.gov/2023053497

FREEDOM IS A PLACE.

—RUTH WILSON GILMORE,
"Abolition Geography and the
Problem of Innocence" (2017)

To the People's Republic of Brooklyn

CONTENTS

Color illustrations appear as an insert following page 80.

CHRONOLOGY

		History	Narrative Timeline
	1790	First US federal census Kings County population equals 4,495; one in every three residents is enslaved	
	1797	John Doughty, Brooklyn's town clerk, manumits Caesar Foster; it is the first recorded manumission in Kings County	
GRADUAL EMANCIPATION	1799	New York State's "Act for the Gradual Abolition of Slavery" All children born to an enslaved mother after July 4, 1799, will be free at the age of 28 if male and 25 if female	
	1808	Slave trade abolished About 250,000 enslaved people (probably an undercount) are brought illegally to the US between 1808 and 1860	(approx.) Croger Family moves from Manhattan to Brooklyn
	1809	Thomas Kirk establishes the *Long Island Star*; it becomes Brooklyn's longest running newspaper in the early nineteenth century	
	1810		Brooklyn African Woolman Benevolent Society founded
	1814	Robert Fulton's steam ferry service begins operations across the East River	
	1815		First private school for Black adults and children opens at Peter and Elenor Croger's home on James Street
	1816	American Colonization Society founded Village of Brooklyn established Richard Allen establishes African Methodist Episcopal Church in Philadelphia	
	1817	Anti-colonization protest in Philadelphia New York State passes a new law stating slavery will officially end on July 4, 1827	Benjamin and Elizabeth Croger's daughter Eliza born
	1818		Brooklyn African Methodist Episcopal Church established
	1820	Missouri Compromise	
	1821	Amendment to New York State Constitution introduces $250 property qualification for Black men to vote; all eliminated for white men	
	1827	*Freedom's Journal* commences publication July 4, Emancipation Day July 5, Black New Yorkers and Brooklynites celebrate Emancipation Day Village of Williamsburgh incorporated	African School in Brooklyn opens to the public

	History	Narrative Timeline
1829	David Walker publishes *An Appeal to the Colored Citizens of the World*	James Pennington arrives in Brooklyn
1831	First annual Black Convention Brooklyn anti-colonization protest	
1833	American Anti-Slavery Society founded	
1834	New York Anti-Slavery Society founded Manhattan anti-Black race riots Brooklyn receives city charter; population increases from 5,000 to 24,000 in three decades	
1836	Congress adopts "gag rule"; any anti-slavery petitions are to be tabled Peck Slip Ferry connects Williamsburg to Lower Manhattan	
1837	Panic of 1837	
1838	Weeksville established Green-Wood Cemetery founded	
1839	Brooklyn City Plan and grid map	William Hodges, wife Mary Ann Tippon, and daughter Julia settle in Williamsburg
1840	First New York State Black Convention, Albany Atlantic Docks established Liberty Party established First recorded West India Day Emancipation Day celebration, Williamsburg	
1841	New York's Personal Liberty Law repealed *Brooklyn Daily Eagle* commences publication	African School in Williamsburg opens; William Hodges is the school's inaugural teacher
1846	3,000 Black people settle on land parceled off by Gerrit Smith in the Adirondacks Referendum to eliminate the property requirement for Black men to vote defeated	Mary, William, and Annie Wilson move from Manhattan to Brooklyn
1847		African School in Weeksville opens William J. Wilson begins teaching at African School, Brooklyn (approx.) Elizabeth and James Gloucester and their family move from Manhattan to Brooklyn
1848	City Hall completed	Peter Croger dies
1849	Siloam Presbyterian Church founded	Sarah and Robert Cousins's home forms part of the Underground Railroad
1850	Compromise of 1850, includes Fugitive Slave Act	Williamsburg resident James Hamlet arrested and accused of being a fugitive

		History	Narrative Timeline
	1852		Mary Wilson opens her crockery store on Atlantic
	1853		Elenor Croger dies
NEW YORK POST EMANCIPATION PERIOD	1854	Kansas-Nebraska Act Republican Party founded Colored Political Association founded	
	1855	Williamsburgh receives city charter Brooklyn annexes city of Williamsburgh and the town of Bushwick Havemeyer, Townsend & Co. Sugar Refinery opens on Williamsburg waterfront	
	1857	*Dred Scott v. Sanford* Supreme Court decision	Pomona Brice fundraises to emancipate her family
	1858	African Civilization Society founded	
	1859	John Brown's raid at Harpers Ferry	Elizabeth Gloucester sends money to John Brown
	1860	South Carolina secedes from the Union Brooklyn is third-largest city in the United States	Elizabeth Gloucester, Mary Wilson, Christiana Freeman fundraise for Colored Orphan Asylum Mary, William, and Annie Wilson move to Fort Greene
CIVIL WAR	1861	Abraham Lincoln sworn in as president Civil War begins	Mary Ann Tippon, William Hodges's wife, dies
	1862	Congress abolishes slavery in DC and federal territories Tobacco Factory Riots, Brooklyn	William Hodges returns to the US South
	1863	Emancipation Proclamation New York City Draft Riots	William, Mary, and Annie Wilson move to Washington, DC, to teach in the Freedmen Schools
	1864		American Freedmen Friend's Society in Brooklyn opens
	1865	Civil War ends Thirteenth Amendment Freedmen's Bureau founded	
RECONSTRUCTION	1866	Brooklyn branch of Freedmen's Bureau opens	
	1867	Prospect Park opens	Willis, Sarah Ann, and their family move to Virginia from Brooklyn
	1868	Fourteenth Amendment	
	1870	Fifteenth Amendment Brooklyn Bridge construction begins	

BROOKLYN'S FAMILIES

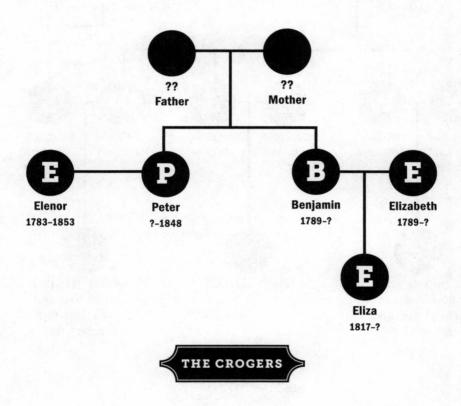

THE CROGERS

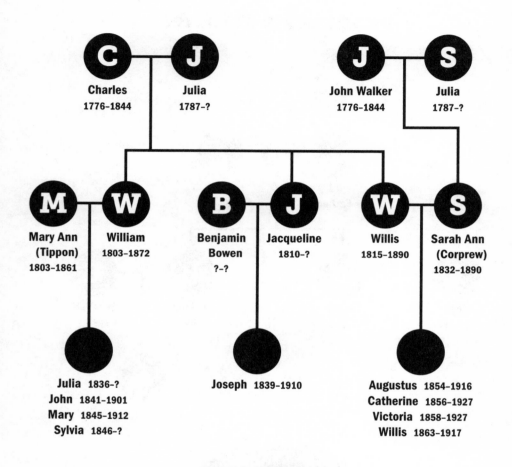

C · Charles 1776–1844

J · Julia 1787–?

J · John Walker 1776–1844

S · Julia 1787–?

M · Mary Ann (Tippon) 1803–1861

W · William 1803–1872

B · Benjamin Bowen ?–?

J · Jacqueline 1810–?

W · Willis 1815–1890

S · Sarah Ann (Corprew) 1832–1890

Julia 1836–?
John 1841–1901
Mary 1845–1912
Sylvia 1846–?

Joseph 1839–1910

Augustus 1854–1916
Catherine 1856–1927
Victoria 1858–1927
Willis 1863–1917

THE HODGESES

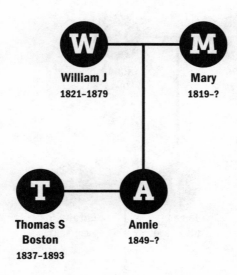

W
William J
1821–1879

M
Mary
1819–?

T
**Thomas S
Boston**
1837–1893

A
Annie
1849–?

THE WILSONS

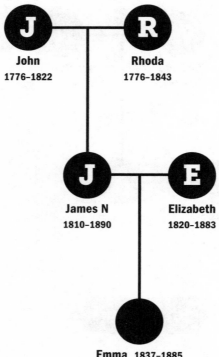

Emma 1837–1885
Stephen 1842–1856
Elizabeth 1845–1915
Louisa 1847–1918
James 1851–1930
Charles 1854–1908
Alfred 1857–1859

THE GLOUCESTERS

PROLOGUE

AN INCOMPLETE REVOLUTION

No man is an island, entire of itself; every man is a piece of the
continent, a part of the main.
　　　—John Donne, from "Meditation XVII,"
　　　Devotions upon Emergent Occasions (1624)

BROOKLYN has a distinct story to tell in the history of social justice. From the end of the American Revolution to the start of the
Civil War, Brooklyn expanded from one of six former colonial agricultural towns that lay on stolen Indigenous land in Kings County to the
third-largest city in the United States. As it did so, Brooklyn's small
but growing free Black community—ordinary people from all walks of
life, including business people, church leaders, educators, homeowners,
journalists, laborers, and writers—sought to grow their city in a radical anti-slavery vision. The nineteenth-century residents of Brooklyn
Heights, Fort Greene, Weeksville, Williamsburg, and the areas we know
today as Downtown Brooklyn, DUMBO, and Vinegar Hill engaged
in a multifaceted struggle as they organized and agitated for racial and
social justice. They did so even as their own freedom was threatened by a
magnitude of injustices including racial violence, systemic and structural
racism, racial capitalism, and the potential for kidnapping into slavery in
the South. These Brooklynites met in the city's churches, schools, parks,
homes, public platforms, and private spaces. In choosing to live in or in
close proximity to an emerging urban landscape surrounded by the vast
New York Harbor, they took advantage of a city on the rise in order to
pursue economic opportunities and build and sustain their communities.

Brooklynites tells the rich story of New York City's second-largest borough and four sets of families from its nineteenth-century free Black community—the Crogers, the Hodgeses, the Wilsons, and the Gloucesters—all of whom called this place home. It is a place-based cultural and social history of Brooklyn, and it is a book about family—traditional biological ones and the ones we intentionally create to strengthen our human bonds ("chosen family"). The book restores the breadth and depth of the work of these four families, along with that of scores of other Brooklynites, who displayed courage and conscience to expand our understanding of freedom, and it explores the ways in which these residents both physically and politically navigated their own city on a daily basis. It centers these families as fully formed persons and ordinary people, first and foremost, and follows the contours and fragility of their own lives through births, marriages, deaths, and kinship, even as they engaged in ambitious radical reforms of their city as political and intellectual thinkers. The book is organized chronologically and thematically, and its scope is bookended by two major chapters of US history: the end of the American Revolution and the beginnings of Reconstruction. Together these represent two profoundly significant moments in this nation's history in which Americans were forced to confront the bleak shortcomings of this country's democratic promise and its founding ideals.

Why Brooklyn? As the third-largest city in the United States for nearly fifty years, entirely independent and separate from Manhattan (or the City of New York), it deserves its own focus. Though once considered just the western tip of Long Island, today it remains, a century after consolidation in 1898, the most populous borough in New York City. For large parts of the mid- to late twentieth century, Brooklyn remained in the shadow of, or as a subchapter to, Manhattan's own history. Brooklyn stands proudly at the heart of this book, as a site of scholarly examination and as a point of celebration and critique through historical analysis. If the capaciousness of the book's title, which points to the history of a people in one of the largest boroughs in New York City, seems at odds with its hyperlocal, or parochial, focus on Brooklyn, the residents from its free Black community saw it otherwise. These Brooklynites and their neighbors radically shaped its streets and neighborhoods into a political ecology so that they, and future generations, could thrive. Keenly aware of global liberation struggles, they created vital local, regional, national, and international networks as part of a social justice program that sought to end slavery immediately in the United States and agitate for political and legal equality for all. These men and women were proud Brooklynites but were also travelers, who connected to the modern Atlantic world in sophisticated ways. To be able to tell a fuller story of their lives and offer a layered social geography of their activism, this book follows the routes they took as they built self-determined grassroots communities of freedom.

Brooklynites builds on and is in dialogue with a rich and groundbreaking range of research on antebellum free Black communities in the Northern United States, from scholars as early as W. E. B. Du Bois, Benjamin Quarles, John Hope Franklin, Leon Litwack, and Dorothy Sterling to relatively more recent historians such as Leslie M. Alexander, Erica Armstrong Dunbar, David W. Blight, Eric Foner, Graham Hodges, Leslie M. Harris, James O. Horton, Lois E. Horton, Gary B. Nash, Richard S. Newman, Carla L. Peterson, Manisha Sinha, Judith Wellman, Craig S. Wilder, and Shirley Yee.[1] This book also owes an intellectual debt to three extraordinary scholars—Ruth Wilson Gilmore, Paul Gilroy, and Stuart Hall—who invite us all to continually and radically reimagine a world "where life is precious, life is precious."[2] Given the enormity of the book's intention—to tell the history of nineteenth-century Brooklyn by centering its free Black community—it owes an interdisciplinary debt to geography, history, genealogy, Black studies, urban studies, and women's studies. It also owes a wave of gratitude to archivist colleagues who have meticulously catalogued, indexed, and processed the kinds of archives that make the telling of this history a possibility. Far from "discovering" or "uncovering" archival items lost in dusty repositories, as clichéd explanations of the historian's craft often go, the book intentionally seeks to amplify the archives' long existence. But it is also a reflection on the capability and nature of the archives to support the telling of stories of New

Yorkers past, especially people of color and particularly those of Black women. Simply put, what do we do as historians and storytellers when the archive does not support the nuance and complexity of Brooklyn's past? The research for this book relies on the traditional archives, which include account books, census records, city directories, contemporary local newspapers and the Black press, engravings and paintings, letters, maps, pamphlets, and probate records. If Black men in Brooklyn are visible at all during the early to mid-nineteenth century, it is because fragments of their lives appear in such archival records. This archival legibility is not always so straightforward for Black women, however, and it is very often the same archives that make Black men's lives legible that simultaneously erase Black women's lives and contributions. Although laboring in equal measure to Black men during this time period, Black women might have done so in less visible ways, for example, by creating spaces in their private homes for community to debate, discuss, and gather or fundraising privately for Black-led institutions or supporting the household financially by bringing in a second income that went unreported in census records. This book, then, is part recovery project dedicated to amplifying the undertold stories of Black women's lives. Theirs might be a life incomplete in the archives, but the pulse of their presence is honored throughout the book, and it assumes that Black women were at the center of radical community building. It therefore also requires reading against structures of power often embedded in the archives. Being attentive to that problem requires being in dialogue and in community with generations of scholars working in other geographical and historical areas. As Saidiya V. Hartman writes, "every historian of the multitude, the dispossessed, the subaltern, and the enslaved is forced to grapple with the power and authority of the archive and the limits it sets on what can be known, whose perspective matters, and who is endowed with the gravity and authority of the historical actor."[3] This book therefore also owes a debt to the brilliance of Michel-Rolph Trouillot and Black feminist scholars such as Erica Armstrong Dunbar, P. Gabrielle Foreman, Marisa J. Fuentes, Saidiya V. Hartman, Tera W. Hunter, Martha S. Jones, Natasha Lightfoot, Jennifer L. Morgan, and Deborah Gray White.[4]

In "The Right to the City," the scholar and geographer David Harvey writes, "The question of what kind of city we want cannot be divorced from the question of what kind of people we want to be, what kinds of social relations we seek. . . . The freedom to make and remake our cities and ourselves is . . . one of the most precious yet most neglected of our human rights."[5] Today, we owe a debt to the activism of these Brooklynites, and the legacy of their work is still immeasurable. Conceptualizing freedom remains essential to our humanity and the ways in which we make life. Our contemporary context for inequality in both New York City and the United States did not arbitrarily begin with redlining, segregation, deindustrialization, broken windows policing, and urban renewal in the twentieth century. How we got here is deeply connected to the history of Brooklyn in the eighteenth and nineteenth centuries. Black Brooklynites and the white allies who would later join them mediated on and broadened the ideology of freedom in deeply profound ways, even as they struggled to secure freedom for themselves. Agitating for social justice in education, housing, safety, and voting and challenging racial capitalism itself were part of their agenda, and these ideas continue to shape our vision of US democracy today. They knew emancipation was not a single historical event but a series of moments in which freedom and liberty would need to be seized and molded in incalculable ways in their own lifetime and beyond. If today's present moment pessimistically reflects this country's long history and legacies of colonialism, genocide, slavery, imperialism, capitalism, gentrification, and displacement through the rise of populism, domestic terrorism through white supremacy, racial violence, and deeply embedded anti-Black racism, I would say Brooklyn's Black communities have lessons to teach us. History has never been one of linear progress—it remains in circular motion, with each revolution inching us (slowly) toward a more just society. *Brooklynites* is a story of necessity; in the stories of Brooklyn's nineteenth-century free Black residents and their activism, history can be one of majestic hope, deep humanity, and love.

This is a story of place-making, of land, home, and labor, of New Yorkers past, and the legacy they left us. This is the story of Brooklyn.

BROOKLYN: A SLAVEHOLDING CAPITAL

The population of the island is estimated about thirty-seven thousand souls, of which number near five thousand are slaves. It is the western part of the island which is the best inhabited; a circumstance to be ascribed, not so much to the fertility of the soil as its contiguity to the city of New York. . . . Brooklynn, the largest of [the towns] is situated just opposite to New York, on the bank of the East River, and forms an agreeable object of the city.

The soil of Long Island is well adapted to the culture of small grain and Indian corn; and the northern part which is hilly, is said to be particularly favourable to the production of fruit.

—Isaac Weld, *Travels through the States of North America, and the Provinces of Upper and Lower Canada during the Years 1795, 1796, and 1797*

RAN away from the subscriber, on Monday the 15th instant; a NEGRO MAN named TOM, about 24 years of age, but appears older; slim built of middling stature, a fear on his face, has a large nose, but not so flat as is common to the African Tribe, speaks both Dutch and English, bred a farmer, and appears very civil. Had on when he went away, a new London brown coat, trimmed, with large yellow buttons, a worsted jacket, and new homespun low shirt and trousers.—It is supposed he is lurking about the city, or gone to some part of the Jersey. Whoever will secure said Negro and return him to the subscriber, living about one mile from Brooklyn Ferry, shall be entitled to the above reward.

—Isaac Cornell, *The Diary or Loudon's Register*, July 19, 1793

It is not probable that slavery ever exhibited its worst features on Long Island. A kindly feeling existed between the owner and the slave. For the protection, the simple fare, and the homespun clothing, which, in accordance with the custom of the age, the master provided, the slave returned generally a cheerful obedience and a reasonable amount of labor.

—Gertrude Lefferts Vanderbilt, "Domestic Service," in *The Social History of Flatbush and Manners and Customs of the Dutch Settlers in Kings County* (1881)

In the disorder and lawlessness that followed the British occupation, the slaves caught the infection, became insubordinate,
and, in search of adventures, abandoned their masters.
—*Brooklyn Daily Eagle*, November 19, 1892

Isabella was just nine years old when the British cartographer Bernard
Ratzer created the *Plan of the Town of Brooklyn and Part of Long
Island* for military purposes in 1766, nine years before the American
Revolution.[6] It is difficult to map her daily routine as a young girl; but
she was almost certainly prohibited from the normality of childhood
curiosity and play, and her mobility was restricted given her enslaved
status. When she did move, she would have done so across a terrain,
as seen in this map, so sublime that it belied the genocidal violence to
which the land was witness. Although little remained of the Lenni-
Lenape collective way of life and its people and the Munsee-speaking
Canarsee had been annihilated some eighty years earlier by Dutch, then
English colonizers, the occupied land still consisted of hills and troughs,
natural waterways with an abundance of oysters, and corn, orchards,
and other crops across expansive agricultural land. The Canarsee of the
Lenape tribe had called this area Sewanhaka, or the island of shells, and
they used it collectively for farming, fishing, and growing wheat, barley,
and corn, allowing the land to speak its usage. Although Isabella would
have been witness to similar annual crop cycles sustained by the same
earth, Indigenous ways of human life existing on this land had largely
disappeared. Whereas Indigenous identities were intricately tied to the
land and places were identified by their Indigenous inhabitants, such as
Canarsee, Keschaeghquerenen, Marechkawieck, Nyack, Techkonis, and
Wichquawanck, the Dutch renamed the whole island Lange Eylandt in
the 1650s, followed by the English, who Anglicized these names. With
its renaming came the erasure of collective land usage, so that many of
our modern concepts of individual or private property ownership have
long roots in the violence of European colonization.

The Brookland Ferry now provided passage to its residents from colonial Kings County to Manhattan, but again it is unlikely that Isabella

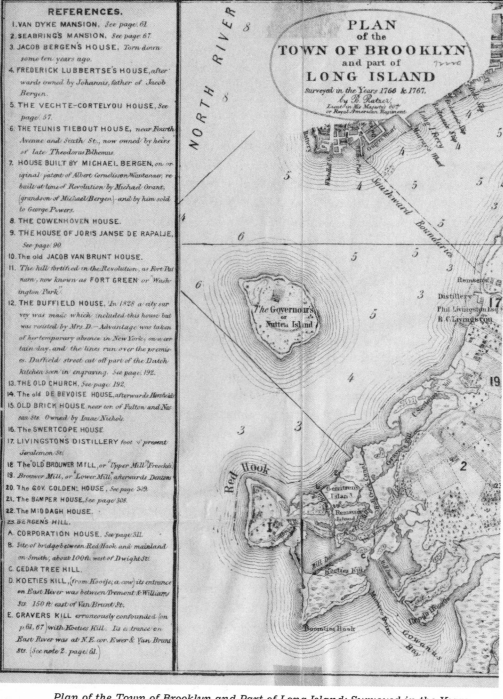

PLAN
of the
TOWN OF BROOKLYN
and part of
LONG ISLAND
Surveyed in the Years 1766 & 1767.
by B. Ratzer,
Lieut. in His Majesty's 60th or Royal American Regiment.

Plan of the Town of Brooklyn and Part of Long Island: Surveyed in the Years 1766 & 1767, by B. Ratzer, Lieut. in His Majesty's 60th or Royal American Regiment, [185?], map. (B A-1766-1767 (185-?).Fl, Map Collection, Center for Brooklyn History, Brooklyn Public Library)

possessed the basic freedom to travel across the East River. Instead, as a child in eighteenth-century Kings County, then part of the British North American colonies, Isabella was expected to work in an agrarian economy mostly led by Dutch and then British farmers until her death. Ratzer's map tells the stories of countless enslaved people of African descent whose labor made possible the discernible large tracts of land you see here. But this map also represents the land that Isabella and others would ultimately liberate themselves from through escape. Like so many people of African descent, Isabella used the chaos of the American Revolution to seize her freedom. Brooklyn was at the tumultuous center of this revolution. It was on this land that the patriots and loyalists fought in the Battle of Brooklyn in 1776 and that George Washington's Continental Army retreated from Brooklyn and New York, resulting in it being loyalist territory for the remainder of the war. It was also the site of Wallabout Bay, where approximately twelve thousand prisoners of war died in horrific conditions on British prisoner ships.

And yet not all enslaved people followed Isabella's journey.

Three blocks from where the Masjid Imam-ul-Bukhari now stands in the Flatlands section of southeastern Brooklyn—home to residents of African American, Caribbean, and Pakistani descent—lies Hubbard Place. Its diagonal irregularity at the intersection of Avenue K, Flatbush Avenue, and Kings Highway is a reminder of the borough's colonial past, when the Dutch and British cared little for neat throughfares and parallel streets. The street, which was originally known as Hubbard Lane, is now a mere fraction of its original length, but its name still pays to tribute to the Hubbard, or Hubard, family. In 1652, they settled in the Flatlands, making them one of the earliest landowning families in Kings County. Over the next two centuries, they amassed enough generational wealth to emerge as prominent landowners, which meant that they were also slaveholders. Elias Hubbard, born in the Flatlands in 1746, cared enough for his own freedom that he joined the patriots during the American Revolution. Having decried his political enslavement at the hands of the British, he conveniently overlooked his own role as a slaveholder. In 1777, just two years into the Revolution, he bought a Black woman named Jin and her children in perpetuity from Isaac Van Brunt, a property owner in neighboring New Utrecht. Exploited and unfree laborers of African descent engaged in candle making, carpentry, cooking, hunting, milling, sewing, shoemaking, tool mending, washing, weaving, and chimney, fireplace, general cleaning, and general farm work. Unlike the US South, where plantation complexes consisted of an ornate home for the slaveholder and separate slave quarters, Northern slaveholders' estates were much smaller. They typically enslaved one to three people within their estate, and the kitchen annexed to the enslaver's home became an intimate site of domestic labor, rest, and surveillance as enslaved people were expected to live and sleep here. In 1782, at the height of the Revolution, Elias sold Jin, presumably in perpetuity, again. He remained the owner of a seventy-seven-acre farm in the Flatlands and a slaveholder long after the war had ended.[7] The Hubards were part of a Brooklyn tradition—Dutch slave-owning families who made enough money in the mid- to late eighteenth century to ensure that they remained prominent Brooklynites well into the nineteenth century. These families included Bergen, Ditmars, Lefferts, Lott, Vanderveer, Van Sicklen, and Voorhees. The Bergens and the Lotts were some of the few families not just of Dutch descent but also of Scandinavian and French Huguenot descent, respectively. Today, their names are still visible on the borough's landscape: Voorhies Avenue in Sheepshead Bay; the Prospect-Lefferts Gardens neighborhood and Lott Street in Flatbush; Van Siclen Avenue in East New York; Bergen Street, which runs east-west from Cobble Hill to East New York; Vanderveer Street in Bushwick; and Remsen Street (named after a descendant of Ram Jansen Vanderbeek) in Brooklyn Heights. Slavery is so entrenched in Brooklyn's history: eighty-two streets are still named after Brooklyn's slaveholding families.[8] There are no streets named for enslaved women like Jin and Isabella whose life and labor made this land possible.

On June 16, 1783, at the end of the American Revolution, Isabella, now twenty-six years old, and her five-year-old daughter, bearing the same name as her mother, joined forty-nine men, women, and children and boarded *Generous Friends*, a British ship bound for St. John's,

Newfoundland and Labrador, Canada. Another one of the many fleeing during this time was forty-year-old James Liverpool, formerly enslaved and described as a "stout fellow," who boarded a ship for Annapolis in Nova Scotia and St. John's. He had run away from his enslaver Christopher Coduise of Brooklyn in 1776, at the very beginning of the American Revolution. *The Book of Negroes*, in which both Isabella and John Liverpool are noted, is a handwritten leather-bound British military ledger that records the name, age, physical appearance, and residence of all three thousand Black passengers who boarded 219 ships that left New York's harbor in 1783 for Canada and sometimes went on to Sierra Leone and the Caribbean. The ledger is, as one scholar has commented, not only a record of escape but also one of the earliest examples of surveillance of Black life and essential to the early formation of the Canada-US border.[9] These Black loyalists had fought alongside the British—they did not do so out of blind loyalty to one oppressor over another but instead risked precious life for the greatest human desire and prize of all: freedom.[10] Their passage was made possible by Lord Dunmore's Proclamation of 1775, in which the colonial governor of Virginia promised liberty in Canada to any person of African descent willing to risk their lives and serve the loyalists. The colossal nature of this event and the violence that engulfed Isabella's life are recorded in two short, handwritten lines in the archives. A "GBC" notation next to her and her daughter's names denotes that they possessed Brigadier General Samuel Birch's Certificate, proof that the adult Isabella probably served as a cook, laundress, nurse, spy, or another type of waged laborer for the British.[11]

This was not the first time Isabella had attempted to escape Brooklyn. Just five years earlier, in 1778, she sought her own dispossession when she ran away from her enslaver Charles Loosley, owner of the town's King's Head Tavern, a drinking and gathering place for Tories. Before Charles Loosley, her enslaver was Resolved Waldron. His family were long-established landowners and slaveholders of Dutch descent who had amassed wealth over a century and a half in Brooklyn and New York, which had been known as New Amsterdam under the Dutch.

Resolved's ancestor was one of the original Dutch colonists who had worked alongside Peter Stuyvesant, New Amsterdam's first director general, as well as serving as sheriff for a few Dutch towns on Long Island. The family expanded their landownership when they married into the family of Ryck Lent, whose land would eventually lend its name to Rikers Island, one of the most notorious sites of the prison-industrial complex in New York City today.[12] After the war, if Charles Loosley proved Isabella had run away from him, as a slaveholder, he would have been compensated under the Provisional Peace Treaty between Britain and the Congress of Confederation in 1783.[13] There would have been no compensation, or reparations, owed to Isabella or her daughter.

The brief two lines in *The Book of Negroes* cannot tell us the conditions of Isabella's escape—whether she ran from her enslaver by day or night, alone, or with assistance from others. During her escape, did she hear the night song of the town's crickets or the daily wrens that flew overhead? Or as the adrenaline consumed her, did she feel the fields of barley, corn, oats, and rye under her feet? Perhaps these details all felt too inconsequential during flight. But we can glean from the archives *why*. On the basis of the two Isabellas' ages and the racist description of the adult Isabella as a "stout wench"—that is, a Black woman of child-bearing age or, in this case, with child—Isabella expressed a basic maternal and human instinct: to protect her unborn child, or possibly a newborn of only a few days or weeks, from a life of traumatic violence that only slavery afforded. As an enslaved woman, Isabella would have automatically passed her status to her daughter. Running away, therefore, represented an act of unconditional love—Isabella's maternal bond was deeply rooted in her humanity, so starkly antithetical to a system that viewed both her and her child as an extension of the land on which they labored. Isabella's act of defiance, like that of countless others who would serve as Black loyalists, and their willingness to risk life for freedom destroyed the fantasy that white Brooklynites would later tell themselves about the borough's past and its "benign" form of slavery, namely, that enslaved people of African descent "caught the infection" of "disorder" and "lawlessness" from loyalist occupation during the American Revolution and, without purpose, simply went in "search of adventures."[14] Isabella did more than just follow the rhetoric of liberty and independence; she used its promise to secure her own actual freedom and that of her daughter. In doing so, she left behind a town whose landscape was utterly transformed by the American Revolution, where "many families fled their homes, never to return, while houses that stood and orchards that had flourished were left smoldering," and a county whose reputation as being unfree grew more notorious as its enslaved population quadrupled between 1703 and 1790.[15]

The dual existence of slavery in a land of freedom was the paradox of the American Revolution.[16] And nowhere was this contradiction more evident than in Brooklyn, where one in three Brooklynites were enslaved. It was in stark contrast to other emerging urban areas in the North. As early as 1773, Black people in Massachusetts petitioned the state legislature to question their enslavement. By 1784, just one year into the young republic's existence, Pennsylvania, Vermont, Massachusetts, Rhode Island, and Connecticut had begun to dismantle slavery. The institution declined for economic reasons, philosophical ideas, religious impulses, and the protest of Black people themselves, who were joined by some white reformers such as the Quakers. Manumissions, anti-slavery societies, and free Black communities grew in the immediate aftermath of the American Revolution across the North, including Manhattan. This was not the case in Kings County. Not all people of African descent were able to make their escape like Isabella. Instead, slavery's numbers strengthened after the Revolution, and the institution formed Brooklyn's geographical and historical milieu. The labor of enslaved people fueled the economic success of Brooklyn, as it transformed from a small town to a sprawling urban space.

In 1783, Brooklyn represented just one of six former colonial towns in Kings County. They were Brooklyn (Breukelen), Bushwick (Boswijck), Flatlands (Nieuw Amersfoort), Flatbush (Midwout), and New Utrecht (Nieuw Utrecht). Breukelen was the oldest of the Dutch towns, established as early as 1651 (only Gravesend came earlier, founded by the English in 1645). When the British evacuated New York in 1783, "the

Brooklyn (Breukelen) (*Brooklyn Eagle*, 1946), booklet. (F129.B7 B766 1946 c.2, Book Collection, Center for Brooklyn History, Brooklyn Public Library)

lands all around [Brooklyn] . . . were divided into fields by post and mail fences, and used for agricultural purposes as farm lands," and it contained no streets, with the exception of the Kings Highway, which was renamed Old Road and later Fulton Street.[17] In 1790, the first US federal census revealed that Kings County's population had doubled in less than a century. Most of this population clustered around the northwestern tip of Kings County, where the Fulton Ferry stood connecting Brooklyn to Manhattan, or New York.[18] Of the approximately forty-four hundred residents in Brooklyn, Bushwick, Flatbush, Flatlands, Gravesend, and New Utrecht, a little more than one-third of its population was of African descent. Of that number, only forty-six were free (i.e., 3 percent). In contrast, free Black people constituted 33 percent of the African diaspora in Manhattan. By 1801, even as the number of enslaved people declined in Boston, Philadelphia, and Manhattan, the number of enslaved people actually increased in Brooklyn, defying trends elsewhere in the North. In Kings County, 60 percent of white families were slaveholders—the numbers were as high as 74 percent and 75 percent in outer areas such as Flatbush and New Utrecht, respectively. Its slaveholding percentages exceeded that of neighboring Manhattan, where 40 percent of white residents were slaveholders. The peculiarity of this history led the historian Harold X. Connolly to label Kings County a "slaveholding capital," given that its numbers exceeded that of any other county in New York State.[19]

How do we account for this anomaly? By the late eighteenth century, Kings County had a thriving agrarian economy long established by the Dutch. Its low, marshy land, together with the area's ponds, meant that the fertile soil could support an abundance of crops, foodstuffs, and produce. As early as 1679, Jasper Danckaerts, a Dutch traveler who would later colonize part of Maryland, commented that he had enjoyed in both Gowanus and Bay Ridge "Gouanes (Gowanus) oysters, which are the best in the country":

They are fully good as those of England, and better than those we ate at Falmouth. I had to try some of them raw. They are large and full,

James Ryder Van Brunt, [Homestead of Cornelius Van Brunt], 1859, watercolor. (Prints and Drawings Collection, M2001.9.1, Center for Brooklyn History, Brooklyn Public Library)

some of them not less than a foot long, and they grow sometimes ten, twelves, sixteen together, and are then like a piece of rock. They pickle the oysters in small casks, and send them to Barbados and other islands. We had for supper a roasted haunch of venison. . . . The meat was exceedingly tender and good. We were also served with wild turkey, . . . a wild goose. . . . Everything we had was the natural production of the country. We saw here, lying in a heap, a whole hill of watermelons, which were as large as pumpkins, and which Symon was going to the city to sell. They were very good, though there is a difference between them and those of the Caribbee Islands. . . .

Continuing onward from there, we came to the plantation of the Najack Indians, which was planted with maize, or Turkish wheat. We soon heard a noise of pounding, like thrashing, and went to the place whence it proceeded, and found there an old Indian woman busily employed beating Turkish beans out of the pods by means of a stick, which she did with astonishing force and dexterity. Gerrit (Evertsen Van Duyn) inquired of her, in the Indian language, which he spoke perfectly well, how old she was, and she answered eighty years; at which we were still more astonished that so old a woman should still have so much strength and courage to work as she did.[20]

Kings County's economy and landscape were strikingly different from adjacent Manhattan. The City of New York had already prestigiously served as the young nation's first capital and, by 1790, had received its city status, surpassing Philadelphia as the largest city in the country. From 1790 to 1810, the port city became the center of North American capitalism.[21] The arrival of investors, bankers, brokers, and lawyers and a rapid increase in the amount of foreign trade resulted in the creation of financial institutions such as the Bank of New York in 1784 and the New York Stock Exchange in 1792. Kings County, however, remained distinctly agricultural. It was responsible for providing fruits, vegetables, and wheat, corn, oats, barley, and rye to its six towns and neighboring New York. After the opening of the Erie Canal in 1825, not only did Brooklynites grow their own foodstuffs, but they were also able to transport them easily to other parts of the country with the advent of the industrialization of the waterways. Médéric Louis Élie Moreau de Saint-Méry, a French lawyer and writer, observed, "the nearness of New York [to Brooklyn] assures a market for all farm products," and as a result, the "Dutch families who form such a large part of the population [in Brooklyn] refuse to sell their holdings."[22] Along with their land, Brooklyn's Dutch families clung to enslaved labor. The lives of enslaved people were "almost too shocking to relate," and the labor "was extremely hard, being obliged to work in the summer from about two o'clock in the morning, till about ten or eleven o'clock at night, and in the winter from four in the morning, till ten at night"; the horses "enjoy[ed] greater privileges than [the enslaved] did."[23] Those who were enslaved included young people like John Jea, who worked as an enslaved child in Flatbush and would find freedom as a teenager when his enslaver manumitted him, as well as countless and nameless others who were never able to escape their slaveholders at the end of the American Revolution.

This story begins at the end of a major chapter of US history. At the end of the American Revolution, Brooklyn was a slaveholding capital. And it was within this context that a free Black community at the town's most northwestern tip would begin to contour the landscape and imbue the land with radical possibilities of freedom. The stories of enslaved women like Isabella and Jin invite us to meditate on the land that became known as Brooklyn, to contemplate it as a series of unwritten spaces, to examine the right to that space and the meaning of place that Brooklynites free and enslaved would assign to it throughout its formation in the early to mid-nineteenth century as it emerged as the City of Brooklyn.

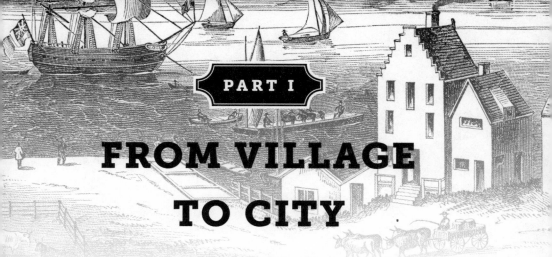

PART I

FROM VILLAGE
TO CITY

1790–1827

AN EMERGING CITY

Brooklyn itself is a beautiful object; and from the opposite shore is seen with great advantage. Several of the streets are straight, and spacious. The houses are generally good; many of them new; many handsome; very many painted white, and therefore cheerful and brilliant. The town contains three churches; a Dutch, an Episcopal, and a Methodist. The inhabitants are, extensively, descendants from the original Dutch settlers: the rest are a casual collection from all quarters.
—Timothy Dwight, *Travels in New England and New York* (1822)

Old Brooklyn Ferry-house of 1746.

N. Orr, *Old Brooklyn Ferry-house of 1746*, ca. 1867, engraving. (M1988.2.2, Prints and Drawings Collection, Center for Brooklyn History, Brooklyn Public Library)

O N a muggy August day, as people traverse the Brooklyn Bridge, families congregate for ice cream in a former twentieth-century fireboat house, and tourists line up outside Grimaldi's Pizzeria where Front Street meets Old Fulton Street. All the while, the cacophony of modern traffic from the Brooklyn and Manhattan Bridges and the much-unloved BQE (the Brooklyn-Queens Expressway, to the unini-tiated) pierces their senses. This is Brooklyn—"Like No Other Place in the World!" The convergence of these people, places, and sounds obscures that here is where the heart of the Village of Brooklyn once stood, home to a "casual collection [of residents] from all quarters" who mostly lived around the Fulton Ferry landing.[1]

THE VILLAGE OF BROOKLYN

Brooklyn was settled along the path leading from Marechkawieck that became known as the road from the ferry in what is today's Brooklyn Heights. In 1704, under an act passed by the General Assembly of the Colony of New York that required the creation, regulation, and mainte-nance of new highways, the road would become the town's main street and be renamed Fulton Street.[2] In the late eighteenth century, one traveler observed that the town of Brooklyn had about one hundred one-story dwellings. Almost all of the village's activity, its structures, and its residents were centered around the northwestern end of town, near the ferry landing where, by 1814, Robert Fulton's steam ferry revo-lutionized travel across the East River by significantly reducing travel time between Brooklyn and Manhattan. Most of Brooklyn's dwell-ings were frame, or made of wood, though some wealthier residents constructed their businesses and homes using more expensive brick or stone. The "unusually healthy" air was otherwise accompanied by the unpaved walkways that frequently became muddy after it rained.[3] Over the next three decades, the one-square-mile village transformed from farmland to an emerging urban development based on land speculation.

The village contained ropewalks, taverns, stores, one-story homes, and unpaved streets (with the exception of Fulton, which was paved in 1822). Whereas in 1800, some foodstuffs, for example, corn (maize), might have still been grown in Brooklyn's fertile soil, by 1822, villagers' diets were not necessarily tied to the local land or weather (though corn long continued in other parts of Kings County, such as New Utrecht, that remained largely agricultural throughout the nineteenth century). Instead, Brooklynites had access to a variety of foodstuffs even in the absence of a singular public market like the thriving Fulton Street Market across the river in the City of New York. The village was home to six butcher stalls (three on Main, three on Brooklyn's Fulton Street) and a fish stall on Fulton near Front, and vegetables and poultry could be found at a number of grocers dotted throughout. One such grocer, G. C. Langdon, who had moved from Manhattan to Brooklyn, sold hams, smoked beef, "Indian currie and other seasonings," white Havana, East India, and brown sugars, Holland gin, teas, and "superior Spanish segars" at his store on Fulton Street next to the Steam Boat Hotel.[4] Myriad regulations governed the behavior of the residents of the small village, from the quiet observance of Sundays to the roaming and use of sheep, bulls, hogs, horses, or carriages to the use of guns, pistols, crackers and fireworks, and firing at marks or targets with ball or shot to businesses of inn holders and cartmen to fires and nuisances, bathing, dirt, and the cleaning of streets (in the absence of central sanitation services, each resident was responsible for their own gutters and the public street in front of their homes).[5]

The English painter Francis Guy arrived in Brooklyn in 1817, just one year after the village was incorporated into the former colonial town of the same name. Brooklyn could not have been more different from Manhattan at this time. Manhattan, or the City of New York, had long established its social and economic status in the United States and in the Atlantic world. In *Tontine Coffee House* (1797), Francis Guy had depicted Manhattan as a modern industrial space (it had already achieved city status, whereas it would take Brooklyn another three-plus decades to do the same). Urbanized and developed, the busy commercial waterfront in the distance makes clear the business of the buildings at the painting's right along Wall Street and the workers at its center. To the left, the grand brick Tontine Coffee House is a gathering place for merchants, brokers, and businessmen whose affairs were intimately tied to the sale of slave commodities such as sugar, rum, and cotton. Manhattan's skyline, already standing so much higher than Brooklyn's, exemplified North American capitalism. When Brooklyn eventually received its city charter in 1834, the mechanics of its own urban operations remained entirely distinct from its East River neighbor, as did its sounds, sights, and smells.

In 1820, Francis Guy captured the village in the dead of winter from his studio on Front Street, in a painting titled *Winter Scene in Brooklyn*. Francis's gray winter sky wraps around the busy village of uneven, diagonal streets lined with frame dwellings—homes, stables, and businesses belonging to its residents, who themselves represented a diverse cross-section of class, gender, and race.[6] These residents included Irish immigrants, transplants from New England, descendants of mostly English colonizers, and to a lesser extent the original Dutch (who lived in larger numbers further out in Kings County), free people of African descent, and in smaller numbers enslaved people of African descent too. By 1820, almost all of the Indigenous Lenni Lenape were either murdered or displaced. In spite of virulent racism, this diverse community of early Brooklynites lived in close quarters and inhabited the same streets and public spaces. They resided in neighborhoods that are known today as Downtown Brooklyn, Brooklyn Heights, DUMBO, and Vinegar Hill.

Scholars have written extensively about the village residents seen and unseen in Francis Guy's *Winter Scene*. The painter identified almost all of the Brooklynites of Dutch and English descent, including Abiel Titus, Mrs. Burnett, Judge Garrison, Jacobs Hicks, and Judge Sands, even as he failed to identify the Black Brooklynites who were also clearly visible.[7] In doing so, Francis makes some Black Brooklynites hypervisible while simultaneously securing their erasure. Henry Stiles, Brooklyn's self-appointed nineteenth-century historian, later identified Samuel Foster, a chimney sweeper who appears on the painting's far right, and

Francis Guy (American, 1760–1820), *Winter Scene in Brooklyn*, ca. 1819–1820, oil on canvas, 58 3/8 × 74 9/16 in. (148.2 × 189.4 cm). (Brooklyn Museum; transferred from the Brooklyn Institute of Arts and Sciences to the Brooklyn Museum, 97.13; photo: Brooklyn Museum, 97.13_colorcorrected_SL1.jpg)

another Black man, Jeff, who stands between his enslaver Abiel Titus, who is feeding chickens, and Mrs. Burnett, who speaks to Abiel's son on horseback.[8] Other Black residents include a man who has fallen on the ice while a dog stares at him and another two engaged in hard, manual labor bent over the logs in the painting's front left. These residents are not afforded the luxury of standing and chatting with their neighbors as the white Brooklynites in the scene do. This "casual collection from all quarters," as Timothy Dwight, who had served as Yale's president from 1795 to 1817, observed, included a thriving free Black community.[9] Its residents included Elenor and Elizabeth Croger and their husbands, brothers Peter and Benjamin Croger, respectively. They lived at a time of both tremendous urban growth for the village and, because of gradual emancipation, formidable challenges too.

THE CROGERS OF THE VILLAGE OF BROOKLYN

The Village of Brooklyn—the town's most built-up area—lay at one square mile in 1816 when Jeremiah Lott created his map. It was bound by the "Public Landing south of Pierpont's Distillery, formerly the property of Philip Livingston, deceased, on the East River; thence running along the public road leading from said Landing, to its intersection with Red-Hook Lane; thence along said Red Hook Lane to where it intersects the Jamaica Turnpike Road; thence a north-east course to the head of the Wallabout Mill-pond; thence through the center of the Mill-pond to the East River; and thence down the East River to the place of the beginning."[10] Members of its small, but significant, free Black community lived among their white neighbors, in an integrated area bound by Bridge Street, Sands Street, Fulton Street, and the East River, with the largest concentration in a triangle that no longer exists between Old Fulton, Main, and Front Streets.[11] This is where the Croger families lived in the early nineteenth century.

Although brothers Peter and Benjamin Croger were born free in Manhattan, their move to Brooklyn around 1806, together with their partners, Elenor and Elizabeth, respectively, signaled new energies in the town. Fragments of their lives appear in census and probate records, city directories, and newspapers. While these records are the fabric of the historian's craft, the archives cannot fully convey the immeasurable impact they had on their city, and relying on them alone offers a cautionary tale, as the lives of sisters-in-law Elenor and Elizabeth Croger are almost entirely erased. This book seeks to honor them in their gifted capacity as "young black women [who were] radical thinkers" and "tirelessly imagined other ways to live and never failed to consider how the world might be otherwise."[12] Peter, Elenor, Benjamin, and Elizabeth would shape the political landscape of Brooklyn through their radical

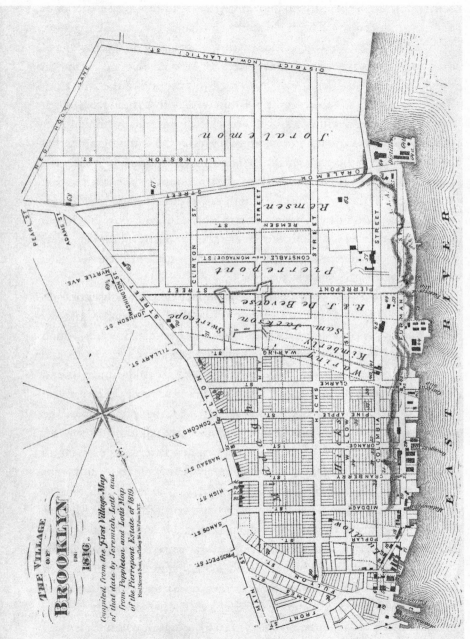

Jeremiah Lott, *The Village of Brooklyn in 1816*, 1816, map. (B P-1816 (1816-?).Fl, Map Collection, Center for Brooklyn History, Brooklyn Public Library)

activism. Though there are no known written birth records for Elenor or her husband, Peter, or Elizabeth and her husband, Benjamin Croger, we know from the 1850 federal census (with the exception of Peter, who had died two years earlier) that they were born at a revolutionary time in the Atlantic world. Elenor was born in 1783, at the end of the American Revolution. And Elizabeth and Benjamin were both born in 1789, which marked both the beginning of the French Revolution and the publication of Olaudah Equiano's *Interesting Narrative*, an autobiography that laid out slavery's horrors and demanded freedom across the Atlantic world. Although we have no written accounts, we can also assume that Peter, Elenor, Benjamin, and Elizabeth heard tales in their childhoods of Black liberation through news of the Haitian Revolution that began in 1799. In other words, they grew up at a time in postrevolutionary New York in which the ripples of radical freedom were being carried back and forth across the ocean's currents.

The first federal census began in 1790, but the Croger households do not appear in the 1800 or 1810 census records. While national events saw the tumultuous passage of the Missouri Compromise in 1820, which admitted Missouri as a slave state, admitted Maine as a free state, and prohibited the expansion of slavery above the 36°30' latitude line in the remainder of the Louisiana Territory, closer to home, the year also marked the earliest federal census detailing the Croger household. The record is interesting for what it does and does not tell us. We know, for example, that there was a free Black man named Peter Croger living in the village of Brooklyn, aged somewhere between twenty-six and forty-five years old, as per the census columns. There were no children listed in the household, and that remained the case until Peter's and Elenor's deaths, according to the couple's will and probate records. We also know from the 1820 census that Peter lived with a free Black woman in the same age bracket. Though there is no name listed, it was more than likely his wife, Elenor. However, we do not know Elenor's maiden name from this census record (later probate records list her as Croger, and no birth or marriage records have been found to date), where Peter and Elenor were born (that would come from later records), or the type of labor the couple engaged in (that appears in other contemporary records). But we do know that the Crogers lived on Pearl Street in 1820, a street that ran from the East River to the long-covered lanes that made up the village's numerous ropewalks, where baskets and rope were made. Today, centuries of urban development have erased the street's original hilly topography, destroyed the bountiful oysters from the nearby East River that lined the village's streets and gave rise to the street's name, and truncated the original Pearl Street that connected the village of Brooklyn north and south. But in 1822, the residents of Pearl Street, according to the city directory, included an eclectic mix of slaveholding families, self-appointed village leaders, white female property owners, and free Black Brooklynites. There were no enslaved people resident on the street, according to census records. Black families along Pearl included the Croger family and neighbors Cornelius (89 Pearl), Samuel Anderson (93 Pearl), Henry Brown (91 Pearl), and Titus Roosevelt (85 Pearl).[13] The street was also home to white families such as William Burnett (a fur dresser at the back of 84 Pearl) and Peter Haley (a mason at 65 Pearl). Peter and Elenor lived at 90 Pearl Street, and Benjamin and Elizabeth lived at number 91, though it is difficult to say if the two residences were next door or opposite to each other, as there was no standardized enumeration of houses at this time.

It is vital to acknowledge a few erasures here. The year 1822 marked the first year that Brooklyn commenced regular publication of its city directories—up until this point, there had been limited sporadic attempts by various village residents. Alden Spooner, a New England transplant, served as the directory's publisher. His print shop, centrally located at 60 Fulton, published a number of small-run pamphlets and was also home to the *Long Island Star* (it would become Brooklyn's oldest and longest-running newspaper), which he had bought in 1811 from fellow local printer Thomas Kirk. Alden also possessed significant power in the village as a publisher and court surrogate and in his leadership positions at central organizations such as the Brooklyn Lyceum and the Brooklyn Gas Light Company. Alden's choice, keeping in line with other city directory conventions at this time, to list alphabetically the head of household (usually the male home owner) and no one else meant that we therefore only have a partial glimpse into the complex class, gender, ethnic, and racial composition of Brooklyn at this time. Boarders, renters, villagers with any housing insecurity, and Black women faced complete erasure from this type of historical record. Moreover, it is important to note that all the white men are listed in the city directory along with their line of work (although they are not designated as white, that is assumed by the publisher). Spooner, for example, is listed with his profession alongside his home address and any visible leadership positions he held in the formal running of the village. Whereas, except for Titus Roosevelt, who is listed in the city directory as a ropemaker—presumably given rope's centrality to Brooklyn's early economy—all of the men of color are listed as "black," and no jobs are printed next to their name.[14] The print strategy in Alden's directory, then, made the racialization of Black men hypervisible, while making invisible the racialization of white men as the default or norm. It also erased from Brooklyn's history how Black labor critically supported the village's economy through everyday low-wage skilled work or its own radical community building.[15]

We know from later census records and advertisements placed in the *Long Island Star* that Peter and Benjamin worked as whitewashers most of their working lives. Whitewashers were essential laborers in a village like Brooklyn, as they mixed and applied a whitewash compound of slated lime and water to barns, fences, gates, walls, or ceiling, resulting in the upkeep of the village's dwellings as they exhibited a bright-white paint. But racism restricted Black Brooklynites to a limited labor market, and no doubt Pearl Street's residents worked low-wage menial jobs that forced them to live on, or below, the poverty line, like so many other Black residents across Brooklyn and New York. From census records, city directory listings, and newspaper advertisements, we know that Black New Yorkers worked as blacksmiths, boot blacks, cartmen, dock workers, general laborers, and whitewashers.

Despite the struggle for a wider variety of jobs that might have showcased their skills and ability to earn higher wages, residents of Brooklyn's free Black community radically organized their labor to serve in an additional public capacity as grassroots church elders, community leaders, educators, and organizational officers. Black Brooklynites embarked on a path of self-determination and created their independent institutions for community building, growth, and celebration. In the "Organizations" section of the 1822 city directory, Peter is listed as a preacher of the African Methodist Church and class leader of the African Methodist Church. In some capacity, print culture such as Spooner's 1822 city directory gave voice to Black Brooklynites' labor and participation in civic life, even as they were excluded from holding formal leadership positions or positions of formal office as clerks, constables, high commissioners, overseers of the poor, and town officers in the growing village. Self-determined participation in civic life would prove to be critical during gradual emancipation in New York from 1799 to 1827, in which Brooklynites and others witnessed the slow dismantling of slavery in New York, the upholding of slaveholders' economic interests, and numerous legal measures that were not designed to improve the economic, political, and social needs of people of African descent, both enslaved and free.

GRADUAL EMANCIPATION, 1799–1827

July 4, 1799, was not a cause for abundant joy and celebration for all. Like so many other Fourth of July commemorations, the date seamlessly intertwined freedom and unfreedom in complex measure. It marked the beginning of a slow and arduous journey from slavery to freedom in New York State. Not only was it the penultimate Northern state to dismantle slavery (neighboring New Jersey being the last), but an "Act for the gradual abolition of slavery" represented the state legislature's third, and ultimately successful, attempt to pass a gradual emancipation law. Previous attempts to end slavery and amend the state constitution were met with resistance in 1777 and 1785 as white New Yorkers remained fearful of emancipation's economic and racial consequences.[16] The law stated that children born to enslaved mothers, after July 4, 1799, would serve a long indenture until the age of twenty-five if female and twenty-eight if male. Slavery had no end date for enslaved people born prior to this date. It was not until 1817 that "An Act relative to slaves and servants" stipulated that all enslaved and indentured people of color, regardless of their date of birth, would be free on July 4, 1827.

On July 11, 1799, the village resident and print shop owner Thomas Kirk, Alden's neighbor, commenced publication of the *Courier, and Long Island Advertiser*. It represented the precursor to a series of nineteenth-century newspapers dedicated to Brooklyn's news and beyond, including the *Long Island Courier*, the *Long Island Star*, *Brooklyn Evening Star*, and the *Brooklyn Daily Eagle*. The inaugural issue of the *Courier* stated, "The present improved and increasing state of the Town of BROOKLYN, and its situation with respect to the rest of LONG ISLAND" meant that a newspaper that would address the needs of its residents was long overdue. In some ways the *Courier* represents a fairly typical example of late eighteenth- and early nineteenth-century North American print culture in its dedication to news and stories from France, Philadelphia, and Long Island, with the interspersal of local advertisements. The first column of the new weekly newspaper stated its commitment to disseminating "intelligence" from the City of New York across Long Island (of which Brooklyn was interchangeably considered a part) and also to providing "accurate and impartial intelligence" on national and international affairs. But the newspaper also promised to pay particular attention to agricultural affairs, which was the backbone of Brooklyn's economy. Given the courting of its local reader—the Brooklyn farmer—it is telling that the only extant copy of the *Courier* is dated July 11, 1799, and it glaringly omits any mention of New York State's Gradual Emancipation Act, which went into effect a week before. It seems that emancipation was not a newsworthy topic for the local press, perhaps owing to the fact that Brooklynites were deeply reluctant to acknowledge slavery's demise, however slow.

Nowhere is this more evident than in the journals of the Kings County farmer John Baxter. Although born in Ireland in 1765, John was a long-term resident of rural Flatlands, and he meticulously recorded agricultural life in the late eighteenth and early nineteenth centuries. His journal entries written just prior to and during the gradual emancipation period demonstrate how deeply slavery had organized social relations in the county, the silence on its trauma, the ways in which enslaved people of African descent seized their freedom during this time, and the existence of a small but growing free Black community. He writes,

JUNE 30, 1790. A. Wyckoff purchased Harry a black and Bett his wife and Peg her Child from widow Lott for £180 I am afraid no Great Bargain.

JANUARY 27, 1791. France the Negro ran away again.

JANUARY 31, 1804. Sold Dion and her two male children for £100.

FEBRUARY 11, 1804. A town meeting concerning the free Black children.

APRIL 21, 1804. The town meeting for Free Blacks the money endue for keeping them I got 24 dollars at 2 Doll. for one month.

AUGUST 12, 1807. Abraham Wyckoff's negro ran off.

MARCH 31, 1812. Cold & freezing weather have load up 64 loads street manure for Barley. Hired my Negro to spread it being Easter yet.

MAY 11, 1815. My thoughts are about my Negro I have petitioned for his non Absconding.

MAY 17, 1815. This morning my negro was to come home. I am afraid he had run away and we can give no account for it.

MAY 19, 1815. My Negro Will ran away.

MAY 20, 1815. Went to Jacobus Voris Gravesend neck about my Negro no Satisfaction 4 negroes gone off at the Holy days.

MAY 22, 1815. Went to morning to New York and published my negro Will John Wyckoff Negro Harry in the Papers—Spectator and Star Reward 80 Dollars.

JUNE 10, 1815. Bought a Negro Jack from J. Mead how he will turn out time will tell.

JUNE 12, 1815. Negro Jack who is free at 21 years or 28 according to Law.

JUNE 26, 1824. Died last night, Jacob Boss, a noted free colored man and a member of the Gravesend Church on Coney Island.[17]

Counterintuitive to its name, New York's Act for the Gradual Emancipation of Slavery of 1799 did little to liberate enslaved people in reality or atrophy their sale or "recapture" in Kings County, nor did the later act of 1817. Rather, it emboldened slaveholders to use the full extent of the law to protect their "property." The *Long Island Star*, Brooklyn's long-running newspaper, frequently featured the sale of people of African descent during gradual emancipation. In 1812, before there was an absolute end date to slavery, an advertisement described a "stout able-bodied" man who "understands all kinds of farming business." The twenty-three-year-old "expresses a wish to be set free at a certain age, but will be sold for life."[18] Born in 1789, this young person had little chance of legal emancipation, as slavery had no end date in New York State for those born prior to 1799. After 1817, if he had survived slavery's traumatic existence, he might have been free on July 4, 1827, had he not already achieved freedom by running away, manumission, or self-purchase. In 1820, after slavery was given an end date, Dutch slaveholders still insisted that their fellow Brooklynites were property. On May 31, 1820, a female slaveholder, Jane Ditmas in Flatbush, "forbid" the "harbor, trust, or employ[ment] under penalty of the law" of Tean, a fifty-year-old Black woman who could speak both Dutch and English and her ten-year-old daughter (no name given).[19] In 1822, with only five years until absolute emancipation, Brooklynite Littelier Cambie, the owner of a public garden that offered "choice" wines and liquors, placed an unusual newspaper advertisement. Littelier labeled David Smith, an indentured twelve-year-old boy, a "great rogue" and was willing to offer the young boy's labor to anyone willing to take him.[20] Even as late as 1825, a certificate for the indenture of Sine, an eight-year-old girl, reveals her harrowing treatment. An indenture document normally required the terms of labor that the person would work for free to be clearly laid out—either as an amount of specific time or after completing a particular work assignment. It was also frequently ignored by slaveholders. Here, Sine was expected to work for Jacob Duryee of Flatbush from the ages of eight to ten, uncompensated. Presumably the short, two-year working period was a formal, legal acknowledgment of state emancipation in 1827. On July 4, 1827, Sine's indenture should have legally ended, according to law. But the law was only effective if Brooklynites upheld it. It is difficult to say whether Sine was eventually emancipated. Outer areas such as Flatbush, Flatlands, Gravesend, and New Utrecht remained deeply agricultural until well into the nineteenth century, and farmers here continued to rely on the unfree labor of Black children and adults, held illegally in bondage and indentured servitude beyond 1827.[21]

In the more developed village and town of Brooklyn, freedom and unfreedom still coexisted in its public spaces in a bundle of contradictions during gradual emancipation. Not all Brooklynites ignored its hypocrisy. On July 22, 1822, the *Long Island Star* published a writer's reflections on that year's Fourth of July celebration: "Can this be a land of liberty? Methinks I detect an inconsistency in the term. How many thousands there are throughout the United States of America, who dedicated yesterday to the commemoration of freedom, and yet hold their fellow creatures in slavery."[22] It is entirely possible that free Black women such as Elenor and Elizabeth Croger might have encountered Margaret, an enslaved woman and street crier who sold hot corn, during their daily travels through the village. Margaret was enslaved by Robert Debevoise, a wealthy landowner whose estate neighbored Hezekiah Beers Pierrepont's land (today's Brooklyn Heights), and profits from her labor one can assume went to Robert. One white Brooklynite recalled that Margaret was known to white Brooklynites as "Debevoise's black Peg," and she would cry, "Hot Corn, Nice Hot Corn, piping hot" at Old Ferry Road or Fulton Street. The writer continues, "and the large bell pears having attained nearly their full size, she stewed them whole until they were soft, and then poured Molasses over them while hot, and cries them through the street as 'Baked Pears' and very palatable they were as I well recollect;—but this cry has gone out of vogue, I have not heard it for years." This was seasonal work for Margaret, as corn was not available during summer ("we had to depend alone upon what was raised in Kings County").[23] Eventually, as Brooklyn's urban expansion continued and slavery ended in New York State, the city began to import its delicious corn instead from the slave economies in the US South and the Caribbean. It is difficult to say if Margaret ever saw compensation for her labor in her lifetime.

It took twenty-eight years for slavery to end in New York. Eighteen of those years had no end date for enslaved people born before 1799. And when an end date was finally given in 1817, it would take another decade of chaos and uncertainty until absolute emancipation. When Emancipation Day did arrive on July 4, 1827, free Black communities were not waiting for this moment to begin building self-determined communities. In spite of the horrors that gradual emancipation had fostered, Black Brooklynites had established strong grassroots institutions that would build political power, secure the community's survival, and create capacity for the community to be able to congregate in spaces that prioritized celebration, mobilization, and joy. Assistance, education, and faith became the pillars of their community, and freedom was theirs to define.

ASSISTANCE, EDUCATION, AND FAITH

In 1810, whitewashers and brothers Peter Croger and Benjamin Croger and Joseph Smith, who worked in the village as a sweep master, established the village's first mutual aid organization, called the Brooklyn African Woolman Benevolent Society.[24] Its name honored the New Jersey Quaker and itinerant preacher John Woolman (1720–1772), a white early anti-slavery advocate. The Brooklyn organization was formed just two years after free Black men in the city of New York in 1808 formed the New York African Society for Mutual Relief, which held similar objectives. The two mutual aid societies represented a vital local network of self-care and economic self-reliance by creating cultural and economic spaces that fostered close familial ties and kinship bonds. In the absence of insurance policies, they also protected and ensured that the family of a deceased member would not be forced into poverty and thereby "alleviate[d] [community] distresses" as long as members "compl[ied] with these articles [of behavior]."[25] Protecting each other from poverty was essential in the new republic. As the historian Gunja SenGupta writes, "the legacy of racial slavery rendered Black New Yorkers even more vulnerable than their white counterparts to the ravages of riot, disease, unemployment, and loss not only of family, but of freedom itself—leaving them in urgent need of relief."[26] Contemporaries often noted that Black New Yorkers were reluctant to seek outside help or assistance and instead preferred forms of mutual aid. However, many Black-led mutual aid societies in the early antebellum period had short histories and eventually dissolved due to financial difficulties or the high demands made of voluntary officers who were already stretched too thin. As the historian Craig S. Wilder notes, "as one dominant association fell, another rose to the center of Black public life." The Brooklyn African Woolman Benevolent Society enjoyed an unusual longevity in its ongoing presence in the village in this context.[27]

Establishing an institutional framework that could address the real material consequences of freedom was a remarkable feat against the chaos of gradual emancipation. While Brooklyn's free Black families organized, mobilized, and created ties with organizations such as the New York African Society for Mutual Relief, manumissions prior to 1817 occurred at a deliberately slow pace, especially compared to Manhattan's, and illegal slave sales continued in Kings County. On March 5, 1797, Ceasar Foster represented the first recorded manumission in Brooklyn. It is difficult to say why Quaker John Doughty, for whom the street in DUMBO is named, decided to manumit.[28] While evidence of anti-slavery activity in Brooklyn's early Quaker community is scant, it is possible that Doughty's decision to manumit was based on religious principle. The Quakers represented one of the earliest anti-slavery groups in Philadelphia and the New York region. And as early as 1767, Quaker residents northeast of Brooklyn in Flushing, Queens County, condemned slavery, and they demonstrated their commitment four years later by rejecting members from their religious circle who were unwilling to manumit.[29] Another group that intervened in Brooklyn's legal manumission cases was the Manhattan-based New-York Manumission Society (N-YMS), an early anti-slavery organization. The organization was formed in 1785 as a direct result of frustration with the second failed attempt to abolish slavery in New York State, and its founders included Governors George Clinton and John Jay, Alexander Hamilton, Mayor James Duane, and two wealthy Quaker businessmen, Robert Bowne and John Murray. Many of these members were also slaveholders. For example, John Jay held six bondspeople in the year of the organization's founding. The contradiction of an anti-slavery organization led by slaveholders was not lost on them, but as members of the wealthy elite, for which property was central to the understanding of freedom and independence in the early American republic, expediency prevailed.[30]

In Kings County, the N-YMS focused on manumissions and illegal slave sales, rather than racial egalitarianism. Although the federal Constitution prohibited the importation of enslaved people into the United States after January 1, 1808, in line with similar legislation enacted in Britain, the N-YMS was compelled to intervene in kidnapping cases. Enslaved people illegally purchased from Canada, the Caribbean, West Africa, and domestically from New Jersey and Virginia were brought to various areas of Long Island and then resold in regions where slavery was still legal. Sometimes, according to N-YMS records, the enslaved person remained in Brooklyn. For example, in 1809, Cornelia was brought to New York by George Bundell of the West Indies and sold to Mr. Coles in Brooklyn (Coles Street is named after this prominent landowning family). The N-YMS also intervened in failed manumissions, as was the case with Harry, who had been promised manumission, money, and an apprenticeship at the age of twenty-one upon the death of his original enslaver, Maria Magdelene Ruble. In 1809, when he was still enslaved at the approximate age of twenty-four, Harry enlisted the help of William Livingston, the surrogate of Kings County, who in turn wrote to the N-YMS to intercede. It is difficult to say whether Harry ever found freedom.[31] The N-YMS was, however, more successful in its work on behalf of Titus. In 1814, he approached the organization to assist with the emancipation of his family, which included his wife, Betsey, a teenage son, a five-year-old daughter, and a baby girl. The bill of sale indicates that they were purchased by the Reverend James

Thompson so he could manumit them. James was a Black Brooklynite who had moved to the neighboring county of Queens. The partnership of Titus and James gives us evidence of an early, informal, self-reliant anti-slavery network, as members of the Black community purchased each other with the clear intention of emancipation.[32]

Education was also vital to freedom—not only was it a basic need in a village that prided itself on its civility, but it also liberated students from the dominant racist discourses that surrounded them. In 1815, Peter Croger opened a private African school at his and Elenor's home. Located on James Street just west of where the neighborhood of DUMBO stands today (the street has long ceased to exist after the area was razed when construction on the Brooklyn Bridge began in 1870), the school offered day and evening classes to both adults and children in the "common branches of education." This was distinctly a secular school, entirely different from a Sunday school attached to the church and rooted in religious instruction (which formed the bulk of educational initiatives in Kings County).[33] The creation of Brooklyn's African school was also critically different from the way education efforts were funded in neighboring Manhattan. In Manhattan, or the City of New York, the white-led New-York Manumission Society, formed in 1785, had been responsible for the financing of the city's African schools. In the village of Brooklyn, it was an entirely Black-led grassroots endeavor, and this necessity soon became clear. In 1816, white trustees including the printer Alden Spooner formed the Village of Brooklyn, contained within the town of the same name, and as residents of James Street, Peter, Elenor, Benjamin, and Elizabeth lived at its most northern point. It had been a difficult year for Brooklynites, after an outbreak of smallpox in the winter of late 1815 and early 1816 resulted in mass deaths across Brooklyn and New York. In spite of these hardships, white trustees stated that the village's new incorporated status meant that the opening of a new district school should proceed. In 1816, Thomas Kirk opened a public school at his printing office on Main Street. If the villagers were excited about their new institution, Black Brooklynites had every right to be wary. Structural racism through educational segregation became ingrained in the village's growth. In a newspaper advertisement for the new district school, the white administrators explicitly stated that "no colored children would be received."[34]

The seamlessness of assistance, education, and faith culminated in the establishment of the African Methodist Episcopal (AME) church in the village in 1818. As the scholar Jasmine Nichole Cobb notes, as many of the Black-led benevolent organizations predated other key institutions in Black organizational life, they were often instrumental in the founding of independent Black churches in their towns and cities.[35] Creating spaces of safety and refuge that might protect the Black community from white supremacy was not new to Peter Croger. The historian Robert J. Swan suggests that Peter, the elder of the two brothers, was originally a member of John Street Methodist Church in Manhattan. Like many churches in the early republic, it was also a site of faith and racism. In 1796, Bishop James Varick led the exodus from John Street, and Black New Yorkers established the Mother African Methodist Episcopal Zion Church in Manhattan. It was this same Black radical tradition that Peter and Benjamin would build on in Brooklyn. Methodism was an old and respected faith in Kings County. In 1787, Woolman Hickson preached his first sermon in the open air in an area overlooking the East River that would eventually become Sands Street. In 1794, residents established the First Methodist Church of Brooklyn, or Sands Street Methodist. It was one of only three churches in the town of Brooklyn for much of the late eighteenth and turn of the nineteenth centuries, and it is believed that its church congregants included Indigenous people and people of European and African descent. But protest took root at the church when Black people renounced their membership after being forced to listen to the proslavery views of the church's Irish pastor, Alexander M'Caine.

The departure of Brooklyn's Black community from Sands Street Methodist, where Thomas Kirk of the *Long Island Star* acted as a class elder and trustee from 1807, coincided with other major religious reforms elsewhere. In Philadelphia, Richard Allen formed the independent African Methodist Episcopal denomination in 1816, the same year that Brooklyn became a village.[36] Just one year later, in 1817, Benjamin and Elizabeth welcomed the birth of their daughter Eliza, and community building continued as Peter and Benjamin Croger came together with their neighbors to discuss fundraising for an AME Church building in the village. Presumably Elenor and Elizabeth Croger fundraised alongside them, though their activism has not been preserved in the archives. Their discussions for a new church took place in the same year that New York State established an end date for slavery and Brooklyn saw the largest number of manumissions in one single year—a total of thirteen, most likely an undercount—presumably as slaveholders looked for quick compensation.[37] While the congregation waited for a pastor from Philadelphia, Richard Allen ordained several of the founders, including Peter and Benjamin, who served as preachers and class leaders, while their neighbors Caesar Springfield, John Corson, Michael Thompson, and Charles Ash served as trustees. This proved necessary, as four years later, the Brooklyn AME Church was still without a resident clergyman, though one was expected shortly.[38]

There were few new public buildings erected in the village in 1818. But on February 7, Brooklyn's free Black community opened the AME Church on High Street near Bridge Street.[39] Although the church was quaint by today's standards, its location was in a bustling part of the village. Along High Street itself was a grocery store belonging to Isaac Moser, a member and officer at Sands Street Church. Beyond Isaac's store were vacant lots that continued until High Street met Fulton and Washington Streets. At this intersection, a continuous poplar grove stood near three to four houses, and then you would encounter a handful of more houses as you headed south. Jacob Titus spoke at the church's opening to members of the African Woolman Benevolent Society about the state of the village: "prejudice, that monster that now stalks about our streets and looks contemptuously upon our unfortunate race, shall ere long hide its head—shall blush at its own deformity, and no longer shed on the mind its wizard darkness." He went on to remind the audience of the country's democratic and spiritual founding ideals: "that men are created equal—that the whole human race are but so many

Eugene L. Armbruster, *Bridge Street African Methodist Church*, 1923, black and white photograph. (V1974.1.1342, Eugene L. Armbruster Photographs and Scrapbooks, Center for Brooklyn History, Brooklyn Public Library)

Façade of what was Bridge Street AWME Church, now part of New York University, 2023. (Author photo)

members of the great family—and that however diversified by mental talents of the gift of fortune, man is every where the brother of men, and the equal object of divine and human beneficence and regard."[40]

The first time the African Woolman Benevolent Society appears in print is in 1819, just one year after the establishment of the village's AME Church and nine years after its own founding. The organization paid seventy-five cents (around fourteen dollars today) for its notice to be included in the *Long Island Star*. It was not an insignificant amount of money, given that the average working wages for a Black man totaled approximately $250 per year, or $21 per month. The newspaper notice appeared on December 28, 1819, and was sandwiched between an advertisement for vendor contract bids for the Brooklyn Navy Yard, founded in 1801 in Wallabout Bay, and a local business advertising the sale of a large assortment of single- and double-barrel guns. But it stood out partly because of the large font size in the advertisement header.

BROOKLYN AFRICAN WOOLMAN BENEVOLENT SOCIETY

The Anniversary of this Society will be celebrated on Saturday next, being New Years day. The members are invited to attend at Mrs Benton's Inn, corner of Fulton and Middagh-streets, at 10 o' clock am, where a procession will be formed and move through some of the principal streets to the African Church at which place an oration and other exercises are expected. The *New-York African Wilberforce Society* will join the procession.
—Peter Croger, president of the Brooklyn African Woolman Benevolent Society, *Long Island Star*, December 28, 1819

As part of the organization's anniversary celebration, its officers and members intended to proudly, and publicly, march from Fulton Street through the center of the village to the AME Church on New Year's Day, 1820. Trustees of the village had embarked on an ambitious street improvement project at the beginning of 1819, in which streets and roadways had been systematically surveyed and mapped, gravel added to throughfares, and sidewalks installed along Fulton.[41] By fall, only Fulton and Main Streets north of Sands Street were paved, accompanied by "narrow imperfect sidewalks" and no street lighting.[42] But the society's procession was not intended to show off the village's streets. It held much wider political significance as part of a growing protest tradition in the North. The decision to print the route, which would take place along the village's main streets—Fulton, Main, Sands, and Front—in the local newspaper was a bold one. In neighboring Manhattan, both the New York African Society for Mutual Relief and the New York African Wilberforce Society began marching through the city's streets to mark the abolition of the slave trade in 1808. In Boston, Black men marched annually from 1808 until the 1820s through the city's streets, and the procession usually ended at the African Meeting House. In Brooklyn, the village's free Black community established and continued a radical tradition that confirmed to their neighbors that they were Brooklynites in equal measure and that they were here to stay. The public formation of spectacle and politics by people of color was antithetical to the legacy of New York's colonial slave laws, which had forbidden Black people from gathering in groups larger than three, other than for the few hours of freedom afforded them on Election Day and the annual Pinkster festival in June.

Beginning in 1810 and in the decade that followed, Brooklyn's free Black community created three independent organizations—a mutual aid society, a school, and a church—that were highly visible throughout their village. They did so even though gradual emancipation created no capacity for what freedom coupled with equality might look like. From 1817 to 1824, even as manumission rates accelerated in Kings County, there still remained a significant number of Black Brooklynites serving indentured terms, in an oppressive labor system.[43] The ability of Black Brooklynites to build and sustain community was therefore remarkable. Brooklyn's AME Church and the independent Black churches that followed in the antebellum period—Concord Baptist, Siloam Presbyterian, Berean Baptist, and Bethel AME—to name just a few, were central to the lives of ordinary people. The churches were not only places of worship but also served as spaces for educational initiatives, political protests, and temperance meetings and assisted new fugitives arriving in Brooklyn. Peter's AME Church that his neighbor Titus spoke at and from which free Black Brooklynites would lead their annual procession has since been renamed Bridge Street AWME. Long relocated from its former land-marked edifice in downtown Brooklyn, today it stands in rapidly gentrify-ing Bedford-Stuyvesant and holds the distinction of remaining the oldest Black church in Brooklyn, still active in matters of faith and politics.[44]

* * *

History embraces origin stories, even when they are sometimes riddled with mistruths. In 1855, James McCune Smith, a Manhattan-based abolitionist, physician, and writer publishing under the pseudonym "Communipaw" for *Frederick Douglass' Paper*, tackled the issue of the history of abolitionism, or the fight to end slavery, in the United States. He wrote,

> The statement of the organ of the American Anti-Slavery Society, "that the colored people have ever kept aloof from the Anti-Slavery movement," would help solve the question, if it were a true state-ment; but it is not. For there was a time when the colored people were identified with that movement—say, they almost began the present movement; they certainly antedated many of its principals. In 1810, while New York was still a slave State, a long array of col-ored men marched through this city, in open day, bearing a banner inscribed with the portrait of a colored man, and the words "Am I not a Man and a Brother."[45]

Originally designed in England as a seal by the Society for the Abolition of the Slave Trade and mass-produced by Josiah Wedgwood in the late eighteenth century, "Am I Not a Man and a Brother" features a kneeling Black man wearing chains and pleading that his audience recognize his humanity. With the man stripped of agency and the image being highly sentimental in its rendering, it nevertheless became ubiquitous in the British abolition movement and was ultimately recycled by American abolitionists. But let us return to the heart of James McCune Smith's argument and his origin story of the abolition movement. Collective memory can sometimes erase historical truths. Today, abolitionism has its familiar faces—William Lloyd Garrison, Frederick Douglass, and sometimes mistakenly even Abraham Lincoln. But as scholars have long shown, the abolition movement that demanded the immediate end to slavery and brought together Black and white political activists toward common purpose for the first time in US history was actually built on decades of Black activism led by ordinary men and women.[46] Across Boston, Philadelphia, New York, and Brooklyn, free Black communities and their unwavering belief in self-reliance and self-determination resulted in the growth of independent churches, schools, and mutual aid organizations. They worked across multiple platforms to secure a foundation on which they could live their lives with dignity and respect. These accomplishments were not without struggle. Many white Americans could not imagine their Black neighbors as equal citizens. Racism and racial violence were widespread in the early republic, and Brooklyn was no exception. But unlike Boston's African Meeting House or Manhattan's African Free Schools, white philanthropy did not play a role in Brooklyn's early Black activism and institution building.[47] It was an entirely independent Black-led movement. Amid the chaos during gradual emancipation, the Crogers and their neighbors, despite their own oppression, strengthened their faith and commitment to equality as they prepared for July 4, 1827, or Emancipation Day.

"THE TIME HAS NOW ARRIVED"

BROOKLYN, 1827

SLAVERY officially ended in New York State—and by extension
Brooklyn and New York—on July 4, 1827. Black New Yorkers and
Brooklynites deliberately chose to celebrate the next day. They did so
to prioritize their own safety—especially given the daily threat of racial
violence in their lives—and to critique the country's own celebratory
discourse. The Fourth of July did not signify freedom for all Americans,
as the Declaration of Independence would have one believe, as long as
slavery continued to exist in the US South. But July 5 in New York was
a day of celebration and joy, and crowds gathered along Manhattan's
Broadway. The doctor and abolitionist James McCune Smith, whose
later insistence on abolitionism's real history we read about in chapter 1,
was just fourteen years old on that day. He fondly recalled, "That was a
celebration! A real, full-souled, shouting for joy, and marching through
the crowded streets, with feet jubilant to songs of freedom!"[1] By this
date, there were very few enslaved people waiting to be emancipated
in Manhattan. A variety of factors had resulted in white New Yorkers
acting earlier on the knowledge that enslaved labor neither made economic sense nor was sustainable. This was not the case in Kings County,
where freedom and unfreedom messily coexisted. There were still 879
enslaved people living in Kings County in 1820 (more than likely an

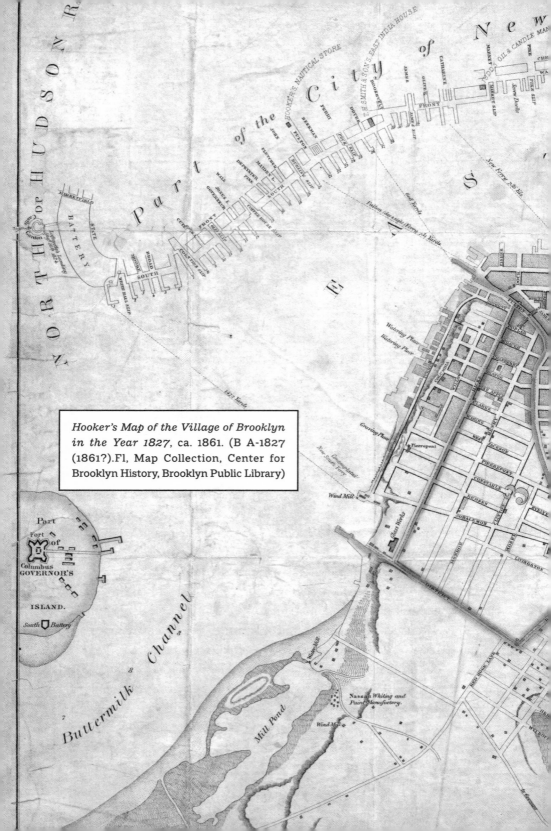

Hooker's Map of the Village of Brooklyn in the Year 1827, ca. 1861. (B A-1827 (1861?).Fl, Map Collection, Center for Brooklyn History, Brooklyn Public Library)

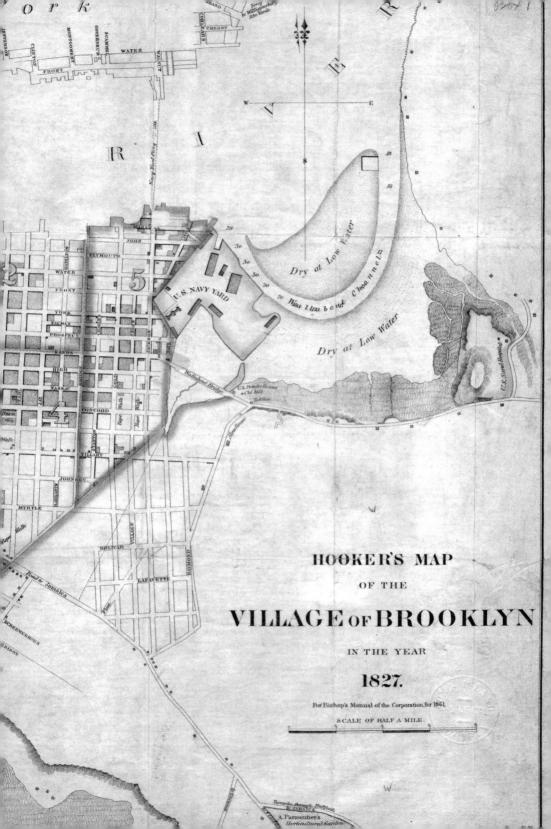

HOOKER'S MAP

OF THE

VILLAGE OF BROOKLYN

IN THE YEAR

1827.

For Bishop's Manual of the Corporation, for 1861.

SCALE OF HALF A MILE.

undercount), so state emancipation should have had a profound impact on their lives, especially for those living in the outer agriculturally dominated areas such as Flatlands, Gravesend, and New Utrecht.[2] Yet, for free Black women and men like Elenor, Elizabeth, Benjamin, and Peter Croger, emancipation would have had little economic impact on their labor or social mobility. Far from it: slavery's demise in Kings County merely confirmed that with freedom did not come equality. Free Black Brooklynites continued to face injustice in areas such as education, voting, and the labor market—while the constant threat of kidnapping to slavery in the South loomed large. Still, Brooklyn celebrated Emancipation Day one week after New York's festivities. Mutual aid organizations from Brooklyn and Manhattan gathered to celebrate and formed a "long and handsome" procession, accompanied by banners and several bands, that culminated in a dinner provided by the oyster merchant Thomas Downing, followed by prayer and an address at the AME Church on High Street. The white-owned *Long Island Star* reflected on the day's festivities, emphasizing the procession's sense of taste and respectability. The article urged its local readers that members of Brooklyn's free Black community were "deserving of much encouragement from their white brethren."[3] In other words, neighborliness was intimately tied to policing Black behavior and ensuring that residents of color acted with decorum.

By this time, however, Northern free Black communities already had a newspaper that addressed their needs. Just three months before New York's Emancipation Day, *Freedom's Journal* commenced publication in Manhattan with the powerful opening, "too long have others spoken for us."[4] Its editors, the Presbyterian minister Samuel Cornish and the journalist John Russwurm, created a print manifesto that reflected the struggles and triumphs of its readership. Its pages were dedicated to the discussion of building Black businesses, community, education, and organizations and mobilizing the right to vote and citizenship, while tackling the legacy of slavery and its impact on the community's material conditions.[5] The newspaper's Long Island (and therefore Brooklyn) agent knew firsthand the importance of citizenship in ensuring full participation in a Western democracy. In 1804, the Calcutta-born, Manhattan-based George DeGrasse appeared before the Court of Common Pleas in New York stating his claim to US citizenship. He was one of the few men of color to be granted it. In the absence of the Fifteenth Amendment, which guaranteed citizenship to anyone born on US soil (which would be ratified in 1868), communities of color were generally excluded from being thought of as citizens, and their loyalties were frequently tested.[6]

Black Brooklynites like Peter Croger also tangibly articulated the right to citizenship through the creation of a mutual aid organization, school, and church. On September 25, 1827, less than three months after state emancipation, the village's African school moved from Peter and Elenor's home on the northern end of the village at James Street and opened at African Hall, a small frame building on Nassau between Bridge and Jay Streets, "under the immediate direction of the African Woolman Benevolent Society." The relocation, intentionally designed to accommodate an increase in students, demonstrated the ways in which Black Brooklynites were ready for the realities of post-emancipation in the village. Henry C. Thompson, a future land investor in Weeksville, served both as president of the mutual aid organization and as a trustee of the school.[7] In spite of the school's more central location, the village was no more tolerant of Black life post-emancipation than it had been in previous years. In 1829, less than half a mile from the Crogers' homes, Christian Brown's print shop on Water Street released the broadside "Brooklyn Boblashun!," part of a long racist print tradition in the early republic that had begun in Boston and quickly gained currency in Philadelphia, New York, and even London. "Brooklyn Boblashun!," supposedly written by a "Long Island Niger," contained all the racist characteristic features of the "Bobalition" print: caricatures of Black identity, with a wood engraving of a Black dandy, a mockery of emancipation, and the belittling of the literacy of Black people. The broadside offered a glimpse into how white Brooklynites regarded the freedom of their fellow residents. They cast that freedom as being utterly meaningless and derided the kind of public roles Peter and Benjamin and their neighbors had created in the village.[8] It is difficult to say when and where the broadside was displayed in the village, but given its dimensions of twelve by seventeen inches, this was a publication intended to be easily hung in the windows of businesses and other public spaces. And it is almost certain given the intimacy of Brooklyn's streets, the proximity of the Crogers' homes to the print shop, and the village's relatively small population of 12,400 people in 1830 that Black Brooklynites would have encountered the racist broadside in the public spaces of their village.

The "Bobalition" print was just one visual manifestation of a larger anti-Black sentiment that was prevalent in the early nineteenth-century United States. The American Colonization Society, founded in 1816, sought to undo decades of community building that free Black communities had struggled to establish. Supporters of the colonization movement, mostly landed white men in positions of influence, did not see African Americans as fellow Americans and argued that that United States would never rid itself of racism and slavery as long as Black people remained here. "What shall we do with the free people of color? What can we do for their happiness consistently with our own?" asked Robert Finley, the organization's founder, in *Thoughts on Colonization of Free Blacks*.[9] The solution was ultimately to rid the United States of people of African descent. Members fundraised through the parent organization of the American Colonization Society, as well as through local auxiliaries, including one in Brooklyn. Adrian Van Sinderen, president of the Brooklyn Savings Bank—one of the earliest financial institutions in the town—also served as president of the local chapter of the American Colonization Society. Adrian and fellow white Brooklynites frequently fundraised to support deportation schemes to the colony of Monrovia on the west coast of Africa. With free Black communities removed from the US, the society's plans concurrently strengthened slaveholding interests in the country. In spite of Adrian's relatively substantial power in the village, free Black men stood up and protested the colonization movement and Adrian's organizing. These free Black men in Brooklyn were part of a national movement that had seen waves of Black people mount anti-colonization protests as early as 1817 in the city of Philadelphia and in which the Black press, like *Freedom's Journal*, frequently published anti-colonization articles and the names of officials belonging to the American Colonization Society.

Two years after the publication of "Brooklyn Boblashun!," Peter and Benjamin Croger, Henry C. Thompson, and their neighbors led Brooklyn's anti-colonization protest, declaring their right to stay on US soil. On June 3, 1831, activists gathered at the African Hall, where Henry chaired the meeting, and George Hogarth, an educator at the African school as well as a pastor at the AME Church, served as secretary. Their address was reprinted in the *Long Island Star*, by now the largest circulating newspaper in Brooklyn. They stated,

> The colored citizens of this village have, with friendly feelings, taken into consideration the objects of the American Colonization Society, together with all of its auxiliary movements, preparatory for our removal to the coast of Africa; and we view them as wholly gratuitous, not called for by us, and not essential to the real welfare of our race. That we know of no other country that we can justly claim, or demand our rights as citizens, whether civil or political, but in the United States of America, our native soil. And, that we shall be active in our endeavors to convince the members of the Colonization Society, and the public generally, that we are *men*, that we are *brethren*, that we are *countrymen* and *fellow-citizens*; and demand an equal share of protection from our Federal Government with any other class of citizens in the community.[10]

Among the many activists who spoke that night was a new arrival to Brooklyn named James W. C. Pennington. He proclaimed, "Brethren, it is time for us to awake to our interests, for the colonization society is straining every nerve for the accomplishment of its objects. They have got the consent of eleven states, who have instructed their senators to do something in the next congress for our removal. Maryland calls imperatively on the general government to send us away, or else they will colonize their own free blacks."[11] James Pennington's life could not have been more different from those of Benjamin and Peter Croger, George Hogarth, or Henry C. Thompson. Just four years earlier, as New York celebrated state emancipation in 1827, an enslaved James prepared to flee Maryland, leaving his family members behind. Quakers initially offered him assistance in Pennsylvania, but by 1829, he ultimately ended up in the free Black community of Newtown, Long Island (today's neighborhood of Elmhurst, Queens), and worked as a coachman for Adrian Van Sinderen in Brooklyn.

That night in 1831, Brooklyn's anti-slavery activists echoed the rhetoric set out by the Boston activist David Walker in his *Appeal* and boldly announced their right to be seen in public life.[12] They pioneered a form of anti-slavery activism that demanded the right to the city and the ability to occupy the same public spaces and streets as white Brooklynites. And in choosing to publish their protest in the local newspaper, they redefined their labor as community builders and citizens. Before the anti-colonization protest, New York State had formally granted the African Woolman Benevolent Society its articles of incorporation on January 28, 1831. The organization was officially part of Brooklyn's social reform movement, which also included sweeping contemporary changes in education, temperance, and religion, which meant attaining spiritual perfection. The Brooklyn anti-colonization protest in June received support from activists in Middletown, Connecticut, who confirmed, "Our brethren in Brooklyn, N.Y. . . . breathe our sentiments in full, . . . and may our voices cheerfully accord with them in protesting against leaving this our native soil."[13]

Later that summer, Robert Gurley, an American Colonization Society secretary for over fifty years, made two visits to Brooklyn to convince local residents of the need to deport the village's free Black community. At the first meeting, Robert spoke to an initial audience of four to five hundred "respectable Afric-Americans in the gallery of the Presbyterian Church," which then dwindled to fifty, despite the speaker urging them to stay. Less than a week later, on July 2, 1831, an undeterred Robert returned to Brooklyn. On this occasion, he spoke to a sparse audience consisting of just one Brooklynite and "two strangers from

Canada." Trustees of the AME Church declined Robert's offer to speak at their venue.[14] The village was emerging as part of a sophisticated Northern anti-slavery space rooted in, and integral to, Brooklyn's own steady growth. Daily improvements could be seen in the town's infrastructure: "new avenues and streets, nearly all of which were regulated and paved, sprang into existence with the suddenness of magic."[15] A new Apprentices' Library, the first free library in Brooklyn, "forming a repository of books, maps, pictures, drawing apparatus, models of machinery, tools and implements, all collected for enlarging knowledge in literature, science and art, and thereby improving the condition of mechanics, manufacturers, artisans and others," stood at the corner of Henry and Cranberry Streets.[16] And a public garden, safe for Black people in the village to engage in simple leisure activities, opened at 116 Front Street at the corner of Jay Street. Edward Haines's mead garden offered the village's residents refreshments and a place to pass the time. Black Brooklynites demanded the right to public space and the freedom to engage one another in those spaces. As the historian Leslie M. Harris notes, "Black entrepreneurs opened pleasure gardens, outdoor cafes where patrons could socialize, drink cool drinks, and eat ice creams," and these places proved especially popular and sought after by residents in the summer months, when they were unable to escape the hot and humid city.[17]

In the fall of 1831, ordinary people took time out from their everyday lives and traveled long distances to advocate and organize for justice. Black Brooklynites joined delegates from all over the North for the first national Black convention, held in Philadelphia in 1831. It signaled the beginning of an ambitious reform movement led by African Americans, among them a number of Brooklynites. James Pennington attended as the Long Island delegate to the inaugural Black convention, and in the following year, the temperance advocate Jacob Deyes, the African school trustee Henry C. Thompson, and the AME Church leader Willis Jones led the Brooklyn auxiliary of the Society for the Improvement of Free People of Color, created as a direct result of the convention. The Black national conventions convened a total of twelve times until 1864 and brought together like-minded activists committed to creating an anti-slavery movement that also combated racial injustice in their own towns and cities. The Black national convention movement had a profound effect on a young printer named William Lloyd Garrison, who eventually became one of the more familiar faces of the radical abolitionist movement. In the 1820s, William, along with other white abolitionists such as Lewis Tappan and Gerrit Smith, believed that slavery was morally reprehensible but also saw a potentially positive outcome in colonization schemes. In 1831, William attended the Black national convention, and the following year, he published *Thoughts on African Colonization*, which showed his newfound disagreement with the colonization movement. William printed the resolutions of Black-led anti-colonization protests, including the Brooklyn protest that had been held just three years prior to his publication. Black activism in public life and print was transformational for William, who declared that of "the whole number of subscribers to the [anti-slavery newspaper] *The Liberator*, only about one-fourth are white. The paper, then, belongs emphatically to the people of color—it is their organ."[18] George Hogarth, secretary at the village's anti-colonization meeting in 1831, served as *The Liberator's* Brooklyn agent. On April 28, 1833, George organized a meeting in Brooklyn to support William Lloyd Garrison's trip to England. The meeting ended with a resolution that would be echoed at the Black conventions: "that we consider the education of our children as one of the most important obligations laid upon us by the moral Governor of the universe, and that it is one of the most efficient means whereby we may effectually emerge out of the state of moral degradation in which we have lain for ages."[19]

Delegates from the village continued to attend each year's Black national convention, including in 1832, despite a cholera pandemic that devastated both Brooklyn and New York that year. Glimpses of hope finally appeared that summer when, as the Brooklyn resident Gabriel Furman observed, he had seen more swallows in one day than in the preceding months, a sign perhaps that the pandemic was on its way out. Birds, he noted, had been all but absent during the height of the pandemic. There was now also an abundance of fruits, grains, potatoes, and vegetables—and for the first time a bounty of peas—growing in the village's soil. That year's hot and humid summer had also brought its own ecology, as Brooklynites could see spiders, mosquitoes, flies, black ants, flying gnats, worms in trees, grasshoppers—again another positive sign, Gabriel believed, that Brooklyn was in a post-pandemic era (as long as residents did not drink cold water even in the unbearable heat, which the village's coroner declared was the cause of the sudden death of several Brooklynites).[20]

James Pennington later recalled that upon his return to Brooklyn from the Black Convention in Philadelphia in 1831, he visited Adrian Van Sinderen's home and the following exchange took place:

A short time afterward, on entering his library, one day [Adrian] . . . carefully drew from his bookcase, the copy of the old *Long Island Star*, containing the addresses and proceedings, and said to me seating himself again in his chair, "James I want you to explain to me your sentiments."

He then questioned, to know, whether my convention sanctioned the positions taken in the documents, giving as a reason that "there is to be today a meeting of the managers of the Brooklyn Colonization Society, and I have been thinking, that if the colored people for whose benefit we intend this society, do not approve it, we had better disband."[21]

Certainly, this is one version of events. But records show that the Brooklyn auxiliary of the American Colonization Society did not disband. By 1834, Adrian Van Sinderen was still the president of the local organization, and members raised over $200 for local operations. That same year, the Black national convention came to New York, across the East River from Brooklyn, and recorded the largest number of Brooklyn delegates in its organizational history. Attendees included residents Abraham Brown, Henry Brown, George Hogarth, James W. C. Pennington, Henry C. Thompson, and Thomas S. Thompson. Black women such as Elenor and Elizabeth Croger might not have been listed in the convention meeting minutes, but it is equally important that we acknowledge their labor. It is entirely likely that sisters-in-law Elenor and Elizabeth Croger were creating space for organizing during this time. The scholar P. Gabrielle Foreman invites us to pay attention to the presence of Black women in these spaces, even with their absence in the archives. We may never know whom these women invited into their homes, what informal spaces they fostered for radical activism, or how the labor of their brothers, husbands, sons, and fathers built on, and in some ways deliberately obscured, the organizing that Black women were also concurrently doing. But it is part of the historian's craft that we recognize the limits of the written archives in the telling of Black women's lives, rather than reforget these women because they do not exist in the traditional archives and thereby undertell their stories altogether.[22]

* * *

In 1834, the same year the Black national convention came to New York, Brooklyn received its city charter. Still, it was an infant city and was not necessarily sympathetic to a radical vision of itself. But the land contained economic, spiritual, and political potential to be imagined anew. It was in this climate that two brothers and free Black men—Willis and William Hodges—arrived in the neighboring village of Williamsburg, while those who had lived in the village of Brooklyn sowed the seeds for Weeksville, an intentional and independent free Black community that would become the second largest in the United States in the pre–Civil War period.

PART II

THE EXPANDING

CITY

1830s–1840s

VILLAGE TO CITY

ANNEXING WILLIAMSBURG(H)

PECK SLIP FERRY. When this ferry came into the hands of
the present Lessees, it was general hoped . . . to persons doing
business in the city of New-York, that not a few New Yorkers
would find it for their advantage to take up their residence in
Williamsburgh; thus advancing the growth and prosperity of
the village.
   —Williamsburgh Gazette and Long-Island
     Advertiser, December 26, 1838

South 8th street has many good brick and wooden buildings,
occupied by private families. The location of these two (9th
and 8th) streets is good. Their commanding situation enables
inhabitants to overlook, from almost all points, the Navy Yard,
Brooklyn, East River, and the city of New York. . . . I would
observe respecting them, that there cannot be found in any city,
or in the neighborhood of any city, so eligible a situation for
residences. It is as near to Wall street as Union place, or that
neighborhood, and the only difference of communication is
steamboat or omnibus; and here gentlemen might locate, with
ground sufficient for a handsome garden, without being con-
fined to 25 by 100 feet, in a moving, dirty city.
—Williamsburgh Gazette and Long-Island Advertiser, July 31, 1839

When in name it was but a village, in extent it was but a mile
square, and in population numbered but a few thousands, when
its streets were ill regulated if regulated at all—neither paved
nor lighted, no side walks, no market, no watch, a police without system, and almost inefficient, a something intended as a
fire department in the shape of a superannuated engine, two
or three hooks and a few ladders, and a government without
the power or the will to strictly enforce its ordinances. At this
period (and many will remember it) everyone having business
to lead him away from his home after night-fall, carried his

own Lanthern; and they will as well remember the mud and mire which at times rendered the streets almost impassable; and calling to mind the state of morals at that time too prevalent, . . . that was the condition of our delightful home about the year 1822.

And now from these small beginnings what have we become? . . . What are we now? Our city covers 12 square miles, and it has upwards of 30,000 inhabitants. We have of streets regulated, paved and lighted, in amount not less than 35 miles, and among them may be found some of the most splendid avenues in the world.

Brooklyn is a most lovely city. In the whole world there is perhaps none which (every thing considered) can equal, certainly not surpass it. . . . *Ours is indeed a city remarkable for its peacefulness and sobriety, and above all others as being the home of beauty—the centre of riches, and seat of health.*
—*Long Island Star*, September 16, 1839

BY 1834, the village of Brooklyn's urban transformation was complete. On April 8, Brooklyn received its city charter, despite neighboring New York's opposition. It was now the City of Brooklyn. The city's population had quadrupled in four decades, and twenty thousand residents now called it home (still dwarfed by Manhattan and its two hundred thousand residents). The city's map was carved up into nine numeral designations or wards, each represented by an alderman. Those officials, in turn, elected Brooklyn's first mayor, George Hall, the son of Irish immigrants. A frenzied pace of development ensued, and Brooklynites witnessed frequent street openings, the announcement of new banks, schools, and churches, the introduction of horse-drawn omnibuses to its streets, and the rise or partial construction of hundreds of residential and commercial buildings, frame and brick, respectively, and twenty-seven shops, or factories. But Brooklyn did not just focus on meeting the needs of the living. Two years before it would become a city, Brooklyn proposed a cemetery on a former Battle of Brooklyn site, near the Gowanus Bay. It was completed sixteen years later and

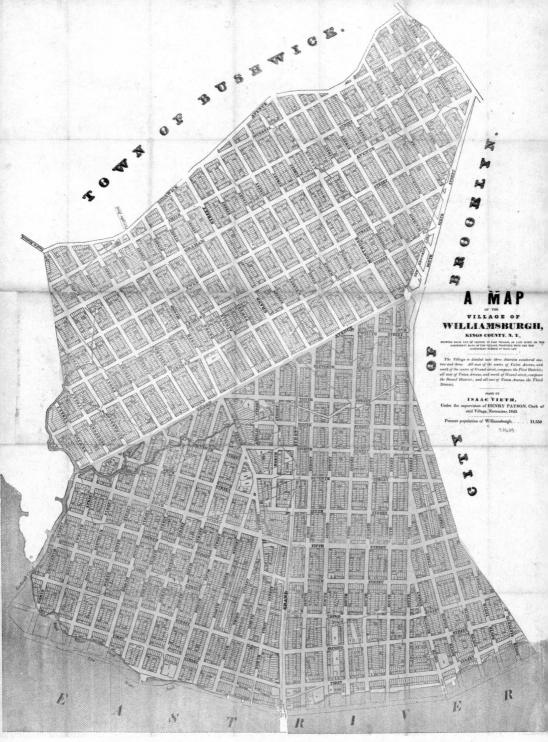

Isaac Vieth, *Map of the Village of Williamsburgh, Kings County, N.Y.*, 1854. (B
A-[1845].Fl, Map Collection, Center for Brooklyn History, Brooklyn Public Library)

named Green-Wood Cemetery. Across Kings County, public and private land was systematically surveyed, divided, and sold to investors at auction—and it was that land speculation that fueled much of the recently incorporated city's urban growth.

Speculation itself was not new to Brooklyn's colonized land, but the phenomenal rate at which it occurred from the 1830s onward certainly was. In 1804, the merchant and New England transplant Hezekiah Pierrepont bought sixty-acres of farmland from the former brewer Robert Benson in what was then Clover Hill. A decade later, with Hezekiah's financial backing, his friend Robert Fulton established the first steam-powered ferry between Brooklyn and New York. By 1817, Hezekiah had bought two other large tracts of farmland, one from the slaveholder Robert De Bevoise in the town's north and another from the slaveholder Joris Remsen in the town's south. While Hezekiah's home stood at what we know today as Pierrepont and Montague Streets, he now owned the land that stretched eight hundred feet along the East River, bounded by Old Fulton Street in the north and Remsen Street in the south.[1] By 1823, this land speculator had subdivided the land into private lots and began selling the parcels to like-minded investors—that is, white bankers and merchants working in Manhattan and looking for more residential space in Brooklyn. This development became Brooklyn Heights, the first modern commuter suburb in the country and today a landmarked historic district.[2] What was once bluffs and a hilly terrain has been replaced by a promenade that continues to offer stunning views of Manhattan, while the cacophony of the BQE accompanies it below. Pierrepont Street still runs east-west, but the narrow sandy road and beach that once ran parallel to the East River, from Joralemon Street to Fulton Street, was replaced by an industrial waterfront that began in the mid-nineteenth century, was then abandoned in the mid- to late twentieth century, and has since been revitalized by a modern urban waterfront park known as Brooklyn Bridge Park.[3]

Just three months after receiving the city charter, the infant city of Brooklyn would receive its first moral and ethical test. In July 1834, mobs of white New Yorkers rampaged through the streets of lower

Manhattan attacking any person or institution they deemed to be tied to radical abolitionism, and the riot eventually descended into a widespread racial assault on ordinary Black New Yorkers. Brooklyn acted as refuge to scores of Black and white New Yorkers escaping the anti-Black or anti-abolition riots in Manhattan. "The New York papers of this morning, give an account of riots and disorders last evening, very disgraceful to the character of the city," the *Long Island Star* reported the next day. It continued, "whatever may be the right in the relative causes of Colonization and Abolition, we are compelled to say that the modes taken by many of the advocates of the former to drive their opponent from the field, is disgraceful to a free country!"[4] The newspaper echoed the sentiments of the city's mayor, George Hall, who was equally keen to frame this as an entirely New York City affair. Less concerned with racial harmony and the safety of the city's own Black residents, Brooklyn's mayor saw this as chance to emphasize the civility and law and order of the city of Brooklyn. It was a convenient characterization but nevertheless a mistruth that would be used again three decades later when the Draft Riots, the worst urban riots in US history, ripped through New York's streets and white Brooklynites deliberately ignored the racial tensions that had been brewing in their own city from the summer before. Still, George Hall was determined, along with the city's Common Council, to keep building and to frame the city as the antidote to the chaos and stress of New York.

George Hall had made significant progress in his short mayoral tenure (he served for only one year), making sure Brooklyn moved beyond its growing reputation as a commuter suburb. The city's infrastructure now included two banks, two insurance companies, fifteen churches, and three public schools. The mayor ensured that hogs were cleared from the streets, and as a temperance advocate, he closed unlicensed liquor stores. In 1835, the city purchased land on the corner of Fulton and Joralemon Streets and proposed a grand City Hall (today's Borough Hall), which opened, partially completed, thirteen years later. Brooklyn was on the rise, as its skyline stretched upward. In 1836, the city's street committee reported that in the preceding twelve months alone, construction had consisted of 321 houses, plus outhouses, and churches, of which thirty-one were one-story frame dwellings, five one-story brick, seventy-eight two-story frame dwellings, twenty-five two-story brick, twenty-five three-story frame dwellings, three three-story brick, and forty-three four-story brick dwellings.[5] The speed and volume of new construction altered the city of Brooklyn's skyline, even as it was still dwarfed by the city of New York's. This rapid pace was also accompanied by an equally rapid population increase, as Brooklyn ballooned from 7,175 residents in 1820 to 12,406 by 1830 and 36,233 by 1840, more than a fivefold increase in just two decades. This was unparalleled in other major US cities. Between 1790 and 1840, Brooklyn's population grew 700 percent, whereas the city of New York's grew 325 percent; Philadelphia, 270 percent; Boston, approximately 150 percent; New Orleans, 600 percent; and Albany, 350 percent.[6] By 1840, land speculation and rampant real estate development resulted in a dramatically different-looking Brooklyn from the one Francis Guy had captured on a winter's day in 1820, even as Kings County from Gowanus all the way south to where the land met the Atlantic Ocean remained largely rural.

Although the village of Williamsburgh was comparatively late to urban development, it still mirrored several elements of Brooklyn's growth until its own annexation to the city in 1855 (when it dropped the *h*). From 1800, developers, speculators, and later the village council created a ferry service, dug wells, opened and then improved new streets that had previously been farmer tracks, established a district school, and offered land to the Dutch Reformed Church to erect a place of worship. In 1827, the same year as state emancipation, Williamsburg was incorporated as a village, and Abraham Meserole, a slaveholder whose French Huguenot family had lived in the area for over 150 years, acted as one of its trustees. It now had a post office, 148 residences, 10 stores and taverns, 5 ropewalks, a distillery, a slaughterhouse, 2 butchers, a Dutch Reformed Church, and a Methodist Episcopal Church. Its population stood at 1,007, which included 72 Black residents. Six years later, there were 72 village streets and approximately 300 houses; the population had tripled to 3,000, and residents were informed of the latest news

Eugene L. Armbruster, *View of Williamsburgh*, 1834, black and white photograph.
(V1974.1.1260, Eugene L. Armbruster Photographs and Scrapbooks, Center for
Brooklyn History, Brooklyn Public Library)

via a new newspaper called the *Williamsburgh Gazette, and Long-Island
Advertiser*.[7]

Williamsburg's growth was made possible by developers, entrepreneurs, and residents recognizing the land's potential. The land stood
forty-five feet above water, which prevented it from flooding; it looked
out at a waterfront that stretched a mile and a half along the East
River; and it stood in close proximity to Manhattan's financial hub. By
1836, two ferries—the Grand Street Ferry and the Peck Slip Ferry—
connected Williamsburg to the city of New York. This was essential for
attracting new residents to the village, especially in the absence of the
Williamsburg Bridge, which would not feature on New York's horizon
until 1903. The influx of merchants, industrialists, and laborers, mostly
from Germany, transformed Williamsburg from a village (1827) to a
town (1840) and finally to a city (1851), before becoming incorporated
into the city of Brooklyn (1855).[8] It was also home to a thriving free

Black community, the second largest in Kings County in 1855, whose anti-slavery activities expanded radical democratic possibilities as Williamsburg morphed from village to city.

THE HODGES FAMILY OF THE VILLAGE OF WILLIAMSBURG(H)

We went out to Long Island, to Carsville, and looked at the farm brother William had engaged. It was a mile outside of the city of Brooklyn, but quite near the New York market. After giving it a good and complete examination, I was dissatisfied with it also. I did not believe that father could make a living upon it.

I saved up my money and in one year's time bought a lot on S. Seventh street, Williamsburgh, LI, within a few minutes walk of Peck's Slip ferry. Brother William bought lots in the same village, on South Eighth street, corner of Fourth street, and built a brick house. Having been a trusted employee in Messrs. Hulbert & Co.'s store for seven years or more years, he had made some money out of speculation besides his salary. He moved to Williamsburg in his new house in 1839, where I believe he now lives.

I made my first public speech at the Troy convention. In it I gave as my opinion that the people of color had to leave the crowded cities and towns of New York, Brooklyn, Syracuse, Albany, Troy, Utica and the rest and move into country and small growing villages like Williamsburg, and grow up with a small town. I believe in that way they would overcome much of the prejudice against them, for, as a rule, there is a fraternal feeling between the people of small towns or places (even in the South) that is unknown in the large cities.
—Willis Hodges, *Free Man of Color* (1848–1849)

Today's Bedford Avenue, the main artery in North Brooklyn's Williamsburg neighborhood, contains the spirits of New Yorkers past. Williamsburg was originally part of the town of Boswijck, or Bushwick, chartered in 1660 by Peter Stuyvesant and home to Dutch, French, and Scandinavian farmers and enslaved African agricultural laborers during the colonial period. From 1827, when Williamsburg became a village, its residents included free Black, Irish, and German communities. In the late nineteenth century, Catholic immigrants from Italy, as part of a second wave of immigration to the US, called the eastern part of the neighborhood home. In 1903, with the opening of the Williamsburg Bridge, eastern Europeans, mostly Jewish communities from Lithuania, Poland, and Russia, left the packed tenements of the Lower East Side of Manhattan for more space in Brooklyn. After World War II, as the housing crisis deepened and redlining took hold, Black, Dominican, and Puerto Rican communities sustained the neighborhood affectionately known as Los Sures, even as the city continued to starve the neighborhood of resources. They lived alongside a Hasidic Jewish community that had escaped the horrors of Nazi Europe. By the 1990s, as corporations took over what had once been local-owned mom-and-pop stores and gentrification displaced historic communities of color, Williamsburg's landscape struggled to tell the stories of its own people. Here once stood the village of Williamsburg, and centered around Bedford Avenue and South Sixth to Eighth Streets was its thriving free Black community.

In 1839, at the height of Williamsburg's speculation, William Johnson Hodges, a thirty-six-year-old free Black man from rural Norfolk, Virginia (today's Virginia Beach), bought his first lot of land in the village. He moved there with his British-born white wife, Mary Ann Tippon, and their toddler, Julia (named for William's mother).[9] The tradition of owning property ran deep in the Hodges family. Described as the "pride of the family, and a mother's son," full of "wit and life," William was the eldest of fourteen children.[10] His father, Charles Augustus Hodges, and mother, Julia Nelson Hodges (née Willis), held ancestral roots in Virginia dating back to the early eighteenth century. As a free Black man, Charles owned approximately fifty acres of land in Virginia in 1815 and two hundred acres by 1840.[11] In spite of their relative wealth, in 1829, a twenty-six-year-old William had to flee Norfolk for Canada after he was accused of forging free papers for an enslaved person and deemed "dangerous" both for his ability to read and for his work as a preacher lecturing free and enslaved Black Virginians. William left an area brewing with revolution. Just two years after his departure, Nat Turner's Rebellion, which saw men and women rise up against their enslaved status, materialized in neighboring Southampton County.

By 1833, William was back in the US. His parents, Charles and Julia, had relocated the entire family to the city of New York, where they rented on Essex Street. The family move might have been prompted by the relative safety that New York provided compared to slaveholding Virginia. As William's younger brother, Willis, suggests in his autobiography *Free Man of Color*, the racism was somewhat easier to bear in the North: "mother . . . felt free from insults under the laws of the state of New York."[12]

The village of Williamsburg was not William's first choice. He had originally looked at investing in real estate in the settlement of Carrsville, sometimes known as Crow Hill, one of the original Bedford Hills, on behalf of his father. These hills were once a typical part of Kings County's landscape—with thick woods and wildlife. What had not already been destroyed by the Dutch, then British, was deforested and then leveled during the American Revolution as troops used the trees for firewood.[13] But it was Willis, twelve years junior to William, who felt that Carrsville would not make a good family investment, as it was too far out. Carrsville lay about one mile south from Weeksville, which had only just been established one year prior, and approximately five miles from the city of Brooklyn.

In Williamsburg, William and Willis were home owners and businessmen, and later William would become an educator and pastor. William lived in a three-story brick home—unusual in its opulence for its time, given that the average working Black man lived in a wood-frame home. It was located on the corner of Fourth Street (modern-day Bedford) and South Eighth Street, a highly desirable part of the village with views of the city and a short walk to the Peck Slip Ferry.[14] Willis later joined his brother and bought a plot of land on parallel South Seventh Street, having initially lived with their sister, Jacqueline, and her husband, Benjamin Bowen, at their home on

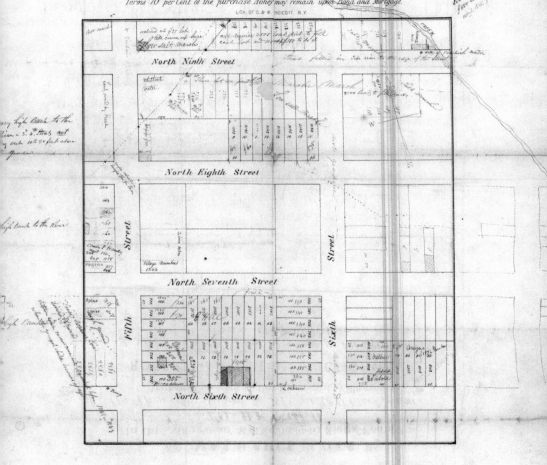

G. & W. Endicott, *48 Valuable Lots in the Village of Williamsburgh, Kings County*, 1845, map. (B P-[1845].Fl, Map Collection, Center for Brooklyn History, Brooklyn Public Library)

York Street in Manhattan's Fifth Ward (today's Tribeca neighborhood) from 1836.[15] In 1840, the brothers jointly ran a store offering "choice family groceries" out of the first floor of William's home. Their stock was typical for its time; it included a selection of teas, coffees, brown sugar, butter, lard, flour, pork, ham, smoked beef, codfish, mackerel, molasses, table salt, rice, tobacco, and soap. For William and Willis, owning a business was a vastly different experience from the menial labor they had done in the city of New York. William had previously found work at E. D. Hulbert & Co., a cotton broker in Manhattan, and remained working there for the next seven years. His brother, Willis, initially worked as a night watchman, responsible for protecting goods held in the docks and stores, for which he was paid $1.50 per shift (approximately $32 today). He then became a porter for E. D. Hulbert, employed by the same company as his brother. But Willis was shocked by the unskilled jobs Black people were forced to take in the city of New York. He remarked, "many tradesmen I knew from the South were now cooks and waiters."[16]

The deliberate choice to live in a small, growing village like Williamsburg was motivated by the brothers' own economic possibilities under racial capitalism but equally focused on safety, political mobilization, and practicality. Willis writes in his autobiography that a "fraternal feeling" existed in small towns that was "unknown in the large cities," such as Albany, Buffalo, and New York, where racial hostilities, he observed, were widespread.[17] When he moved to Williamsburg, Willis was already a seasoned activist. He had been introduced to fellow organizers at Abyssinian Baptist Church in Manhattan by his sister, Jacqueline, whose own home stood just blocks from the church.[18] In December 1837, a "W. Hodges," referring either to Willis or William, was listed as a manager of the auxiliary of the American Anti-Slavery Society, a radical abolitionist organization calling for the immediate end to slavery.[19] In the 1830s, Willis noted that there was only one abolition society in Williamsburg, and the brothers were the only members of color.[20] The possibilities of a village meant that its free Black community could organize quickly. In the decades that followed, William, Willis, and their neighbors built local institutions that echoed much of the earlier community building that had occurred in the village of Brooklyn two decades prior. And on a practical note, the village also offered them an opportunity to buy land that was affordable but accessible to the city of New York with a quick ferry commute.

From Weeksville to Williamsburg, buying land signified freedom in myriad ways. Private landownership—the antithesis of Lenape collective notions of land use and steeped in the legacy of European colonization—was a symbol of status, political power, and generational wealth. For scores of Black Brooklynites and New Yorkers, it meant they could choose to house boarders, or renters, especially when working-class wages made their own lives financially precarious. Sometimes, these boarders might even be newly arrived fugitives from the South looking to rebuild their lives, and these homes were the first step toward care and assistance. From 1821 onward, however, owning $250 worth of land also meant the right for Black men in New York to be able to vote and therefore to lay rightful claim to citizenship. It was *the* political struggle that would define the lives of Black men in Brooklyn and the city of New York for the nineteenth century, a struggle that was rooted in racism and became a quintessential New York story: one of real estate, voting, and citizenship. Its momentum took root in city of Brooklyn at the same time as the frenzied pace of construction across the city came to an abrupt halt. Following the financial crisis known as the Panic of 1837 and in the economic depression that followed, property prices plunged and stayed low for a subsequent fifteen-year period in Brooklyn. Total real estate values that were worth $32,000,000 in 1836 rose slowly to only $40,242,999 by 1851. These historically low property prices brought a new energy to the activism of Brooklyn's free Black communities.[21]

LAND, VOTING, CITIZENSHIP

The minds of the blacks are not competent to vote. They are too much degraded to estimate the value, or exercise with fidelity and discretion that important right. It would be unsafe in their hands.

—Samuel Young, *Reports of the Proceedings and Debates of the Convention of 1821, Assembled for the Purpose of Amending the Constitution of the State of New York*

Finally, brethren, we are not strangers; neither do we come under the alien law. Our constitution does not call upon us to become naturalized; we are already American citizens; our fathers were among the first that peopled this county; their sweat and their tears have been the means, in a measure, of raising our country to its present standing. Many of them fought, and bled, and died for the gaining of her liberties.

—Henry C. Thompson and George Hogarth, anti-colonization meeting in Brooklyn, 1831

Structural racism in the guise of federal and state constitutional frameworks meant that nineteenth-century free Black Brooklynites and New Yorkers were extended neither natural voting rights nor automatic citizenship, even as their ancestors had laid foundation to the modern United States. The Naturalization Bill of 1790 had restricted citizenship to free white persons, automatically excluding Indigenous, Asian, and Black communities. And in the absence of the Fourteenth and Fifteenth Amendments to the federal Constitution, which granted citizenship to anyone born in the US and automatic voting rights to citizens, respectively (they would not be passed until 1868 and 1870), Black Brooklynites and New Yorkers were forced to engage in an almost-eight-decade struggle for citizenship and voting rights. All of this was compounded by changes to New York's state constitution. Prior to 1821, less than two in five adult men could vote in New York State, but all men, regardless of race, had to be at least twenty-one years old and possess $100 worth of property in order to vote. In 1821, the state legislature passed an amendment to its state constitution that eliminated property qualifications for white voters, while it introduced a $250 property requirement for Black voters. Part of a larger Jacksonian electoral reform that sought to extend the vote to white men only, neither the timing of the constitutional amendment nor the dollar amount associated with the voting qualification was arbitrary. By 1817, New York State had determined an end date for slavery: July 4, 1827. Changing the voting laws in 1821 was part and parcel of structural racism intentionally designed to disenfranchise Black men. The $250 requirement was not an insignificant amount—it represented about the average working-class man's annual salary. Moreover, whereas white men had to have only resided in New York State for a year and in one town and county consistently for six months to be eligible to vote, Black men needed to be a resident of the state for three years and in the town or county where he planned to vote for at least one year.[22]

The magnitude of these injustices was not lost on the Black New Yorkers who founded the intentional free Black community of Seneca Village beyond New York City's official borders in 1825, just two years before state emancipation. Andrew Williams, a twenty-five-year-old shoe shiner, became that community's first land investor when he bought one hundred lots in what is today's midwest section of Central Park. Other New Yorkers, many of them former residents of the crowded and well-known Five Points neighborhood in lower Manhattan, soon followed. The African Methodist Episcopal Zion Church became the single largest landlord in the area, and its land purchase paved the way for the creation of a church and a cemetery so that residents could be honored in life and in death. Seneca Village thrived over eight hundred acres of land for over three decades as a mixed Black, Irish, and German community until the city razed it and displaced its residents in the first historic example of eminent domain, in order to create a park intended to "rival the Champs Elysees of Paris and Corso of Rome."[23] In 1859, it opened as Central Park. Many of the displaced residents did not receive adequate compensation despite Seneca Village being one of the largest landowning Black communities in New York (and its residents by extension possessing the right to vote).[24]

The desire to own land and therefore have the right to vote and affect policy was also mirrored in Weeksville, Brooklyn. From its inception, Weeksville was a political project designed to create a land-owning community that would recognize Black people as full citizens with voting rights and to offer safety and refuge in Brooklyn's secluded Ninth Ward, which meant that it was also developed alongside anti-colonization resistance. Just one year following the Panic of 1837 and during the subsequent economic depression, entrepreneurial Black New Yorkers intentionally founded the village of Weeksville, buying small, private lots of land at auction that had been divided from larger parcels of former farmland belonging to the slaveholding Lefferts family. They then sold these to fellow like-minded investors by advertising in the Black press. As early as 1832, William Thomas, a chimney sweeper, purchased thirty acres along Hunterfly Road. Samuel Anderson, who had been formerly enslaved, also bought seven acres. By 1835, Henry C. Thompson, a resident of the village of Brooklyn, bought thirty-two lots. Three years later, a stevedore named James Weeks purchased two lots from Henry C. Thompson. According to the historian Judith Wellman, James would go onto buy four more properties in 1839, 1845, 1849, and 1853 and was, of the seven original land investors, the only one to actually live in Weeksville. Its development was accelerated by the Brooklyn and Jamaica Railroad. Incorporated in 1832, the train line ran east-west along Atlantic Avenue and connected passengers via horse-drawn streetcars and steam trains from the East River in the northwestern tip of Brooklyn to Jamaica, Queens, in the east, while running north past the village of Bedford.[25] In 1850, just twelve years after the founding of Weeksville, it boasted higher percentages of property ownership than any other free Black community in fifteen other Northern US cities and centered around an urban, rather than rural, base. As scholars have discussed extensively, like the early village community of Brooklyn, the residents of Weeksville established numerous liberatory institutions, including Colored School No. 2, the Howard Colored Orphan Asylum, the Zion Home for the Colored Aged, two churches,

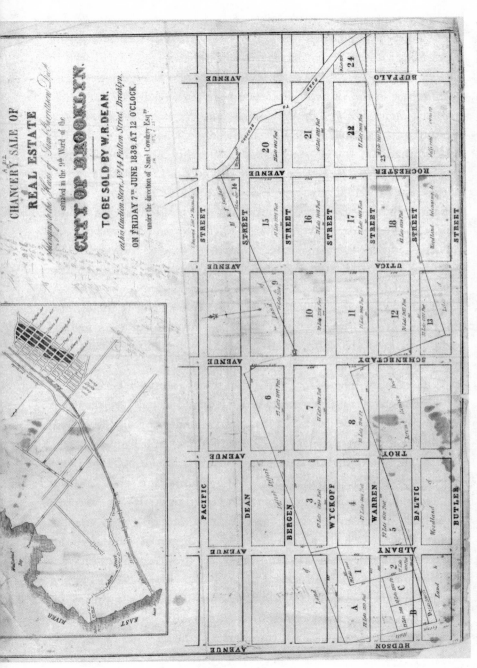

George Hayward, *Chancery Sale of Real Estate Belonging to the Heirs of Samuel Garrittsen, Decd., Situated in the 9th Ward of the City of Brooklyn,* 1839, map. (B P-[1839].F1, Map Collection, Center for Brooklyn History, Brooklyn Public Library)

two newspapers (*Freedman's Torchlight* and the *People's Journal*), and the national headquarters of the African Civilization Society. It was one of the United States' earliest and most successful Northern independent free Black communities and the second-largest free Black community in the United States before the Civil War.[26]

Black men of Brooklyn, Weeksville, and Williamsburg engaged in a multifaceted campaign throughout the 1830s, 1840s, and 1850s to buy land so that they could vote. And if they could vote, who could deny that they were in fact citizens of the United States? This was the rallying call of the first Black state convention held in August 1840 in Albany, where rhetoric was combined with tangible action. Willis Hodges attended the convention as the delegate for Williamsburg and was charged with getting signatures for a petition on voting rights that would be sent to the state legislature.[27] The minutes from the convention recorded, "The principal legal disability which affects us is, our deprivation of free exercise, in common with other men, of the elective franchise. A free suffrage is the basis of a free government, the safeguard of a free people." That same month, William, Willis, and their neighbors met at the Colored Methodist Meeting House on North Second Street in Williamsburg, where they stated that their protest was a "Christian duty, as well as a political one," and they vowed to lend their support to the newly formed Liberty Party.[28] Intended to break the federal deadlock between the two-party system of Whigs and Democrats, the Liberty Party, founded in 1840, was committed to ending slavery, promoting a free labor market, and opposing colonization schemes. Prior to its founding, Brooklynites were among the thousands who exercised their First Amendment rights to petition the federal government to redress their grievances. One such petition, signed by Peter, Eleanor, and Benjamin Croger in 1838, demanded that the government prohibit the "commerce of slaves in several states."[29] But by 1836, Congress had responded to the onslaught of anti-slavery petitions by instituting a "gag rule," which meant thousands of these documents were simply tabled between 1836 and 1844 and not considered for discussion or debate, including a petition signed by William and Willis in 1841 demanding that

James Ryder Van Brunt,
[Homestead of Cornelius Van Brunt], 1859, watercolor (Brooklyn Public Library)

HOOKER'S MAP
OF THE
VILLAGE OF BROOKLYN
IN THE YEAR
1827.

SCALE OF HALF A MILE.

Hooker's Map of the Village of Brooklyn in the Year 1827, ca. 1861. (Brooklyn Public Library)

Isaac Vieth, *Map of the Village of Williamsburgh,*
Kings County, N.Y., 1854. (Brooklyn Public Library)

CITY OF NEW YORK

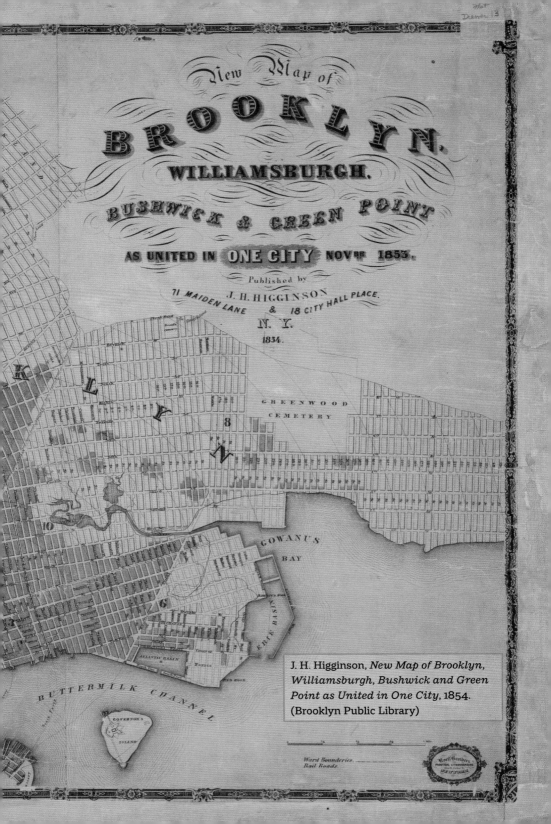

New Map of

BROOKLYN.

WILLIAMSBURGH.

BUSHWICK & GREEN POINT

AS UNITED IN **ONE CITY** NOVᵉʳ 1853.

Published by

J. H. HIGGINSON

71 MAIDEN LANE & 18 CITY HALL PLACE.

N. Y.

1854.

GREENWOOD CEMETERY

GOWANUS BAY

ERIE BASIN

ATLANTIC BASIN

RED HOOK

BUTTERMILK CHANNEL

GOVERNOR'S ISLAND

Ward Boundaries
Rail Roads

J. H. Higginson, *New Map of Brooklyn, Williamsburgh, Bushwick and Green Point as United in One City*, 1854. (Brooklyn Public Library)

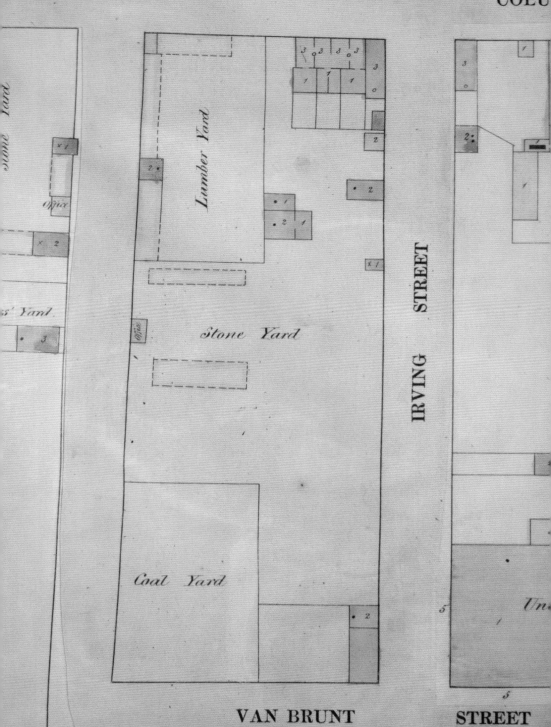

COLU

Lumber Yard

Stone Yard

Coal Yard

IRVING STREET

VAN BRUNT   STREET

William Perris, detail from *Maps of the City of Brooklyn,* (Brooklyn Public Library)

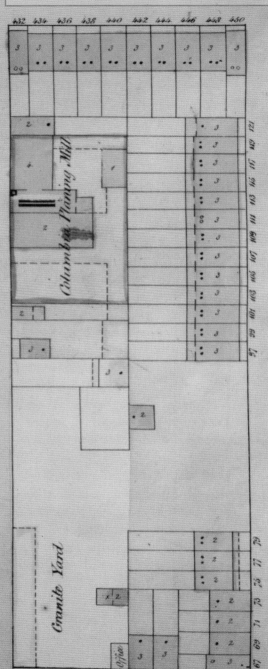

SEDGWICK STREET

Columbia Planing Mill

Granite Yard

7

M. Dripps, *Map of Brooklyn and Vicinity*, 1862.
(Brooklyn Public Library)

Congress remove the gag rule.[30] Although ultimately unsuccessful in the 1840 election, the Liberty Party formally infused anti-slavery organizing into electoral politics in the United States, and its presence confirmed that abolition debates could no longer be simply sidelined, tabled, or gagged.[31]

Electoral organizing brought together Brooklynites old and new. On December 7, 1840, George Hogarth, an educator and the leader of Brooklyn's AME Church, appeared on a platform urging suffrage reform and "unrestricted use of the Elective Franchise to all citizens irrespective of color or condition," at the Baptist church on Antony Street in New York. Petitions were again circulated for the collection of signatures to submit to the state legislature.[32] Just over a month later, another meeting was held at Brooklyn's AME Church on High Street, led by Benjamin Croger. The Reverend George Hogarth offered the prayer, and a young Augustus Washington served on the committee of arrangements. Attendees passed a resolution stating,

Whereas our brethren in our sister city and in other sections of this state, are now making active and vigorous efforts to petition most respectfully the legislature of this state, to repeal an unjust and odious section of a statute which demands a certain amount of freehold property, as the qualification of a colored voter, and by that course are thus showing to the nation and the world, their love for freedom and genuine republicanism—their patriotism and philanthropy—their love of free institutions, of justice and impartial laws. Therefore Resolved, That we, the colored citizens of Brooklyn, feel it our incumbent duty to participate in this grand moral work, and in every other cause which has for its object the moral, the social, the political and religious elevation of our oppressed and down trodden citizens. Resolved, That the spirit of liberty and justice which cheered the hearts, and animated the hopes of the heroes of the revolution and pressed them into deeds sublime, of noble daring, now hovers like an angel of mercy over the legislative halls of our state, and we believe that it needs but a moral effort on our part to enable her to extend her influence like a zone of mercy around our state, and bring all of her citizens irrespective of color under the wide canopy. Resolved, That a committee of five persons be immediately appointed, with power to appoint sub-committees, whose business it shall be to make immediate and active efforts to obtain the signature of every colored citizen of this city, vicinity and county, and also those of our white citizens. Jan 5, 1841.[33]

The meeting was recorded in the *Colored American*, a widely distributed Black newspaper run from 1836 to 1842 by Samuel Cornish, who founded it along with Philip Bell and Charles B. Ray after *Freedom's Journal* had folded. William acted as the village's distribution agent for the *Colored American* and regularly advertised in the newspaper for rooms to let at his home.

By 1846, just before the state referendum that might have potentially removed all property requirements for New Yorkers, William and Mary Hodges's family had expanded. Their eldest daughter, eleven-year-old Julia, was now an older sister to five-year-old John Quincy, one-year-old Mary, and baby sister Sylvia. William had also widened his political circle beyond Williamsburg and joined his colleagues in the city of New York. In January 1846, residents from Williamsburg, Weeksville, Fort Greene, and downtown Brooklyn stood alongside New York's antislavery activists. William J. Wilson, George Hogarth, Benjamin Croger, Augustus Washington, Lewis H. Nelson, Willis Hodges, and Isaac and Jupiter Reed met with New Yorkers James McCune Smith, Charles B. Ray, Theodore S. Wright, Thomas Van Renssalaer, John Zuille, and Patrick Reason to discuss strategies for extending the vote.[34] In April of that year, they convened at Lexington Hall, Manhattan, and demanded to be "fully acknowledged" as citizens with "strong religious attachments" and advanced education. They argued, "We do not feel that it is the *man* who votes, it is the *property* which votes. The disqualification of others because of their color, robs this man of the noble and inspiring consciousness of voting as a man, on equal grounds as a citizen, with his fellow-citizens."[35]

In that same month, Brooklynites gathered again at a schoolhouse in Carrsville. James Weeks chaired the meeting, James Gloucester acted as secretary, and George Hogarth again offered a prayer. Their resolutions included forming a committee of five members who could create a manifesto of voting rights—its membership included the educator William J. Wilson and the Weeksville resident Francis P. Graham. The meeting's organizers chose to publish their proceedings in the newly renamed *Brooklyn Evening Star* (formerly *Long Island Star*) to have a formal recording of the protest and presumably to reach out to a wider readership but also to be in direct dialogue with the racist anti-Black rhetoric that otherwise filled the pages of their local newspapers.[36] A few days after the Carrsville meeting, the Democratic Convention convened in Flatbush and nominated Henry C. Murphy, former mayor of Brooklyn, and Tunis C. Bergen to attend the State Constitutional Convention. On whether the property qualifications should be dropped for Black men, William's local newspaper reprinted the convention's debates: "[On] extending the elective franchise to the negro; because the elective franchise is a political right founded on the social equality of those who have delegated some of their individual rights to the representatives of those who are politically associated; and until we are prepared to associate with the negro race, we shall oppose that mistaken and mischievous fanaticism and political maneuvering which must lead either to an amalgamation between the white and African race, or to a dissolution of our cherished union."[37]

Ultimately that November, the chance to eliminate property requirements and introduce universal male suffrage failed when the proposal to amend the state constitution was defeated by fifty-three to thirty. Frustrated by the constitutional failure, several Black families left the city and moved to Timbuctoo between 1846 and 1853. Inspired in part by the utopian communities movement, the abolitionist Gerrit Smith parceled off 120,000 acres of land that he owned in the Adirondacks into smaller forty- to sixty-acre lots, selling them for a nominal sum or giving them free to various Black families, thereby affording the men the right to vote. They were also expected to live off the land (although it is not clear if all families actually moved there). In Hamilton County, William J. Wilson, Peter Vogelsang, and Elijah B. Bundick acquired land. In Franklin County, James Holly, Lewis H. Nelson, Benjamin Croger, Willis Hodges, Robert H. Cousins, Abraham Brown, Isaac H. Hunter, Eli N. Hall, Bristor N. B. Worrick, and Junius Morel held land too. Intended as an oasis for Black families to escape the racism they encountered daily while supporting them as voters with full citizenship rights, Timbuctoo eventually fell short of those ambitions. The utopian experiment proved difficult for many of its former city residents—they were unprepared as farmers and lacked basic supplies, and their difficulties were exacerbated by the lack of fertile soil.

Willis Hodges was among those who moved to Timbuctoo. Although he had felt relatively shielded in the village of Williamsburg, the place had not altogether been a panacea to New York's racism. He responded to the state's failure to redress suffrage rights in New York by submitting an article to the *New York Sun* and paying $15 to have it published. When it was featured among the paid advertisements, Willis questioned the article's placement and was told by the editor, "The Sun shines for all white men, not black men. You must get up a paper of your own if you want to tell your side of the story to the public."[38] On January 1, 1847, Willis and the Manhattan-based abolitionist Thomas Van Rensselaer launched the *Ram's Horn*. "We hope, like Joshua of old, to blow the Ram's horn, until the walls of slavery and injustice fall," opened the inaugural issue. The newspaper's contributors included Frederick Douglass, who would launch the *North Star* later that year. Although today only one issue of the *Ram's Horn* survives, at its height, the publication had fifteen hundred subscribers—including the radical abolitionist John Brown. This was a substantial number for the Black press, given its chronic and consistent underfunding.[39] Willis had praised the Timbuctoo experiment in the *Ram's Horn*, and on May 12, 1848, he received a deed of forty acres on Gerrit Smith's land in Franklin County, just weeks before his newspaper folded. Scholars think that it was during this time that Willis began drafting his autobiography, in which he recalls his childhood in Virginia and early adult life in New York and

Williamsburg (it would be published posthumously in 1896). Once there, he was also comforted by old friendships that he had made through the publication, especially when life proved hard in the rural, barren Adirondacks. He received rations of pork and flour from his friend John Brown, to be shared among various families in order to "make all as happy and comfortable as possible."[40] By the mid-1850s, Timbuctoo was no longer operational. Willis left the Adirondacks to return to his brother, William, who was still serving as the main educator at the local African school in Williamsburg—a school they had both helped create. Education continued to provide a path to liberation.

AN ANTI-SLAVERY PICNIC

The blessings in which you, this day, rejoice, are not enjoyed in
common. The rich inheritance of justice, liberty, prosperity and
independence, bequeathed by your fathers, is shared by you, not
by me. The sunlight that brought light and healing to you, has
brought stripes and death to me. This Fourth July is yours, not
mine. You may rejoice, I must mourn.
—Frederick Douglass, "What to the Slave Is the Fourth of
July?," address delivered in Rochester, New York, July 5, 1852

Ferry Landing, Grand Street, Williamsburgh, 1835, illustration from *The Eastern
District of Brooklyn with Illustrations and Maps*, 1912. (NYC Municipal Library)

O N a cooler August afternoon than most New Yorkers are accustomed to, students attending Sabbath and African schools in New York, Brooklyn, and Williamsburg gathered at one of the many groves in the quiet village of Williamsburg. Its tall trees were not required to provide shade and respite that day, as a gentle breeze ensured that the convening children and adults were comfortable. "The day was calm and beautiful," according to one report published in the *Colored American*.[1] Attendees were treated to a children's choir that sang three songs including "Hail to the brightness of freedoms' glad morning! Join, all the earth, in an anthem of praise!" And several speakers meditated on meanings of freedom and liberty both in the US and abroad for the large crowds of attendees. One thousand to twelve hundred people had gathered on Monday, August 2, 1841, to celebrate August 1, or West India Emancipation Day, and the recent repeal of New York's nine months law. The removal of the nine months residency rule meant that any enslaved people brought to Brooklyn or New York, or indeed any part of the state—as was the norm for Southern slaveholders to do when vacationing here in the summer months—would be immediately emancipated. They no longer had to wait the obligatory nine months of continuous residency in New York before declaring their freedom. These were monumental reasons to celebrate, and William and Willis Hodges, who served on the celebration's organizing committee, along with their neighbor Lewis H. Nelson and Samuel Ricks, were praised for their "judicious arrangements, and their untiring exertions to accommodate visitors."[2] This was the first recorded West India Emancipation Day celebration in Brooklyn and New York, and the city's African schools were at the center of this Kings County tradition.

The majestic August 1 or West India Emancipation Day celebrations were created by Black educators for Black communities, and Black joy was at its heart. The date had assumed special significance for Black diasporic communities throughout the Atlantic world. On August 1, 1834, centuries of chattel slavery came to an end in the British West Indies.

An act of British Parliament passed a year earlier came into effect, thereby emancipating enslaved people in Barbados, Guyana, Jamaica, and Trinidad and Tobago, even as they entered a subsequent four-year brutal period of indentured servitude. After 1838, anti-slavery activists in the US used slavery's demise in the British Caribbean to mobilize the abolition movement in the United States and collectively demonstrate that the "peculiar institution" had no place in the modern Western world. The celebrations crucially also acted as a political critique of the Fourth of July. For Black diasporic communities, West India Emancipation Day celebrations were a show of early pan-African consciousness and transatlantic solidarity in which organizers and participants renewed their commitment to the freedom of others and their own, and they usually took place in vast, open spaces that could accommodate large crowds and provide shade during the hot summer months, with easy transportation links. In the three decades that followed the first recorded West India Emancipation Day celebration in Kings County in 1841, public displays of joy continued in a mix of rural and urban spaces in Carrsville and Weeksville (1851), Morris Grove, Queens (1855 and 1858), Brooklyn's AME Church (1855), Williamsburg (1861), and Flushing and Westbury, Long Island (1862), as well as in western Canada, Britain, and other Northern US cities.[3] Scores of ordinary Brooklynites attended and spoke at these events, in which education and activism were their heart. The archives confirm the presence of educators, church leaders, and entrepreneurs such as William and Willis Hodges, Amos Freeman, James N. Gloucester, Junius C. Morel, and William J. Wilson and white men such as Simeon C. Jocelyn and Erastus D. Culver (a prominent Republican congressman and then a judge in Brooklyn's city court).[4]

It is no coincidence that many of the educators were also anti-slavery activists, including George Hogarth, Augustus Washington, William J. Wilson, William Hodges, Maria Stewart, Sarah Smith Tompkins Garnet, and Junius C. Morel. Although Black women are not listed in the written archives, their presence as co-organizers and attendees is still felt, especially given their immeasurable contribution to the city's African schools. In the history of Brooklyn's African School system, two things are evident: many of these educators were women, though the archives make it difficult to fully recover their stories, and they were also responsible for building and contributing to Brooklyn's rich educational history.

BROOKLYN'S AFRICAN SCHOOLS

It is the duty of every friend of the colored people to use every lawful effort to advance the cause of education among the rising generation.
—*Colored American*, July 3, 1841

Our Colored Public Schools are legitimately a part of our Public Schools system. They are conducted under the same regulations, pursue the same studies, and are under as good tutorship as the rest of them. [They are] No. 1 in the W[estern] D[istrict], No. 2 at the village of Weeksville, and No. 3 in the E[astern] D[istrict].
—William J. Wilson to Henry R. Stiles, ca. 1863 (folder 4, box 1, Henry Reed Stiles Correspondence, ARC.218, Center for Brooklyn History, Brooklyn Public Library)

Literacy had liberated generations of Brooklynites. In 1829, after James Pennington escaped his enslavement in Maryland and soon after his arrival to Brooklyn, he joined a Sabbath school in Newtown, Long Island (today's Elmhurst neighborhood in Queens). Just like John Jea before him, having been deprived of the right to literacy under slavery, the effect that an education had on the newly arrived fugitive was profound. James wrote that the "rare privileges" of an education stirred an anti-slavery consciousness within him, and the thought of those still enslaved "entered into the deep chambers of [his] soul, and stirred the most agitating emotions [he] had ever felt."[5] Sabbath schools attached to Black churches were one way in which people of African descent were able to educate and emancipate themselves of the racist discourses that surrounded them. But it was the formal African school system where Black self-determination shone.

Education was central to Brooklyn's formation. As early as 1661, Carel de Beauvois, a Huguenot, or French Protestant, became

Breuckelen's first schoolmaster. The colonial government offered him an annual salary and housing in exchange for educating the town's children, and the school operated within a local church near the intersection of today's Bridge Street and Fulton Street. The town of Brooklyn was not alone in its educational efforts. Two years later, Boudwyn Manout agreed to serve as schoolmaster and court clerk in the town of Bushwick, in exchange for a salary, housing, and firewood. That school stood at the current intersection of Bushwick Avenue and Skillman Street.[6] But the history of educating Black children differed in Brooklyn and Manhattan. In neighboring Manhattan, the white-led New-York Manumission Society funded the first African Free School in 1787 with forty-seven students, and an array of other formal sites in lower Manhattan soon followed. The African Free School system in New York was responsible for educating some twenty-three hundred students by 1814 and had illustrious alumni including the abolitionist Henry Highland Garnet, the actor Ira Aldridge, the businessman George T. Downing, and Dr. James McCune Smith. The genesis of Brooklyn's schools for Black children was entirely different. Between 1827 and 1841, Kings County's free Black community established three African schools in Brooklyn, Weeksville, and Williamsburg—none of them were the result of white benevolence but founded entirely through private grassroots efforts of its free Black community, beginning with the first, housed at Peter and Elenor Croger's home on James Street. In locating the school in their small home, Peter rejected the contemporary British Lancastrian system of education. This popular method of teaching prioritized economics over pedagogy, as one teacher was responsible for educating students in a crammed classroom, thereby keeping costs low. The importance of Peter's investment in Black education was made clear when the village announced that thirty-five to forty children would be temporarily taught at Thomas Kirk's print shop, and "no colored children would be received" until a formal building opened.[7] When the school did open on Concord and Adams Streets on May 6, 1816, one room was allocated to Black children, if they were taught at all.

If gradual emancipation had allowed structural racism to flourish, post-emancipation did not improve conditions for the education of Black children in the village. In May 1830, the colonizationist Adrian Van Sinderen, serving as director, and a "few benevolent and spirited individuals in that village" created an African infant school for the "poor and laboring population." Not one member of the village's thriving free Black community was invited to collaborate on its structuring. "As this society is designed for the moral and intellectual improvement of our colored population, why is it that the ministers and members of the African church are not admitted to a participation of its management?" rightly asked one resident in the *Long Island Star*.[8] The newspaper's contributor might have been the Reverend George Hogarth, who served as both pastor at the AME Church and the first educator at the African school in Brooklyn long after it had moved out of Peter and Elenor Croger's home.

In 1841, trustees George Hogarth, Sylvanus Smith, and Henry C. Thompson placed an ad looking for teachers to work at Colored School No. 1 (formerly the African school).[9] While they served in similar self-determined senior leadership capacities for the school and at the AME Church, the daily lives of the three trustees in the city were markedly different. Sylvanus Smith worked in Brooklyn as a hog driver, a crucial job intended to keep the city's streets safe and clear from wandering animals. Henry C. Thompson, just like Peter and Benjamin Croger, worked as a whitewasher. Both Sylvanus and Henry would become early land investors in Weeksville. George Hogarth, born around 1805 in Maryland, arrived in Brooklyn to serve as pastor of the village's AME Church, where his fellow trustees Henry C. Thompson and Sylvanus Smith were elders. Together with his wife, Ellen, who was born in Queens, George lived initially at 108 Sands Street and then moved to Navy and Myrtle Streets around the Navy Yard when the family expanded with children Ellen, George, and Henry. There they rented out the upper part of their home, presumably to supplement the family's income, although George owned a substantive $4,500 of property, according to census records.[10] In addition to his duties at the AME Church,

George contributed to Black institutional life as the manager of the Brooklyn Temperance Association. His colleagues included Benjamin Croger (president), James Pennington (secretary), Austin Isaacs (treasurer), and fellow managers Willis Jones, Joseph Titus, and Jacob Deyou, all Brooklyn residents. The temperance movement sprung out of the antebellum moral reform movement in its pursuit of godly perfection. The Brooklyn Temperance Association and later William Hodges's Williamsburgh Union Temperance Benevolent Society combined sobriety and anti-slavery activism, by virtue of the fact that members were committed to both causes. However, it is important to underline that while most anti-slavery activists were temperance advocates, all temperance supporters were not anti-slavery activists or even sympathizers. The Brooklyn Temperance Society, for example, was established in 1819, and its president was Adrian Van Sinderen.

In 1863, Henry Reed Stiles, a cofounder of the Long Island Historical Society and the city's unofficial historian (he was compiling his three-volume book on the history of Brooklyn), invited the long-serving educator William J. Wilson to write a history of the African schools. William remembered the chronological order of educators at the Brooklyn school as being Benjamin Croger (not his brother, Peter), then George Hogarth, L. Brooks (who he notes had a very short tenure), Augustus Washington, and finally himself. The reason for George, Sylvanus, and Henry placing an ad for a new teacher in 1841 is explained in William's letter detailing the history of Brooklyn's African schools. That year, having taught at the school "for some time with much success," George Hogarth had "finally resigned to engage into trade with Hayti and at length became quite an extensive merchant."[11] He had also risen up the ranks at the AME Church. By 1840, George served as the general book steward of the AME Church, an extremely prestigious position, and a year later, he began publishing *Doctrine, Economy and Usages to Practical Religion and Monthly Reform*, the first Black monthly magazine in the United States.

During George's tenure as the school's teacher and a trustee, Rosetta Morrison, born in Hartford, Connecticut, and a graduate of the Female

Domestic Institute in Clinton, New York, opened a primary school for the city's Black children in the basement of the AME Church on High Street, assisted by her friend and classmate Ursula James, where she promised to teach the "branches usually taught in primary schools [with] particular attention paid to the morals and manners."[12] Rosetta was described as a "stranger, singlehanded, and alone, with an ardent desire of usefulness to her people," and the school was said to have been "entirely the result of female enterprise and effort."[13] But the gainful employment of being an educator in the city did little to protect people from racism or the threat of kidnapping. Rosetta was known in activist circles—the prominent abolitionist Charles B. Ray officiated her marriage to Isaac Wright, a free man from Philadelphia. But her introduction to these local abolitionist circles in Brooklyn and New York was harrowing. Her husband, Isaac, who worked at L. & L. H. Parker, a Manhattan-based furniture shop and "decidedly abolitionist" business, was kidnapped around 1837 and sold into slavery in New Orleans. Under the leadership of the abolitionist David Ruggles, the Manhattan-based Vigilance Committee raised enough money for his emancipation. When Isaac returned to New York, he donated money to the Vigilance Committee.[14] Isaac and Rosetta's daughters would eventually teach in New York City's public schools.

By the time George was replaced by Augustus Washington in 1842, Brooklyn's Colored School No. 1 had one department, with a male teacher who taught eighty students.[15] Issues of overcrowding were prevalent. The upper room of the Woolman Society Hall on Nassau Street between Bridge and Jay Streets was too small for the number of enrolled students, and Rosetta's primary department, located in the basement of the AME Church and designed for the education of girls, also closed after eight months due to overcrowding and lack of resources.[16] Augustus Washington, born in Trenton, New Jersey, soon left his position and moved to Hartford, Connecticut, where he became a successful daguerreotypist and eventually relocated to Liberia. His successor was a fellow New Jerseyan, William J. Wilson, who began teaching at the school now located in a new two-story brick building on Willoughby Street on October 18, 1847.[17] That same year, a second school opened in Weeksville on the corner of Troy Avenue and Bergen Street (it would later be renamed Colored School No. 2).[18] William's departure on November 20, 1863, to teach in the Freedmen Schools in the South meant that he earned the distinction of being the longest serving educator at Brooklyn's African school in the pre–Civil War period. His colleague the educator, journalist, and abolitionist Junius C. Morel, likewise, would serve at the Weeksville school for twenty-seven years. The two schools in Brooklyn and Weeksville were complemented by a third—an African school in Williamsburg.

A year before state emancipation, and Williamsburg's incorporation as a village, the first public school opened in Williamsburg on what is today North First Street between Berry Street and Bedford Avenue. Willis would remark in his autobiography, "I found that there were forty colored children in the village of Williamsburg between the ages of five and sixteen, who did not attend school; many of whom could neither read nor write. At this time there was but one free school in the village, and I tried to get several of our children in it. They were refused, and I called a public meeting to take the subject into consideration."[19] Shortly thereafter, William, Willis, and their neighbors Samuel Ricks, Lewis H. Nelson, Thomas Wilson, and Henry Davis formed a committee to begin planning for the opening an African school in Williamsburg. They were perhaps inspired by the debates on education that had dominated the New York State Black Convention just one year earlier in 1840, which all of the men had attended. William had also grown up in a family that placed a great deal of importance on education. His father, Charles, had insisted that William receive a proper education in Norfolk, Virginia, so that he could in turn teach the rest of his siblings.[20] It was a natural choice, therefore, that William would become the lead educator at the proposed school. On June 29, 1841, just two years after William's arrival in the village and the same year George Hogarth was looking for someone to replace him in Brooklyn, William resolved to organize a weekly donation paid by the village's free Black community that would provide initial financial support. The Williamsburg African

Above: Eugene L. Armbruster, *Public School 191 or Colored School #3 in Williamsburg*, 1929, gelatin silver print. (V1991.106.125, Eugene L. Armbruster Photograph and Scrapbook Collection, Center for Brooklyn History, Brooklyn Public Library). *Below:* The building in 2023. (Author's photo)

school officially opened that year and had approximately sixty to seventy students. (Today, the later façade of the school still stands as a land-marked protected site on the corner of Union Avenue and Stagg Street). Approximately one month later, the committee placed advertisements in both the *Long Island Star* and *Williamsburg Gazette*, appealing to the larger community for funding and for the donation of books for its students.[21] The *Long Island Star* revealed the omnipresent racism that surrounded free Black Brooklynites when the newspaper chose to place an editorial around the committee's appeal with the headline, "Educate the Colored People—Education Is Less Expensive than Crime."[22]

Despite William's centrality to the founding of the village of Williamsburg's school and its running as its main educator, he was not able to escape the racism of his neighbors. The Reverend Samuel H. Cox, a professed abolitionist and therefore a white ally to Black activists, had fled Manhattan during the 1834 anti-Black race riots in which mobs attacked anyone associated with those who were demanding an imme-diate end to slavery. In Williamsburg, Samuel became the pastor of First Presbyterian Church. William was less than a year into his educator position when Samuel recommended William be fired for his insolence during a meeting of the trustees. William had proposed the building of a new schoolhouse to accommodate the "large number of children now in the district; and also [for] its necessity to the respectability and rapid march of improvement in the village." Samuel Cox recommended that a tax be levied against local residents without their knowledge. William highlighted the moral dubiousness of Samuel's plan and was told, "Only keep quiet, Hodges." When plans for the new school were to be pushed back to 1843, William "expressed himself very freely on the subject be-fore the meeting, when he was informed by Samuel Cox that unless he asked pardon of him for his insolence he could expect nothing further of them."[23] Samuel Cox saw no contradiction in his work as an abo-litionist and in his policing the behavior of his Black neighbors and activist colleagues.

By 1842, Willis, William, and their neighbors formed a committee to campaign to incorporate the African school into Williamsburg's

Common School System. Trustees of the Common School accepted responsibility on the basis that William resign as teacher. The Common School won.[24] It is difficult to say when William's position at the African school in Williamsburg was reinstated, as he appears and disappears from the archives. In 1847, acting as the school's principal, he requested $1,900 in funds from the Board of Supervisors to pay for a new schoolhouse.[25] But by 1850, William was no longer associated with the school, which now had "on register 194 children, average attendance, 99." Instead, Maria Stewart, who had been a vocal women's rights activist in Boston, was now listed as a teacher at the Williamsburg school.[26] Just nine years later, Weeksville investor Sylvanus Smith's daughter Sarah Smith Tompkins Garnet was listed as a teacher in the Female Department, where Georgiana Putnam served as head under the overall leadership of Samuel S. Rankins.[27]

In 1845, Brooklyn's newly formed Board of Education possessed considerable power inside and outside the classroom. It was responsible for the division of the city into school districts, and the result was the creation of fourteen public school districts in Brooklyn, with one of those dedicated to the African schools (renamed Colored School No. 1 in Brooklyn, No. 2 in Weeksville, and No. 3 in Williamsburg). The Board of Education also oversaw purchasing real estate and interior furniture for schools; maintaining all existing school buildings; handling the construction of newer ones; employing teachers, clerks, janitors, superintendents, and other officers; determining courses; selecting textbooks; establishing a training school for teachers; and applying state funds to both schools and the city's libraries.[28] But financial troubles soon hit the former African schools when the Board of Education absorbed their management. This was not new: as early as 1831, of the $100 quarterly allowance allocated to the African school in Brooklyn, only $43.25 was paid, and it was later reduced to $30. This meant that the school's trustees were forced to raise the rest of the funds. These systemic issues, which the Board of Education was expected to alleviate, continued under its management, so that issues of overcrowding, the nonarrival of allocated funds, poorly paid educational staff, inadequate books and teaching supplies, and the lack of general resources were never addressed.[29]

Despite these problems, these three African schools, together with their educators and students, remained central to public displays of celebration and joy. They were at the center of the West India Emancipation Day celebrations, and they also honored the school's achievements through exhibitions. Exhibitions, or examination days, were common events across Brooklyn and New York. Advertised in the local and Black press, these events were open to the public, showcasing the schools' academic achievements, and they served as part open house, part fundraiser. They were therefore crucial to the city's Black-led schools as a way of elevating their profiles in the city, and they served as one way of addressing a systemic and chronic lack of funding and resources (though the city's Board of Education rarely attended). Black educators and students appeared at exhibitions held at the AME Church when George Hogarth and then Augustus Washington were the lead educators (March 31, 1831, and September 3, 1841, respectively). On those occasions, "there were aged parents, who had never enjoyed the advantages of education, listening with delight and wonder to the attainments of their own children."[30] Exhibitions continued in Williamsburg (June 2, 1842), where Maria Stewart led student recitations in geography, arithmetic, and astronomy; at the Brooklyn Institute on Washington Street (August 4, 1845); at the Tabernacle on Pierrepont Street (January 26, 1850), led by William J. Wilson, in which the children displayed their proficiency in spelling, reading, geography, grammar, arithmetic, and astronomy and exhibited "beautiful specimens of worsted work, flower painting, drawing, map coloring, &c"; and finally at Colored School No. 1 (1851), where students showcased their achievements in English, natural philosophy, and history.[31] But these events were also politically motivated. Brooklynites publicly demonstrated their readiness for full citizenship, while disabling racist stereotypes and creating a new generation of young activists ready to tackle structural racism. As one scholar notes, the ability of these young students, "never seeming afraid," in front of mixed audiences "gave black adults an opportunity to rethink their own position in the social fabric."[32]

The names and faces of the city's Black activists and prominent residents were changing, even if their struggles were not. Peter Croger, part of Brooklyn's first wave of activism, died in December 1848. He bequeathed his property to his wife, Elenor Croger, thereby making her a property owner in nineteenth-century Brooklyn—although she would still lack the right to vote. His brother, Benjamin, acted as executor of the estate, and their neighbor Willis Jones was appointed as coexecutor.[33] It was not the first time Benjamin would act as executor within the community. A decade earlier, Benjamin and George Hogarth were listed as executors of the late couple Mary and Joseph Johnson. They placed an advertisement in the *Long Island Star* asking all creditors to come forward so that the couple's debts could be cleared.[34] Capitalism, which centered credit, debt, labor, and production, was firmly entrenched in Brooklyn. Starting in 1840 and in the two decades that followed, land developers and industrialists aggressively pursued profits over people as they focused on the untapped commercial potential of the city's waterfront. By the 1850s, Brooklyn was well on its way to becoming the third-largest city in the United States and intricately tied to the economies of slavery once again.

PART III

THE CITY IN CRISIS

1850s

CITY OF COMMERCE

I had brought up into Fulton Avenue, one of the great out-
lets of Brooklyn, and destined yet to become one of its leading
business streets. Three years ago, lots in this street might have
been purchased for three hundred dollars, now they cannot be,
for three thousand.

I am fully persuaded that what few capitalists we have,
have greatly erred, in not taking advantage of the infant condition of the growing Town by securing good business localities especially, not only as a source of profit to themselves,
but as a great means of inducting African America into the
business world.

> —William J. Wilson, writing as Ethiop,
> *Frederick Douglass' Paper*, May 27, 1852

Throughout the State of New York, colored men are occupied
or employed as farmers, blacksmiths, engineers, inventors, carpenters, machinists, cabinet makers, engravers, masons, type
founders, brass founders, merchant tailors, hair dressers, hatters,
painters, coopers, tinsmiths, printers, shoemakers, silver platers,
jewelers, musicians, watch makers, chemists, grocers, drug store
keepers, professors, clergymen, editors, teachers, physicians,
stock and land brokers, stone cutters, ship builders, lumber
dealers, sail makers, wheelwrights, traders, &c., &c.

The cities of New York, Brooklyn and Williamsburgh
contain more than a third of the entire colored population of the State. A hurried investigation, in which
many instances have been overlooked, and all the es-
timates rendered low, show that colored persons
have invested in business, carried on by themselves—

> In New York City, $775,000
> In the City of Brooklyn, 76,200
> In the City of Williamsburg, 4,900
> Total, $836,100

> —James McCune Smith, in William C. Nell's
> *Property Qualifications or No Property*
> *Qualifications: A Few Facts* (1860)

FULTON STREET, FROM THE FERRY, BROOKLYN, N. Y.

Fulton Street, from the Ferry, Brooklyn, N.Y., 1857, engraving. (M1975.763.1.1, Prints and Drawings Collection, Center for Brooklyn History, Brooklyn Public Library)

Each fall, Brooklyn's busy Atlantic Avenue closes to one of the borough's oldest and largest annual street festivals. Since 1974, Atlantic Antic has celebrated the long history of capitalism and commerce along its thoroughfare. Crafts, food, and market stalls line the street during the festival, partly against the backdrop of Cobble Hill's landmarked historic district. The earth that forms Atlantic Avenue once belonged to the Livingston and Remsen families on stolen Indigenous ancestral land. The Livingstons and Remsens would slowly parcel it off and sell it to private investors. In the eighteenth century, it morphed into a dirt road that ended at Ralph Patchen's farm, which overlooked the East River. In the Battle of Brooklyn, this site served as a fortification for George Washington's army. Eventually, Patchen's private dirt road became District Street and formed the southern boundary of the village of Brooklyn. In 1855, District Street was renamed Atlantic Street, ultimately transforming into an avenue in the 1870s, and by the late nineteenth century, both Atlantic and Fulton Street were established commercial thoroughfares.[1] By the early to mid-twentieth century, Atlantic was an economic hub for the Arab American community displaced from lower Manhattan's Little Syria. Today, the conglomeration of architectural styles and big and small businesses is captured in the triangle formed by the long locally owned Sahadis and the Damascus Bread and Bakery Shop next door, which sit diagonally opposite the retail chain grocer Trader Joe's, housed in the former South Brooklyn Savings Bank, built in 1924. The bustle of this part of Atlantic Avenue is markedly different from its west end, where the street meets the East River and car traffic impedes pedestrian flow due to the BQE's baffling design. But it was precisely here, at Atlantic and Hicks Street, that a Black-owned business once thrived.

In 1852, Atlantic was still two decades away from morphing into an avenue, but its radical transformation from dirt road surrounded by cornfields to busy thoroughfare in less than a decade provided new opportunities.[2] That year, thirty-year-old Mary Wilson opened her crockery store at 66 Atlantic Street.[3] Located in a fashionable shop-ping district, her store was in a busy area of the city with further commercial and industrial activity as you headed westward. Here along the waterfront, the smells and noises from the factory of the glass manufacturer John L. Gilliland & Co. (it would eventually become Corning, maker of Corningware) would have been familiar to Mary and her customers, and the South Ferry, which began shuttling passengers from Brooklyn's Atlantic to Manhattan's Whitehall Street in 1836, ensured good foot traffic to the store. Given these factors, it is more than likely that Mary's store served Brooklynites and New Yorkers of all races and ethnicities. As a crockery store owner, Mary was part of a long history of entrepreneurial Brooklynites fulfilling their neighbors' every dining needs. Crockery, particularly china, once a luxury of the rich, was especially in demand by middle- and upper-middle-class New Yorkers and Brooklynites in the mid-nineteenth century. Today, New York City's archeologists rely on crockery shards and their remnants long buried deep in the city's soil as the single most retrievable product in digs to piece together the lives of New Yorkers past.[4]

The nature of Mary's business and its prime location would have been lucrative for her and her family, which included her educator husband, William, and in 1852, their then eight-year-old daughter, Annie. But the existence of Mary's business also indicates the ways in which ordinary Black women experienced capitalism and patriarchy and how they navigated the city's changing political economy in their day-to-day lives. We know about Mary's store today because she is listed in the city directory for 1853, which was unusual even at that time. Although the city directory follows contemporary naming conventions and lists her as "Mrs. William J. Wilson," with the usual asterisk to indicate race, these directories normally only captured heads of households (which could also include widows). It rarely listed married women regardless of race, even less so businesswomen, and even rarer than that a Black woman. But it is crucial to remind ourselves that rather than treating the exception as the norm, there were probably hundreds of Black women just like Mary sustaining the city's economy in more informal ways. And while there might not be any written record of their commercial activities, they still deserve to be honored.

Despite Mary's business standing, she was still susceptible to gendered politics. Ten doors down from Mary, at 56 Atlantic Street, John N. Still, an acquaintance of her educator husband, William, operated his retail and wholesale secondhand clothing business with a "large and rapidly increasing run of good cash customers—a fine store on as good business street as any city can afford, and a good credit with some of the most respectable firms in the city of New York."[5] John was looking for a business partner and made it clear that he sought a Black man only to infuse cash capital into the store; no Black women were invited. Given the gendered politics of the Victorian era, an advertisement that reimagined Black women at the center of commerce might have been impossible, even as Mary was organizing in similar radical activist circles alongside her husband, William, and her commercial neighbor John. Still, while William was working as an educator at Colored School No. 1, he was also the *Frederick Douglass' Paper* Brooklyn correspondent, writing under the pseudonym Ethiop, offering news and reflections on business, education, the Black conventions, and politics in general and mocking his New York rival "Communipaw," the pen name for James McCune Smith, who was also a columnist for the same paper. Here William writes a touching tribute to the blossoming of Black-owned businesses along Atlantic and Fulton and refers directly to the separate businesses of John Still and his wife, Mary:

Taking a circuit towards the "Heights," I missed Fulton street, (which I intend to visit some day) but, fetched up into Atlantic street; coursing downward towards the Ferry with the multitude I crossed another extensive *clothing house*; and had I not known that the proprietors were colored, I certainly believe I should have doubted my own eyes. Such activity, such promptness, such business like air and tact is rarely found in any one House, certainly not in Atlantic street; and with all such a crowd of eager customers. More than one white man extensively engaged in business has stepped in this house for consultation and advise, and gone out profiting thereby. In fact, the best business man in the street is at the head of this establishment.

Next door to this, number fifty-eight I think, I found a very respectable little business conducted entirely by a female. Truly, thought I, as I retired to my lodging, these are beginnings not to be despised; if encouraged and fostered they will grow to great results; yet but *Oasis*, they may with care and attention, flourish and spread over the whole surface. May I not be disappointed.[6]

William, Mary, and their daughter Annie Wilson lived in Brooklyn at a time of rapid commercial expansion, and they were determined to grow with it.

THE WILSONS OF THE CITY OF BROOKLYN

More anon, ETHIOP. Brooklyn Heights.
—"From Our Brooklyn Correspondent," *Frederick Douglass' Paper*, December 25, 1851

Mary Ann Wilson was born in New York around 1822, and her husband, William J. Wilson, was born in Trenton, New Jersey, around 1818; but both would dedicate their thirties toward institutional and community building in the city of Brooklyn. The couple were married by the abolitionist and rector of St. Philip's Church Peter Williams Jr. on November 2, 1837, in Manhattan, where William worked at a bootblacking business at 15 Ann Street.[7] By 1845, the Wilsons and their eight-year-old daughter, Annie, had relocated to Brooklyn's Fifth Ward so William could take over educator duties at Colored School No. 1, as the previous teacher, Augustus Washington, had departed for Dartmouth College. William was also now writing for *Frederick Douglass' Paper*.[8] Their home was in the area where DUMBO and downtown Brooklyn meet today, neighboring the Navy Yard and the newly emerging neighborhood of Fort Greene to the east. According to the 1850 federal census, the Wilsons lived in a mixed immigrant working-class neighborhood—their immediate neighbors were listed as white and from Barbados, England,

Germany, Ireland, and, closer to home, New Jersey and New York and were engaged in work as bakers, coachmen, farmers, porters, rope makers, silversmiths, and tailors. Only one other Black family lived close by. By this time, William was listed on the census as owning $600 worth of property, meaning he could vote, and his occupation was listed as "educator." But he had not forgotten his entrepreneurial roots. William was one of the founding members of the national American League of Colored Laborers, one of the first Black-led unions in the country; he served alongside members including Frederick Douglass and Henry Bibb.[9]

By 1855, the family had relocated to 4 Greene Avenue in the city's Eleventh Ward, known today as Fort Greene. Like so many other Brooklynites, the Wilsons moved east to a rapidly developing residential neighborhood on the fringes of the city as Brooklyn. Originally farmlands owned by the Ryerson, Post, Spader, and Jackson estates, Fort Greene was, like most of Brooklyn, sold into smaller lots to private investors. The Wilson family moved at a time when Fort Greene was slowly shedding its working-class roots and morphing into a middle-class neighborhood—animals were cleared from the streets, and residents of the shanties were displaced so that their homes could be replaced by frame and modest row houses.[10] The Wilsons would have had access to Washington Park (today's Fort Greene Park) and been within walking distance of Siloam Presbyterian Church, then located at Prince Street near Myrtle Avenue, where they were active members.

As the longest serving educator in Brooklyn's African schools in the pre–Civil War period and a gifted and prolific writer, William made a series of valuable recorded observations about the history of the African school system in Brooklyn, specifically its golden era in the early nineteenth century and then subsequent abandonment after its acquisition by the Board of Education. In a letter to Henry Stiles, serving as librarian of the Long Island Historical Society (later Brooklyn Historical Society and now Center for Brooklyn History at Brooklyn Public Library), William, knowing the value placed on the written word, corrected a number of misinformed racist narratives about the history of the African schools.[11] In 1850, Colored School No. 1 consisted of a primary and grammar department. In 1854, the school also opened a library. The connection between literacy and liberation was made clear by an "Observer" (possibly William himself) writing in *Frederick Douglass' Paper*: "The conclusion forced upon our mind was, if such little guardian care may have raised a youth from degradation to respectable manhood, how many are lost for the need of such; and how much may such an institution as we are now forming, do to help them, and not only to manhood, but to worth and honor!"[12]

In 1847, according to the *Brooklyn Daily Eagle*, only 4,345 children aged between five and sixteen out of a total of 13,955 white children in Kings County attended school. Yet 255 of 387 registered Black children went to the African schools in Brooklyn, meaning that the Black community boasted a higher rate of attendance.[13] In 1851, John J. Zuille, acting on the Committee for Education, presented the following landscape of the city's African schools:

In the city of Brooklyn, there is a public school capable of seating 450 children, having on register 300 and an average attendance of 200. Taught by Mr. William J. Wilson and Miss Wilson.

A Public School at Carsville, 60 on register—average attendance 40, 12 of whom are white. Mr. Junius C. Morel, Teacher.

At Williamsburg, there is a public School having on register 194 children, average attendance 99. Mr. E. Jinnings and Mrs. M. W. Stewart, Teachers. An Evening School, 69 on register, 16 average attendance. Private School by Miss Jane Williams, 40 on register, 27 average attendance.[14]

Despite the schools' growth, sustaining enrollment, attendance, and then retention became an ongoing issue. For William, the success of the African schools depended on funding, which was continually lacking and was also hindered by the general racism that Black educators faced. James Pennington, who had contributed to the city's first wave of anti-slavery activism, recalled the trouble he encountered as a teacher at a mainly white school in Long Island. He writes,

When I entered my field of labor as a teacher, I was soon made sensible of the necessity of having the confidence of the parents of the children I was to teach. Having previously visited the place and engaged with the trustees, I went on the day appointed (5th of March), on foot from Brooklyn seven miles and a half in the snow ankle deep. I arrived at my school house door, teacher-like, at half past eight in the morning. . . . The parents had in advance, to some extent, imbibed a prejudice against a colored teacher: and some had so little idea of a colored teacher, that they were astounded when I appeared, supposing that I had been a white man. On the seventh day of March, I found myself seated in the room with nine scholars to begin with. But here comes the first difficulty in the school room—scholars but no books. I made the best I could of my little visitants, by spelling them all off one book, making out a list, cultivating acquaintances, &c. I found the little rogues very shy—very shy indeed, doubtless they participated in the disappointment of their parents in not seeing a white man in their stead. The gentleman who founded this school founded also a school for poor white children. He furnished a quantity of books, slates, &c., for both schools; but the white school went into operation first, and took all the books and slates, which left us destitute. I repaired to Brooklyn that evening and laid out several dollars of my own money for books and other school stuff. And by the third day I found myself quite snuggly underway with twelve little Long Island Dutch chaps for my company. (The school was situated on the Dutch lane too, if you please). . . . In the discharge of my duty, I soon had occasion to see what the character of Long Island slavery had been. It was perhaps the vilest the sun ever shone upon. The slaveholders of the Island were principally Dutch and reprobate Quakers. And all the world knows that when these combine to do wrong we have the subtlety of the serpent and the sullen perseverance of him that begun his quest in heaven![15]

William's concern was also the lack of commitment from Black parents to send their children to Black-led schools. The editors of the

Brooklyn Daily Eagle blamed the carelessness of Black parents for their children's lack of education. But this racist take was to be expected from the Democratic newspaper founded in 1841, which had a long history of deriding the city's Black residents.[16] William's concerns were slightly different. He criticized Black parents for sending their children to the main public school and thereby, in his view, fostering a mediocre education. He argued, "Those who have charge of education matters among us here, instead of encouraging and, if need be, compelling our youth to attend within their own district and school, especially to train them up to and beget within them stable habits, act as though wholly ignorant of the matter, or as indifferently as though it were entirely without their province."[17] He echoed the same concern again two and a half years later. William writes in the *Frederick Douglass' Paper*,

> Thousands of children hereabouts have commenced their *Autumn School Term*, and not a few colored ones among the number. But the Institution, our branch of it as a whole, how different from the white one! Instead of a vigorous Institution, in which are being fitted our sons and daughters for the real duties of life, we find it a languishing, sickly thing; while those whose business is to make it what it ought to be, are found whining and fawning round the doors of the white branch, and hankering after the crumbs that fall there—such as even their beggars refuse to snap up. Instead of being like a forest in which are being grown fine thrifty *oaks*, which are to compose some day, (not far distant,) a part of our country's *ships*, our branch of the Institution, as a whole resembles more a neglected patch, in which the seeds had been good and the husbandmen faithful, but the nutriment lacking. *Parents*, *Guardians*, *and Sponsors*, you are that nutriment so much needed. In your longings for this change, from the black flock to the white flock, you say in extenuation more can be gained there; better pasture for your little lambs. Ah! Is it so? Let me tell you something. You may neglect your own schools, and cringingly crowd or clandestinely slide your little ones into white schools, and slink away from the white presence with a satisfaction

wonderfully astonishing; but if you have ever heard of or know anything of a condition of a toad under a harrow, then in the comparison
you may draw a very faint outline of their condition.[18]

William's views were not shared by everyone in his circle. Although
he served as an elder at Siloam Presbyterian, the pastor of the church,
Amos N. Freeman, argued that William's focus should be on addressing
structural inequality rather than blaming individuals, and he highlights
William's hypocrisy:

> I will say it is true that Ethiop did say that he did not blame anyone
> for sending where the higher branches are taught, and that he would
> do the same thing; and, sir, I think that it can be shown that he has
> been known to express the wish, that he could send his little daughter
> to a white school, on account, merely, of better association. Will he
> deny this? But how strange it is, that white schools should prove to be
> degrading to colored children, and yet be the means of producing such
> a man as Ethiop, who told me himself that he never attended a colored
> school! And yet don't deny his people. Now, let me say here, that I am
> not for abandoning our colored schools, nor never have been. I should
> as soon think of giving up our colored churches as our schools.[19]

The city's educational frameworks presented a genuine economic
dilemma for working-class families and especially for Black people in
Brooklyn and New York, where an education came with no guarantee
of economic or social mobility. In a city where racial capitalism ensured that many families lived in a poverty trap, all potential wage earn-
ers, even children, might contribute to the household's finances, making
a formal education a second priority. Moreover, there were only three
major African schools across the city, all with lengthy distances between
them. For a child living in Gowanus, commuting to either the downtown
Brooklyn, Weeksville, or Williamsburg school would have been an enormous undertaking—if they were allowed on public transit at all. It was
in these scenarios that Sabbath schools played a major role in educating

Brooklyn's children, and there was one attached to each of the city's major Black churches: Bridge Street, Siloam, and Concord. In 1830, Brooklyn's Black churches, given the popularity of the Sabbath schools, formed the Union African Sabbath School for Adults and Children, located at the Apprentices' Library.[20] Students were not required to be members of the congregation to attend classes, and teacher-to-student ratios were often smaller and therefore more favorable.[21] Sabbath schools engaged in public exhibitions, or open days, like the African school system, to celebrate student achievement and often brought together the city's white and Black churches. On a warm and sunny day in May 1859, schools attached to Plymouth Church, Concord Baptist, the Bridge Street AME Church (renamed after its relocation), First Presbyterian, Second Presbyterian, and Siloam Presbyterian came together in public procession. "The juveniles," who were "dressed in their best," gathered on Brooklyn's streets, and at 1 p.m., "the different schools marched forth. . . . The city was alive with juveniles,—young men and young ladies, and with the numerous school banners, presented a most agreeable and attractive spectacle."[22]

Brooklynites continued to take to the streets in celebration, but Brooklyn's Black residents were rightly concerned about the right to the city. The city's rapid urban transformation meant new public transit networks, with their own legal frameworks that focused more on policing than transportation. As the historian Darryl M. Heller writes, "According to legal precedents, urban streets at this time were unquestionably public property, meaning that they belonged to everyone and no one. Private individuals were thus prohibited from infringing upon this public space on behalf of their personal interests. Street railway corporations, however, were the distinct exception to this rule."[23] For the educator and New Yorker Elizabeth Jennings, boarding the Third Avenue Railway Company's horsecar at Pearl and Chatham Streets in Manhattan without the car having the designation "colored persons allowed" resulted in her violent removal in 1854. Elizabeth was represented by a young Chester Arthur, and the trial moved to Brooklyn, where a judge ruled in her favor and she was awarded compensation plus court costs. For James Pennington, however, being removed just a year before from a ferry that crossed the East River had no such justice. James relied on the Fulton Ferry as part of his commute from his home in South Brooklyn (today's Cobble Hill) and his workplace at Shiloh Presbyterian in Manhattan, where he served as pastor. "These boats run as a fast as possible all the while both day and night," observed William M. Bobo, a Southerner vacationing in New York in 1852. "There are always many passengers and that at particular hours at morning and night they are literally crowded."[24] These packed ferries were separated into male and female cabins, but the male cabin had a particular reputation for its poor appearance, which often included a filthy floor usually wet with seaweed and a general strong smell of stale tobacco. It was custom, therefore, for commuting Brooklynites and New Yorkers to stand temporarily in the women's cabin. On a hot July day in 1853, James waited in the women's cabin but was the only person asked to leave.[25] Tired of the daily racism that people of color faced on public transit, James formed the Legal Rights Association with Amos Freeman and the New York activist T. Joiner White. They sued the Union Ferry Company, which operated the Fulton Ferry, but ultimately lost the case.

Movement across New York's waters formed the backdrop to other, more sinister occurrences. Over half a century after the slave trade was made illegal in the US in 1808 (even as slavery itself remained legal in the country), New York's harbor reminded its residents otherwise. On September 15, 1860, the *Friends' Intelligencer*, an anti-slavery newspaper, reported that a "suspicious-looking fast sailing brig, having on board a large quantity of rice and water-casks," left the Atlantic Dock in Red Hook, Brooklyn, where it was "reported that she took her departure for the coast of Africa, for the purpose of returning to the Western shores of the Atlantic with a cargo of negroes." The rumor was that "vessels that line up regularly in Brooklyn are constantly engaged in the African slave trade."[26] But it was not just the activities in the water but also those along the waterfront itself. While residents campaigned for a more just city, a growing waterfront economy that relied solely on unfree labor would secure the city's fortunes into the decades that followed. Brooklyn was central to the business of slavery.

THE WALLED CITY

Construction workers pierce the morning quiet along Williamsburg's long-disused waterfront as hammer takes to sheet metal. Today's residents wince at the noise as development continues at a frenzied pace, and a serenity one might expect when jogging or walking the dog is drowned by a monotonous and continuous bang-bang-bang-bang. But the echo of that banging sound is a reminder of how little sometimes things change in Brooklyn. Before the manicured turf and promenade now called Domino Park existed, nineteenth-century Williamsburg was a place of industry, bellowing factory smoke, giant warehouses, frenzied waterfront activity, and all the trappings of environmental pollution that would have disrupted the morning calm for its past residents, dwelling in their modest frame houses, too.

Brooklyn's access to water—the Red Hook peninsula, Gowanus Creek, Newtown Creek, Gravesend Bay, and, of course, the East River—together with the abundance of open space had long contributed to its prosperity. The Lenape, Long Island's Indigenous peoples, lived off the land's fertile soil and fished in its creeks. In Marechkawieck and Nayack (now Brooklyn Heights and Fort Hamilton, respectively), they planted corn and tobacco. In Gowanus, they had access to an abundance of oysters. Toward the southern end of Kings County, the Canarsee had grown maize, beans, squash, and gourds. As Europeans colonized Long Island during the seventeenth century, decimating most of Its indigenous population, the Dutch built their farms and small villages close to the shoreline and retained close communication with neighboring New Amsterdam. By the end of the eighteenth century, market farming stretched from Bushwick to the Flatlands, and a number of cottage industries emerged out of this development. Long, cavernous ropewalks for the manufacture of rope lay in close proximity to the Fulton Ferry, reflective of the county's economic reliance on water. After the opening of the Erie Canal in 1825, new waterfront warehouses, tanneries, and factories manufacturing such commodities as paint, glass, and glue opened in Brooklyn.[27] By 1848, salt marshes, which had once been the envy of the Dutch, had dried out, and the Gowanus Creek had been turned into the Gowanus Canal for the purpose of establishing "a conduit for sewage and storm water."[28] In 1855, the city of Brooklyn absorbed the city of Williamsburg. The annexation presented industrialists with an unrivaled economic opportunity along a waterfront stretching approximately fourteen undeveloped miles.

Yet few could have predicted the city's rapid industrial development in the mid-nineteenth century. During gradual emancipation, the local resident Gabriel Furman recalled hearing the street cries of Margaret selling hot corn, depending on that season's locally grown yield. That romanticized scene was replaced just two decades later by an abundance of the crop, as corn was shipped from the US South and the West Indies in the latter part of May and June and from the North in September.[29] The importation of crops that had once been native to Brooklyn's soil was made possible by the rapid development of the city's waterfront, which began with the construction of the Atlantic Docks. In 1840, the businessman Daniel Richards looked to Brooklyn's Twelfth Ward for commercial opportunity. The area was an obvious choice for Daniel especially as Manhattan's warehouses were expensive and overcrowded. In Brooklyn, merchants could store their commodities cheaply, while they negotiated prices and taxes at the nearby Merchants' Exchange and New York Custom House on Wall Street in Manhattan. Daniel Richards was not the first to recognize Brooklyn's commercial potential. The Dutch had marveled at the area, as it was known for its distinct red clay soil and marshland, and named it Roode Hoek (meaning "point" or "corner"). The Red Hook peninsula, which became part of a general area that nineteenth-century Brooklynites called South Brooklyn, stood between Buttermilk Channel, Gowanus Bay, and the Gowanus Canal. Originally settled by Dutch colonists in 1636, by 1839, the peninsula and the surrounding area were central to the city's urbanization plans. As a result, developers filled in ponds, leveled the area, and created new streets. Daniel Richards transformed Red Hook's swampland by creating a mammoth docking and warehousing district that he would name the Atlantic Docks.

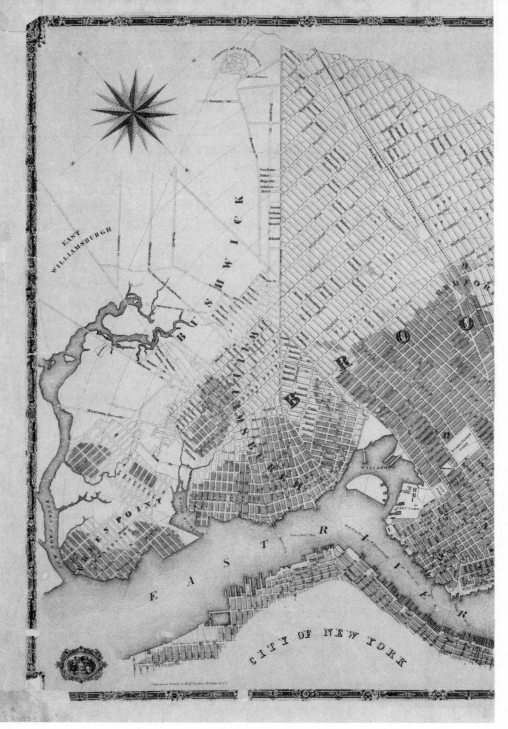

J. H. Higginson, *New Map of Brooklyn, Williamsburgh, Bushwick and Green Point as United in One City*, 1854. (B A-1854.Fl, Map Collection, Center for Brooklyn History, Brooklyn Public Library)

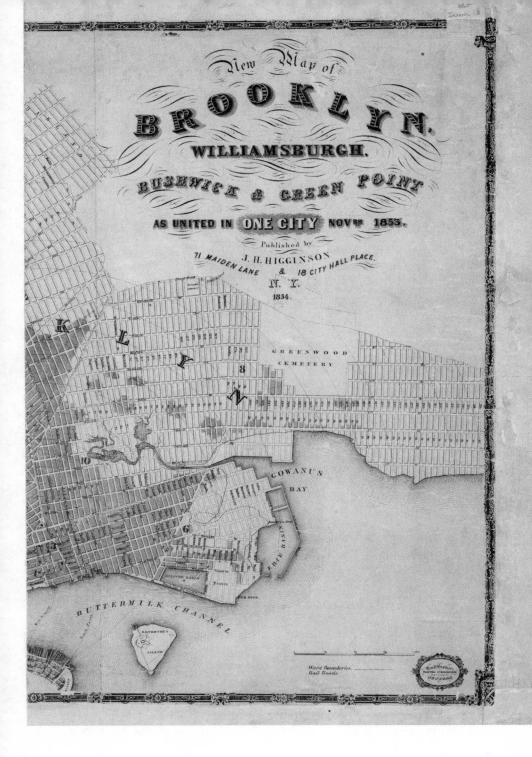

New Map of

BROOKLYN,

WILLIAMSBURGH,

BUSHWICK & GREEN POINT

AS UNITED IN ONE CITY NOVbr 1853.

Published by

J. H. HIGGINSON

71 MAIDEN LANE & 18 CITY HALL PLACE.

N. Y.

1854.

GREENWOOD CEMETERY

GOWANUS BAY

ERIE BASIN

ATLANTIC BASIN

RED HOOK

BUTTERMILK CHANNEL

GOVERNOR'S ISLAND

Ward Boundaries.
Rail Roads.

The Atlantic Dock Company permanently changed Red Hook, which lost its distinctive red soil, marshland, and working-class dwellers. "The object of the [Atlantic Dock] company," wrote Daniel and the company's fellow founders, "is to construct *Docks*, *Bulkheads*, and *Piers* forming a *Basin* to embrace a surface of about 42 acres, and a Hydraulic Dock within the same."[30] The deep Atlantic Basin and its surrounding warehouses were completed by 1847 and housed industrial ingenuities like a steam-powered grain elevator, while the surrounding water's depth allowed both brigs and small ocean steamers to pass through, opening the waterfront to international trade. The Hamilton Avenue Ferry, established in 1846 and located west of the basin, transported laborers and merchants between Manhattan and the docks in Brooklyn.

Developers were confident that the creation of the Atlantic Docks would act as a catalyst to fully industrializing the economy of the city of Brooklyn and result in Brooklyn mirroring the prosperity of another famous port city: Liverpool, England. A long-established site in the Atlantic world, Liverpool, according to the Atlantic Docks' marketing brochure, was once an "inconsiderable town" but now enjoyed an "extraordinary increase in commerce, population, and wealth."[31] What the promotional materials conveniently omitted was that Liverpool had also built its wealth through the exploitation of unfree laborers in the Caribbean and across its British colonies. The brigs that would soon transport slavery's valuable products to Brooklyn—cotton, molasses, sugar, and tobacco—so they could line the city's warehouses intricately tied the economies of the "free" North and the "slave" South.

BROOKLYN'S SWEET PROFIT

The city of New York's interest in sugar began in the colonial period, when the British transported liquid molasses and muscovado, or unrefined brown sugar, from the Caribbean colonies. But Britain was not the only colonial power to prosper from sugar. The sugar industry's sweet profits had also resulted in the creation of vast empires for France, Portugal, and Spain, which all relied on the brutal plantation system in

13

S is the Sugar, that the slave
Is toiling hard to make,
To put into your pie and tea,
Your candy, and your cake.

Detail from *The Anti-Slavery Alphabet*, by Hannah Townsend and Mary Townsend, 1846. (Collection of the Historical Society of Pennsylvania)

the Americas.[32] After the American Revolution, the industry continued to expand in Manhattan. And by the 1850s, Brooklyn's industrialists sought to emulate this exploitative yet profitable business practice by developing their city's waterfront and inviting Manhattan-based companies that traded with Cuba, Puerto Rico, and the US South to store molasses, rum, sugar, and tobacco in their vast warehouses. The business of slavery created immense generational wealth for a new set of Brooklynites including the Pierreponts and Havemeyers, who profited from the nation's sweet tooth. And it was this exploitation of land and labor, whether on the Southern slave plantations of Louisiana or the cane fields of Cuba, that allowed Brooklyn to rapidly expand and become the third-largest city in the United States on the eve of the Civil War. As the historian Craig Wilder notes, "if cotton was King in New York, Queen Sugar reigned across the East River."[33]

William and Henry Pierrepont were the sons of Hezekiah Beers Pierrepont, Brooklyn's first prominent land developer. By 1857, the brothers from this elite family opened the Pierrepont stores (or warehouses) on Furman Street near Montague Street in Brooklyn Heights, about a century before the BQE would split the neighborhood into two. The stores were designed to house commodities until their duties or taxes were paid at the Customs House in New York, and once the sale was completed, a broker could easily travel from Wall Street to

Montague Street on the Wall Street Ferry. One of the major commodities stored at the Pierrepont warehouses was sugar, and the city was at the center of a trading hub that connected domestic and international sugar markets. In 1855, the state census confirmed that commodities that had contributed to the town's early development, such as cordage, rope, and market produce, were still important to the city's economy, but the city's single-largest manufacture was sugar. The commodity arrived in Brooklyn on ships from Cuba, Puerto Rico, and the English, French, and Dutch West Indies. Occasionally the goods remained at the warehouse for long periods of time, especially after the Warehousing Act of 1846, which stipulated that taxes did not have to be paid until a sale was confirmed. But following the economic Panic of 1857, which saw a decline in international trade and an overexpansion of the domestic economy, sugar packed Brooklyn's warehouses. Nevertheless, the city's fortunes multiplied as industrialists found other ways to increase their profit margins.

In 1807, during gradual emancipation, German immigrants William Havemeyer and his brother, Frederick, hired five workers and opened a sugar-refining business on Vandam Street in Manhattan, where the commodity was already big business. Although it had largely been a luxury commodity relegated to upper-class consumption, technological changes, including the inventor Norbert Rillieux's Multiple Effect Evaporator under Vacuum, meant that sugar could now be mass-produced, refined quickly and cheaply, and sold at more affordable prices. By the 1830s, sugar was consumed on a mass basis, but the greater demand for it coincided with crowding along New York's waterfront. By the 1850s, Manhattan's waterfront was congested by the coal, cotton, ice, iron, stone, and wood that were transported across its docks, piers, and wharves. The ports could barely accommodate the canal boats, ferries, steamers, and yachts that moved in and out, and passengers and omnibuses clamored for space, contributing to the ruckus along the waterfront.

In 1855, Frederick's grandson William Osborne Havemeyer relocated the family's sugar business to Brooklyn to avoid overcrowded

Pierrepont Stores.

Pierrepont Stores, ca. 1890, gelatin silver print. (V1973.5.854, Brooklyn Photograph and Illustration Collection, ARC.202, Center for Brooklyn History, Brooklyn Public Library)

Manhattan. He and his business partner, William Townsend, opened the formidable-looking Havemeyer, Townsend & Co. factory on South Third Street along Williamsburg's waterfront. Most of Brooklyn's domination of the sugar industry was made possible by the Havemeyer family, which continued the tradition of importing and then storing sugar in the city. But they took that process a step further and began refining the sugar on-site, thereby increasing their profits. In 1857, the Havemeyer plant produced three hundred thousand pounds of sugar per day, which rapidly increased to one million pounds per day by the close of the Civil War. Once refined, the sugar was packed and then sent domestically via rail or shipped internationally via New York's ports. Even as the Havemeyer family dominated the market, a dozen other sugar refineries soon followed and transformed Brooklyn into a sugar capital. By the late nineteenth century, some of the largest sugar refineries in the world lined Williamsburg's waterfront. Their

Atlantic Publishing and Engraving Company, *Havemeyer and Elder Sugar Refinery*, ca. 1870, engraving. (M1979.1.1, Prints and Drawings Collection, Center for Brooklyn History, Brooklyn Public Library)

Development at Domino Sugar factory at Domino Park, 2023. (Author photo)

success resulted in the creation of the Sugar Refineries Company in Brooklyn, which controlled 98 percent of US sugar output. In 1900, the Havemeyer company changed its name to the more familiar brand we know today: Domino Sugar.[34]

While sugar was sweet for Brooklyn's consumers and industrialists, it was a death trap for enslaved laborers in the US South and the Caribbean. Generations of people of African descent lost their lives working in the sugar plantations of Cuba, Puerto Rico, Louisiana, and South Carolina, as groups of unfree laborers were forced to work in dangerous and exhausting conditions in a relentless and intensive year-round process. The season began in late December with the prolonged backbreaking task of planting the sugar crop. By spring and early summer, workers removed weeds from the growing canes. During the summer months, laborers built canals and ditches to ensure that the fields had sufficient drainage. By early November—when the crop was in harvest—men, women, and children were expected to work with speed nonstop. Enslaved laborers cut sugar canes, stripped the leaves, and transported them to the mill for processing. At the mill, a burning furnace fired up four huge open, boiling-hot kettles so that the cane's extracted juice could be evaporated. Lime was then added to the boiling juice to remove impurities. The workers removed the lime and ladled the sugar into another kettle for evaporation. After the semimolten sugar was checked, enslaved people filled wooden vats, allowing the product to crystallize. Finally, the sugar was packed into large casks with holes at the bottom, allowing the molasses to separate from the brown sugar. Planters then shipped the casks of molasses to domestic and international markets, and the raw sugar was loaded onto ships bound for Brooklyn and beyond for further refining. Once the year's work was complete, enslaved laborers had a few days rest before starting the crop planting again for the upcoming year—that is, if the enslaved person survived the process. The average life expectancy for an enslaved person laboring on a sugar plantation was about eighteen years old.[35]

In 1855, for fifty-one-year-old William Hodges; his wife, Mary Ann Tippon; and their children, nineteen-year-old Julia, fourteen-year old

John Quincy, ten-year old Mary, and nine-year old Sylvia, witnessing the changes to the city's waterfront must have been overwhelming. When William had bought his home as a man in his midthirties in 1839, the lack of development meant that the family would have enjoyed pristine views of the shore and Manhattan. Now Williamsburg, or the Eastern District's waterfront, was home to noise and environmental pollutants that were part and parcel of mass production and the city's global industry. Boat makers, boatmen, brokers, caulkers, dockworkers, dock builders, laborers, merchants, sailors, and ship carpenters lined the city's waterfront. The unprecedented seven miles of factories, ferries, shipyards, sugar-refining plants, and warehouses from Greenpoint in the north of the city to Red Hook in the south placed Brooklyn firmly on the map, as it emerged as a prominent port city vital to domestic and international trade. And in a beautiful development, "this new industrial waterfront created the conditions that allowed queer lives to flourish in Brooklyn."[36] By 1860, Brooklyn became the third-largest city in the United States. And yet, even under racial capitalism's confines, there were plenty of Brooklynites for whom ethical consumerism, consumption, and production were central to their vision for the city.

CONSCIENCE AND COMMERCE

Residents of Brooklyn's past, like residents today, made ordinary— even mundane—daily choices that held deep political repercussions, especially under racial capitalism. A nineteenth-century Brooklynite could choose to support slavery in the churches they attended, the newspapers they read, in whom they voted for, and in their daily consumer choices. In neighboring Manhattan, white Quakers led the short-lived free produce movement, borrowed from a tradition in Boston, Philadelphia, and Wilmington. Their store at 377 Pearl Street deliberately did not stock coffee, cotton, rice, sugar, or tobacco—the popular consumer products made by enslaved labor.[37] But the business ultimately failed due to a lack of popularity and sustainability.

According to written records, there was no such store in Brooklyn. In spite of William Hodges's strong anti-slavery activism and political beliefs, his grocery store in Williamsburg offered a selection of teas, coffees, brown sugar, butter, lard, flour, pork, ham, smoked beef, codfish, mackerel, molasses, table salt, rice, tobacco and soap. But there was a dignity in being able to define the type of work he wanted to engage in. Contemporary census records are lined with residents of African descent engaging in low-wage manual labor, forced to work through economic necessity, and reflective of neither their talents nor their capabilities.

This legacy of slavery was laid bare by Brooklyn's residents and their labor. In 1831, just four years after state emancipation, Henry C. Thompson, George Hogarth, James Pennington, and George Woods questioned Brooklyn's economic inequity at the village's anti-colonization meeting. "In our village and vicinity, how many of us," they asked, "have been educated in colleges, and advanced in different branches of business" and yet were forced to work in the "drudgery of the streets[?]"[38] It was an observation also made by Willis Hodges, who noted that many skilled workers from Virginia now worked in a limited labor market in New York. In capitalist cities like Brooklyn and New York that marginalized Black people and their labor to cart men, domestics, manual laborers, porters, and whitewashers, setting up your own business was a bold proposition but also meant the consolidation of political power. William J. Wilson encouraged self-determination, self-sufficiency, and community networks as a means of fighting economic oppression. "'Try, try again,' must we say to our young men: by trying only will you succeed," he urged. As Ethiop, he wrote, "I am fully persuaded that what few capitalists we have, have greatly erred, in not taking advantage of the infant condition of the growing Town by securing good business localities especially, not only as a source of profit to themselves, but as a great means of inducting African America into the business world."[39] Mary Wilson's store on Atlantic was a powerful reminder of their endeavors, as were the businesses of other like-minded entrepreneurs.

THE SHOEMAKER, BARBER, AND INVENTOR

Less than a mile from Mary's store was the bustling Fulton Ferry commercial area. At one of its intersections at Fulton and Orange Streets, you might have seen all manner of activity. Today the intersection no longer exists, as it was razed to make way for Cadman Plaza Park in 1935 on previously condemned land. But in the 1840s, this area was busy, loud, and vibrant with storefronts, market sellers, passengers, and public transportation. And it was precisely at the intersection of Fulton and Orange that you could find Isaac H. Hunter's shoe business. Born enslaved in Raleigh, North Carolina, around 1809, Isaac had saved enough money from his nightly work making and repairing shoes to emancipate himself through self-purchase, or "by his own labor," for $1,200 (or about $33,000 in today's money).[40] He then saved another $432 to emancipate his wife and children, but it was not enough. Isaac was forced to leave his family behind when his free status triggered a North Carolina law that meant a free person of color had to leave the state or risk reenslavement. He reached out to anti-slavery networks in New York, Philadelphia, and Washington, DC, to raise a further $1,757.60 (or $48,500 today), which also included compounded annual interest, so that he could free his family.

On November 29, 1842, Isaac detailed his family's experience in the *Brooklyn Evening Star*. Isaac explained that once the family was free, they relied on "humane and sympathizing persons" in Brooklyn and Manhattan to adjust to Northern urban life. And at the very bottom of the letter, Isaac describes the economic opportunity he seized upon his arrival in Brooklyn. He set up shop as a shoemaker at the busy commercial corner of Fulton and Orange Streets. There he worked "as an industrious and honest mechanic, and a good workman in endeavoring to support his family in a way honorable to himself, and serviceable to the community."[41] The phrases "by his own labor" and "honorable to himself" are incredibly powerful rhetorical and political devices. Slavery had deliberately dehumanized the Hunter family and countless other enslaved people, only some of whom were able to escape the US South. In Brooklyn, Isaac demanded the ability to express his basic right of a fair exchange of wages and labor through self-employment. But the fact that Isaac chose to have his story published in the city's main newspaper is also significant. Certainly his letter represented an advertising opportunity for his business, but an advertisement in the prolific city directories might have also served the same purpose. Isaac's boldness in sharing his story with the wider public reflects some of the city's own standing by the early 1840s. Brooklyn was an established destination, not just a stopover, for formerly enslaved people to start their lives anew and seek economic opportunity.

By 1847, presumably to make himself an eligible voter, Isaac acquired property on Gerrit Smith's land in the Adirondacks. And by 1850, the family was back in Brooklyn, according to the federal census. Eight years after first arriving in Brooklyn, the Hunter family—Isaac (forty-one years old); his wife, Emaly (thirty-five years old); and their children, Elizabeth (sixteen years old), Hisekiah (fifteen years old), Isaac (twelve years old), Mathias (nine years old), Emaly (five years old), Romulus (three years old), Theophulus (two years old), and Catharine (eight months old)—lived in the city's Fourth Ward (today's downtown Brooklyn), not far from Isaac's original place of work. While most of the family had been born in North Carolina, the youngest four children were born in New York. Isaac had left the shoemaking profession and was now listed in the federal census as a physician, another economic and professional expression of his capabilities.[42]

Given the lack of uniformity in medical training and the ubiquitous racism of US medical schools in their unwillingness to admit Black people in the nineteenth century, it is entirely possible that Isaac was not a formally trained doctor as we might associate with the word "physician" today. However, these professionals served critical roles in the Black community in ensuring the good health of the patients who visited them. Black men, women, and children could choose to visit these healers in their community, or they could go to see their local barber, as most barbers often doubled as physicians. The barbering profession was a critical one in the community, offering Black men "power, prestige, and status," as they tended to own their own business. This political and economic independence placed them among the occupational elite within the Black community.[43]

Just north of where the Hunters lived was Lewis H. Nelson's residence and workplace. Of similar age to Isaac, Lewis was born in Pennsylvania around 1810 and had moved to New York, where he initially ran a grocery and tea store at 53 Anthony Street, New York, with "goods free from slave labor." By 1837, he also served as one of the original publishers for Samuel Cornish's *Colored American*.[44] Around 1841, Lewis relocated to Kings County, and for the next twenty years, according to the federal census, he operated a "Hair Dressing & Shaving Saloon" from his home at 45 Fourth Street, Williamsburg. There otherwise remains very little archival material on Lewis's business and his customer base, although it is entirely possible that Lewis may have been forced through economic necessity to cater to Black and white customers. In an article written by "Long Island Scribe," James Pennington's pseudonym, he remarked that sometimes barbers ignored their Black clients and courted white ones for financial reasons. He asked, "Is it not time that an effort should be made to change the anti-abolition policy of our colored barbers? What can you and I say to rebuke and persuade a white barber, when our own colored men of the same business have as much prejudice as they?"[45] Samuel Cornish, the newspaper's editor, commented that "allowances" should be made, especially as barbers did not always have the luxury to choose their clients, and therefore, economic survival, rather than personal or political choice, often informed their decision.

In 1852, Lewis placed a full-page advertisement in the Williamsburg city directory, and the ad offers a small glimpse into his business persona. He self-identifies as a professor and seeks customers who "are losing their hair, and are on the road to baldness." The business might have gone through a recent refurbishment, as Lewis urges the return of his "old patrons," who, according to the advertisement, consisted of men, women, and children.[46] Two years later, in 1854, the business was still thriving, and Lewis Nelson placed another advertisement in the city directory.

In the same year that Lewis placed his first advertisement in the city directory, Willis Hodges and his growing family returned to a markedly

PROFESSOR NELSON'S
FASHIONABLE
HAIR DRESSING AND SHAVING
SALOON,
No. 45 Fourth Street, Williamsburgh. L. I.,

HAS been enlarged and beautified for the convenience and comfort of the Public—where may be found an extensive assorment of

PERFUMERY,

and where Gentlemen may be relieved of their Beards in the easiest and most scientific manner. Those having never tried his new apparatus for Shampooing, will enjoy a treat by calling and testing it. He hereby invites the attention of all to his new and fashionable style of Gentlemen's and Boys' HAIR CUTTING. Strict attention will be paid to Cutting and Dressing Young Misses' Hair.

NELSON'S
TRICOPHEROUS, OR HAIR INVIGORATOR,

for freeing the head from dandruff, and disposing the hair to curl. Its frequent use will preserve the hair in beauty and health, to the latest period of life.   For sale at

PROF. NELSON'S, 45 Fourth Street,
Between South 7th and South 8th.

Samuel & T. F. Reynolds, *Reynolds' Directory of the City of Williamsburgh, 1854.* (Center for Brooklyn History, Brooklyn Public Library)

different Williamsburg after short stints in the Adirondacks and Virginia. Their neighbors included Willis's older brother, William, and his family; their younger brother, Charles Hodges; and Lewis Nelson. Willis was now married to Sarah Ann Corprew, some seventeen years his junior, and their eldest son, Augustus Michael, was born two years later. Sarah Ann Corprew was born free in New York, but her parents were both formerly enslaved in Princess County, Virginia, where the Hodges family had also lived. One newspaper reported that her father, John Walker Corprew, worked nights as a cooper, making masks and barrels, in order to save enough money to eventually emancipate himself and Sarah's mother. They then moved to New York City in the early 1830s and eventually became Weeksville residents.[47]

By the time Lewis Nelson placed these city directory advertisements, he was more than a hair and health professional. His long career as an activist is well documented. Lewis was a contemporary of David Ruggles, a mostly Manhattan-based abolitionist who founded one of the first Black-owned bookstores. Lewis was also an officer, along with David, in the Garrison Literary and Benevolent Association, which was dedicated to the "diffusion of knowledge, mental assistance, moral and intellectual improvement" and was named for the Boston abolitionist William Lloyd Garrison.[48] In 1841, he joined William, Willis, and Samuel Ricks and opened the African school in Williamsburg that would become Colored School No. 2.[49] And he was a long-term advocate for expanding the vote, along with other activists in Brooklyn and Williamsburg; in 1846, he convened a meeting at Lexington Hall and appeared on a platform to fight voter discrimination with Simon Jocelyn, Alexander Crummell, and James McCune Smith. Lewis's political work built on the activist struggles of early Brooklynites such as the whitewashers Peter and Benjamin Croger.

While whitewashers were considered laborers, they were critical workers in the village and city, as they maintained the city's buildings, even as the work was grueling partly because of their cumbersome equipment. All of that changed with the invention of Freeman Murrow's adjustable brush. Freeman, a fellow Williamsburg resident, lived at 90 Meserole Street and had invented an adjustable brush for whitewashing, painting, and varnishing. "This invention," stated Freeman, "remedies the defects of brushes in common use, having fixed and immovable handles, and consists in so connecting the handle and the brush, by means of adjustable joints, that the brush can be adjusted to any desired position and angle with its handle." Like Lewis Nelson, he targeted male and female customers.[50] Freeman's invention appeared again in an article titled "Great Inventions by Colored Men." He had secured a patent, but "owing to the strong prejudices and indifference of scientific societies and scientific men," he was unable to accompany his invention to the American Institute Fair, a precursor to the World Fair, and instead "had to have it presented by a white man." "Though an inventor," the article continued, Freeman Murrows was "incapable of negotiating for funds, or controlling the business department of its operation." But in "England or France, Mr. M's invention would have secured him an independent fortune, and redounded to the honor of himself, his family, and his people."[51] The invention won a silver medal at the American Institute Fair in October 1853.[52]

After securing a patent, Freeman formed the Brooklyn Brush Manufacturing Company. Henry Davis served as president, and Bristor Worrick, a whitewasher originally from North Carolina, served as president of supervisors. They held their investor meetings at Battermans Hall, near the corner of North Second and Sixth Streets, Granada Hall at 94 Myrtle Avenue, and at 356 Broadway in Manhattan. The company's Rules of Association included a poem titled "Tornado." Through its many Masonic references, the men declared that the company stood for the "welfare of Civil Rights and not bloodshed," which included the right to vote without restriction and to enjoy the privileges of citizenship without question. They also declared that the company's intention was to liberate the women and girls in their family from menial labor by providing "other means of support for [their] wives and daughters than perpetual servitude as scrubbers and washing servants to others."[53] This was a powerful political statement—few women of color had the choice of rejecting paid work, and many were forced to take positions as washerwomen and domestic servants in order to provide a second or sometimes even a primary income to support themselves and their families. Freeman challenged popular racist assumptions about the capabilities of Black men with his labor and eventually created a context for his own.

Against this backdrop of Black entrepreneurial excellence, in which individuals and collectives created and pursued economic opportunities that showcased their own ambitions in a capitalist economy, also came some of the greatest challenges to Brooklyn's and New York's free Black communities. The 1850s tested their safety in unprecedented ways, with the catalyst being the passage of the federal Fugitive Slave Act. In the decade that followed, the law's devastating aftermath was felt in Brooklyn and beyond.

BROOKLYN, 1850

It is estimated that there are over three thousand fugitive slaves in the Northern and Eastern States; and the excitement among the colored population of these States is at present very great. The most of these fugitives have families, and many are engaged in profitable industry, and live very comfortably in their free homes.

In every quarter of the North and the East, the colored people are holding meetings, and the conclusions arrived at by them are, generally, that they will organize for armed resistance to the execution of the [Fugitive Slave] law, and rescue any fugitive who may be arrested in their midst.

Now, however unpalatable this law may be to individuals (and our own dislike to it has been heretofore expressed) . . . our laws must be maintained and that they *will be* maintained, whatever may be the cost.
—*Brooklyn Daily Eagle*, October 2, 1850

I fled from Brooklyn, because I could not sleep, as I was so near the Slaveholding country. I thought I could not be safe until I had got to the other side of the globe.

(Unnamed fugitive who walked from Louisiana to Brooklyn, found employment in the city, and left shortly afterwards. He wrote these words from a whale-ship in the Pacific Ocean).
—William M. Mitchell, *The Underground Railroad* (1860)

Must Runaway Slaves Be Delivered Back?
They must. Many things may have the go-by, but good faith shall never have the go-by.
—Walt Whitman, "The Eighteenth Presidency!" (1856)

The passage of the infamous Fugitive Slave Law incited a flame of resentment which scorched the souls of those whose lives has been one of protest against the foul injustice of a disregard of the consciousness of human brotherhood. Unknown except to the initiated, a committee of thirteen was formed in our city, each member of which was pledged to keep the letter but to violate the spirit of unholy enactment. Without officers, headquarters, passwords or treasury, this band was liberally supported. Aid was given to escaping slaves, financially or otherwise, by those who required no other details save that such help was needed.

—Maritcha Lyons, *Memories of Yesterdays: All of Which I Saw and Part of Which I Was* (1928)

THIRTY-YEAR-OLD James Hamlet, like many of his neighbors, took the Peck Slip Ferry that left Division Street in Williamsburg in the city of Brooklyn to Peck Slip in the city of New York. From there, he would have walked less than a mile to his job as a porter at the Tilton and Maloney general store, located at 58 Water Street, with clear but not necessarily tranquil views of the East River. With an overdeveloped waterfront, Manhattan no longer offered pristine views of the New York harbor that had once attracted the original European colonizers to Lenape land. But the water still provided economic ties to the South and reminded New Yorkers and Brooklynites that freedom for some was a fragile thing. On Saturday, September 26, 1850, James left Tilton and Maloney and was arrested under the provisions of the Fugitive Slave Act, passed by Congress just eight days earlier—meaning that it was a Brooklynite who was the first casualty of a draconian federal law that obscured the neat distinctions of the "free" North and "slave" South. Professional slave catchers had approached the porter, stating that he was wanted as a witness in a criminal case. He was subsequently accused of being a fugitive who had run away from the enslaver Mary Brown, a resident of Baltimore, Maryland. All it took was a sighting by Mary's son

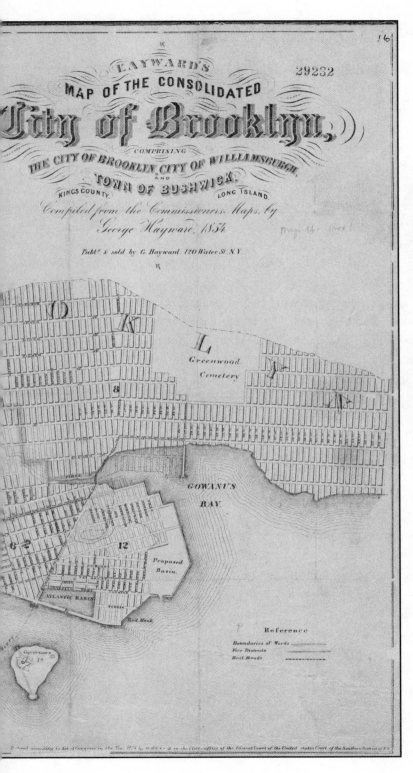

George Hayward, *Map of the Consolidated City of Brooklyn, Comprising the City of Brooklyn, City of Williamsburgh and Town of Bushwick, Kings County, Long Island*, 1854. (B A-1854a.Fl, Map Collection, Center for Brooklyn History, Brooklyn Public Library)

Gustavas, who claimed he had spotted James Hamlet in Manhattan in the six months prior to his arrest. James protested that he was a free man, but under the new Fugitive Slave Act, his testimony was not permitted. He was instead immediately taken to Baltimore amid fears of a rescue attempt by the city's abolitionists.[1] While the Black press and a Sunday newspaper, the *New York Atlas*, covered the incident extensively, the *Brooklyn Evening Star* dedicated just six lines of print after the Williamsburg resident "arrived safe" in Baltimore.[2] On brand for the *Brooklyn Daily Eagle*, the city's Democratic newspaper detailed the terrifying arrest in Manhattan and minimized the organized protest of Black New Yorkers to "threats" by "excited blacks."[3] Neither city newspaper identified James as one of their own, and his story did not even manage to make the *Eagle*'s "City News & Gossip" column, which had been introduced earlier that year. But the danger to Black lives in Brooklyn and New York was not new. Kidnapping and racial violence were a constant threat in the lives of the cities' free Black communities, which made places of safety and refuge like Weeksville resemble an oasis.

In the 1830s, the Manhattan abolitionist David Ruggles warned of bird catchers who would roam Manhattan's streets in order to kidnap free Black people and send them south into slavery. Unprotected by legal frameworks at the city, state, or national level, free Black communities created self-determined systems of safety and welfare. But even those failed against the intense Fugitive Slave Act. James's arrest was the direct result of the federal government's appeasement of Southern Democrats in Congress, to ease sectional tensions that arose from the new land annexed during westward expansion. As the United States expanded following the Mexican-American War (1846–1848), Congress passed the Compromise of 1850—it allowed California, where residents and explorers had struck gold, to enter as a free state; abolished the slave trade in the nation's capital; and intentionally strengthened slaveholders' national interests with one of its bills, the Fugitive Slave Act. The law legalized the kidnapping of any person of color accused of being a fugitive. It was not without precedent. The 1793 Fugitive Slave Act required any fugitive to be returned to their slaveholder, but it was vague in the obligations of its participants. The 1850 version explicitly framed it as one of the many duties of being a good American—anyone found assisting a fugitive would face fines or imprisonment. Any person of color suspected of being a fugitive could be "returned" to slavery in the South, there was no trial by jury, and the accused's testimony was not permitted in court. Moreover, the act created a group of special federal commissioners who were entitled to cross state lines to assist in the arrest of a fugitive, while judges were often given special financial incentives to rule in favor of slaveholders.

On October 2, six days after the arrest, activists packed the Mother African Methodist Episcopal Zion Church in Manhattan, where James had been a congregant, beyond its fifteen-hundred-person capacity. Many of the attendees were Black women—and it is not difficult to imagine Mary Wilson leaving her crockery store on Atlantic in Brooklyn, making her way across the East River, and being present at the protest that night. The audience listened to organizers from New York, such as Samuel Cornish and Albro Lyons, and Brooklynites Junius C. Morel and Robert H. Cousins. James's fellow Williamsburg resident Lewis H. Nelson also appeared on the platform. Just sixteen days after the fundraiser, James was released from a Baltimore jail, as activists had rallied together to raise the $800 needed for his emancipation.

The written archives are often silent on the emotional and economic trauma inflicted on Black families when men were kidnapped from the streets, especially as they were often the main source of income, but we do know that it was James's wife, Harriet, who showed profound strength following his arrest and led much of the fundraising in Williamsburg.[4] Crowds of four to five thousand New Yorkers all gathered at Broadway and City Park awaiting James' return to the city and to hear him speak.[5] Articulating the horror he had faced during his arrest and imprisonment was too much for James, and the Williamsburg resident "regretted his inability to express his feeling to the audience." He was separated from Harriet and their three young children, Cath, Elijah, and Alvord, all born in Maryland but residents of Williamsburg, and the details of his arrest were equally harrowing. He stated,

> Men came where he was to buy slaves; but they were cautioned against buying *him*, as he was a New Yorker, and they would lose their money. It was an intimation that he had tasted liberty, and therefore could never be held again in chains. He expected to be, one day, in his Father's house above, where there would be no more child-stealing. He expected to meet the woman there who had falsely, wickedly claimed him as her slave, when, with his parents, he had been formerly been manumitted, but, through the neglect of his grandmother, had lost his papers and had been retained in slavery. He hoped Millard Fillmore would be brought to repent of his crime of signing the Fugitive Bill, before he is called to render an account before a more fearful tribunal than that of his country.[6]

James returned to the village of Williamsburg on October 5, and a final celebration for his return took place at the AME Church on High Street in Brooklyn.[7] It was a white Brooklyn resident, William Harned, living initially at 130 Bridge Street and then at the intersection of Duffield and Willoughby Streets, who published James's full ordeal in print form. It is William Harned's name that appears on a small handheld-sized pamphlet titled *The Fugitive Slave Bill: Its Unconstitutionality—with an Account of the Seizure and Enslavement of James Hamlet, and his subsequent restoration to Liberty*. The pamphlet form allowed frequently financially troubled anti-slavery organizations to take advantage of a print market where materials could be produced with the widest, cheapest, and largest circulation possible.

At a cost of two dollars for every hundred pamphlets, or five cents for an individual copy, the American and Foreign Anti-Slavery Society printed three editions of the James Hamlet pamphlet in less than six weeks, having sold thirteen thousand copies in the first three weeks of initial publication alone. The third edition included the statement of Judge Samuel E. Johnson, a county judge in Kings County who had refused the position of special commissioner. Despite the attractive financial incentives to law enforcers, the judge deemed the Fugitive Slave Act unconstitutional.[8]

By 1850, Brooklyn had earned the title "city of churches" due to the relatively disproportionate number of sites of faith to the city's population. Though the majority were Protestant (111 in total in 1855), the city also boasted fifteen Catholic churches and one synagogue (today this is Kane Street Synagogue, located in Cobble Hill, which originally stood on Atlantic Avenue and Clinton Street not far from Mary Wilson's store). It was at the Protestant churches that enforcement of the Fugitive Slave Act became a divisive issue for its pastors and congregations. At the still relatively young Plymouth Church, organized in 1847, the newly arrived pastor, Henry Ward Beecher, argued, "the Bible is heavier than the statute-book," and demanded his congregants follow their moral conscience and the attainment of individual perfection, rather than the law that compelled Brooklynites to hand over a suspected fugitive, or their neighbor, to authorities.[9] Less than half a mile away, at Church of the Pilgrims, the pastor, Richard S. Storrs, compelled congregants to do the same. At South Presbyterian Church on Clinton and Amity Streets, the pastor, Samuel T. Spear, was more ambivalent, urging the preservation of the Union but also acknowledging that slavery was a sin. But a mile and a half away at Second Presbyterian Church, on Clinton and Fulton Streets, Ichabod Spencer was clear in his stance: "The question is not, whether slavery is right, or the Fugitive Slave Law right. It draws deeper. The question is, shall Law be put in force, and the government of the country stand; or shall Law be resisted, and the government of the country disobeyed, and the nation plunged into all the horrors of civil war? If Law cannot be executed, it is time to write the epitaph of your country!"[10] Ichabod certainly knew his audience—parishioners at Second Presbyterian, in spite of its location, were mostly wealthy merchants living in Brooklyn Heights and had significant leadership roles in the city, including Isaac Otis, a trustee of the Brooklyn Savings Bank. Nevertheless, for white Brooklynites, the Fugitive Slave Act remained in the moral abstract. Members of the city's free Black community were forced to organize in new practical ways in order to protect and secure their freedom.

BROOKLYN'S GUARDIANS

Imagine to yourself, my dear Douglass, a group of twelve men, seated in a neatly furnished, well warmed, and well-lighted room, in a respectable, but retired part of the TOWN, on a cold December night. The fierce storm and howling wind are ranging without, and the rain comes tapping against the window, as though seeking admission. They draw closer, seemingly in expectation of someone. Presently the door opens, a man enters, the Committee of Thirteen are before you. Near the center of the group, is seated one scarcely of middle height, and of slight stature; and were it not for his massive head and broad forehead, the large arm-chair in which he sits would almost bury him. But there is a countenance indicating that you are in the presence of a superior man, of a master mind. He is quiet, and commands others to be so.

A tall young man of good appearance rises, and commences to speak. His manner is vehement, his style is logical and determined; he is bent on his purpose.

But there is (and I should have mentioned it) another massive head in the room; one that a phrenologist would be proud to pronounce upon. The possessor is perched upon a stool with his head inclined forward. Beneath an overhanging and expressive brow, a pair of small piercing black eyes occasionally from out of their half-closed lids fore-shadowing what is working within. He seems intent rather upon his own thoughts than upon the argument of the member who has just taken his seat.

By the table, taking notes, is a young man, seemingly a youth of gentle manners and pleasant bearing. He has learnt the important lesson, that a young man at the end of his college-journey has but taken the initiatory step in the journey of life.

But stop! Who is this in the background? Faith, he is a handsome man! "mustaches," "imperial," and all, to have been unobserved!

A few of the prominent features of the renowned Committee of Thirteen my dear Douglass, are now before you; I have been rather hiding their presence and power, than exposing them. I shall, on another occasion, speak of the causes of the formation of this Committee and the honorary members, &c as I deem such matters, a portion of the history of the people of color here.

—Ethiop, *Frederick Douglass' Paper*, February 12, 1852

At James's welcome-home celebration in 1850, New York's Mayor Caleb Smith Woodhull gave his word that the city's police force would not participate in the arrest of a fugitive.[11] Just under two years later, James Martin, a police officer in New York's Sixth Ward, arrested Horace Preston. His case was depressingly similar to James Hamlet's: born in Maryland, a resident of Williamsburg, Brooklyn, where he lived with his wife and child, Horace was accused of escaping Baltimore in 1847, around the same time as James. The incidents of police misconduct were not unique to Manhattan alone. In 1839, the *Long Island Star* announced that the young city of Brooklyn had "a police already proverbial for its watchfulness," after factions of Brooklynites pushed for greater police protection and a city police force that could match that of the city of New York.[12] Instead, it would repeat the mistakes of New York—policing its Black communities rather than protecting them.

In 1842—eight years before the Fugitive Slave Act would come to pass—the Brooklyn resident Edward Saxton was accused of being a fugitive from Mobile, Alabama. His captor, J. C. Gantz, also from

Mobile, approached a New York court with an affidavit claiming that Edward had forged his freedom papers. As Edward resided in Brooklyn, J. C. Gantz needed an arrest warrant endorsed by a Brooklyn court. He had little difficulty in obtaining it. An officer named Barkaloo of Brooklyn and J. C. Gantz arrested Edward at Mansion House, a hotel located on Hicks Street between Pierrepont and Clark Streets, and he was taken to a Baltimore jail. The case came before a grand jury for two reasons: Edward's enslavement was deemed illegal without a trial; and no judge of a police court had the power to issue a warrant for the arrest of a fugitive. Edward should have been paid $500 in damages, but he pleaded guilty to being a fugitive—more than likely under duress—and was enslaved again under Alabama law. Officer Barkaloo stated that he had "frequently known warrants for the arrest of alleged fugitive slaves, issued by the Justices of the Police Court, and had himself assisted in arresting several negroes under such warrants, who were delivered to the claimants and taken off." An editorial line in the abolitionist newspaper *The Liberator* aptly commented, "How many similar cases there may have been, we know not."[13]

While there were probably numerous others, the next recorded incident in Brooklyn occurred in 1848. Just five days before Christmas, two free Black men, Joseph Belt and Thomas Peck, were walking along Duane Street in Manhattan when Joseph was kidnapped by the slave catchers Sydney Clayton and Charles Bird, who had been sent by John Lee, a slaveholder in Maryland. Joseph Belt was imprisoned in a house in Gravesend, located at Kings County's most southeastern tip. When Officers Hulse and Wolven were sent to rescue Joseph, they discovered that he had been held in two different houses over three days. Joseph was ultimately returned to freedom, but the rescue was not without incident. The city of Brooklyn did not offer Joseph any compensation for his unlawful imprisonment. Instead, the New York Vigilance Committee, for which William Harned acted as treasurer, was expected to reimburse the police officers for their work; plus any other funds the committee had raised were to be donated as a reward to members of the public who might have offered a tip. William Harned would later highlight in an editorial that the safety and protection of all of Brooklyn's residents should be a basic part of police duty, for which no extra compensation was required.[14]

In the aftermath of the 1850 Fugitive Slave Act, other Brooklynites took on vigilance roles. William J. Wilson's duties as educator at Colored School No. 1 and as an elder at Siloam Presbyterian Church expanded further still. He contributed to local debates on the potential creation of an independent Black-led militia to provide physical protection to New Yorkers and Brooklynites (although one never came to fruition), created emergency fundraising systems as the number of abductions of free men and women of color escalated, and joined a vigilance committee known as the Committee of Thirteen. There were three known vigilance committees at this time.[15] William's Committee of Thirteen consisted of prominent abolitionists from both Manhattan and Brooklyn, and they offered financial assistance to freedom seekers, offered protection from slave catchers, and sustained the protest against colonization. The printer John Zuille chaired the committee, whose members included the journalist Phillip Bell, the doctor James McCune Smith, the restaurateur George T. Downing, all from Manhattan; the educators William J. Wilson and Junius Morel from Brooklyn; and the doctor T. Joiner White from Williamsburg. Information is otherwise scarce on the two other two committees: the Brooklyn-based Committee of Nine and the Williamsburg-based Committee of Five. We do know that all three committees worked together in 1851 to collectively raise funds for the high-profile Christiana Patriots case, in which fugitive defendants in Christiana, Pennsylvania, had been charged with murder, riot, and treason for killing the slave catcher who had come to arrest them and resisting the Fugitive Slave Act. Beyond that, relations between the three vigilance committees appears to have been strained. Writing for *Frederick Douglass' Paper*, William claimed that the needs of Black communities across Brooklyn and New York were met by the Committee of Thirteen alone and questioned the need for a further two vigilance committees. In 1852, when neither the Committee of Nine nor the Committee of Five sent any delegates to that year's state convention in Albany, William criticized them for their notable absence. "Where are they?" he asked, "What are they doing? What are their intentions?"[16]

* * *

The Fugitive Slave Act foreshadowed the cataclysmal decade ahead. In quick succession, Congress passed the Kansas-Nebraska Act, which allowed for the expansion of slavery in the United States (1854); the Supreme Court ruled that Black people were not US citizens in the *Dred Scott* decision (1857); and authorities executed John Brown and his army of men for raiding Harpers Ferry (1859). As the country entered a new chapter of brutality on Black lives and the sectional crisis deepened, the families that had shaped Brooklyn were in transition. Residents such as Peter Croger and George Hogarth died in 1848 and 1850, respectively. Elenor Croger, now sixty-seven years old and Peter's widow, was living with her brother-in-law, Benjamin, and his family, which included his wife, Elizabeth; their daughter, Eliza; and a number of other residents, possibly boarders, relatives, or kith and kin: thirty-eight-year-old Sarah Lane and her daughter, thirteen-year-old Phoebe, and forty-year-old Susan Galser, from Massachusetts, and her children, fifteen-year-old Joseph Galser and four-year-old Lucretia Galser. Benjamin was still working as a whitewasher, according to the 1850 federal census, and fifteen-year-old boarder Joseph was working as a mariner. There are no jobs listed for any of the women or children. Elenor was certainly financially independent of her brother-in-law. Peter had left their home on Pearl Street to her, meaning that she was a property owner in the city of Brooklyn. It is entirely possible that Benjamin and his family had moved into Elenor's home or combined the two homes (the brothers had been neighbors throughout the 1830s and 1840s) or that Elenor sold the property and was living with her brother-in-law's family as she entered old age.[17]

While one generation of Brooklynites was growing old together, new residents to the city continued to pour in—including James and Elizabeth Gloucester—and they were determined to meet the brutality of white supremacy with militant action.

CITY OF REFUGE

It is now nearly twenty one years since I was called by the Common Council to preside over the affairs of the late City of Brooklyn then first ushered into existence.

The population of the City at that time [1834] consisted of about 20,000 persons residing for the most part within the distance of about three quarters of a mile from the Fulton Ferry. Beyond the limit, no streets of any consequence were laid out, and the ground was chiefly occupied for agricultural purposes.

The shores throughout nearly their whole extent were in their natural condition, washed by the waters of the East River and the Bay.

Within the comparatively short period of twenty one years, what vast changes have taken place. . . . Williamsburgh from a hamlet became a City with about 50,000 inhabitants—Brooklyn, judging from its past increase, yesterday contained a population of at least 145,000 persons and on this day . . . takes its stand as a the second City in the Empire State, with an aggregate population of about 200,000 inhabitants.

The superficial extent of the area included within the City limits is about 16,000 acres—The extent in length of the city along the water front is 8½ miles, along the inland bounds 13½ miles, and between the two most distant points in a straight line 7¾ miles and its greatest width 5 miles.

Within these limits 516 streets have been opened for public use, old roads have been discontinued and closed, hills have been levelled, valleys and low lands filled up, old landmarks have disappeared, and almost the whole surface of the City has been completely changed.

A large tract of land in the 8th Ward, containing 360 acres, has been set apart and adorned as the last resting place of the dead, and internments have been made therein, to the number of 38,000; another Cemetery has been more recently laid out and established on the Eastern borders of and partly included within the City. . . .

There are 27 public schools, containing 317 teachers, and about 35,000 scholars, the greater portion of whom are regular attendants.

    —Mayor George Hall, message to Brooklyn's Common
       Council, *Brooklyn Evening Star*, January 2, 1855 (Hall
         served as mayor in 1834 and again 1855–1859)

Build high your forge fires, and cast out your manacles—man your slave ships, and freight over not by hundreds now by thousands, but millions of victims from Africa's coast. Annex Cuba, subjugate Haiti, grasp Mexico, and enlarge your boundaries. Oh, my country! Oh, noble! Oh, patriotic! Oh, liberty-loving republic.

Let the tocsin be sounded, and to arms every man whose skin is not whitened with the curse of God; and let our motto be, "hands off, or death." Instant death.—'Tis useless to delay.

    —Ethiop, *Frederick Douglass' Paper*, June 5, 1854

On Saturday last, a fugitive slave whose name is of no consequence, (not being a citizen according to the Dred Scott decision) arrived at the port of New York . . . from Savannah. On landing here the fugitive was placed in charge of two New York officers, who conducted him to Red Hook Point. [He] is now supposed to be on his way to Canada on the underground railroad.

    —*Brooklyn Daily Eagle*, December 2, 1857

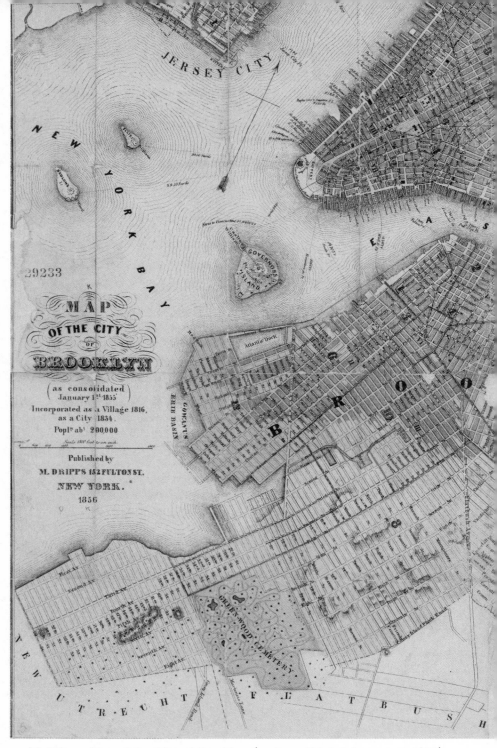

M. Dripps, *Map of the City of Brooklyn (as Consolidated January 1, 1855),
Incorporated as a Village 1816, as a City 1834, Popln. abt. 200,000*, 1856. (B
A-1856a.Fl, Map Collection, Center for Brooklyn History, Brooklyn Public Library)

THE 1850s marked the end of a chapter in Brooklyn's history. In 1853, Elenor Croger passed away and left her property (that Peter had bequeathed to her) and her "best feather bed, one pair of pillows, one bolster, and six silver teaspoons" to her brother-in-law, Benjamin Croger, and his heirs. With the exception of the property, Elenor's estate was fairly small, but she left her worldly possessions equally divided among family and friends, revealing the familial networks that Black women had fostered in the village of Brooklyn. Elenor left her sister-in-law, Elizabeth Croger, "one metallic tea pot, one brass kettle, one castor, two metallic tumblers, two glass desert dishes, one large earthen dish, and one flower dish waiter." For her niece, Eliza Simpson, Elizabeth and Benjamin's daughter, Elenor left one mahogany bureau, one feather bed, a pair of pillows, and one bolster. Left without biological children of her own but having created family, Elenor also left Jane Alice Boerum, "who has been principally brought up" by Elenor, the contents of a trunk and the trunk itself, her Bible, "two bed spreads, six china teacups and saucers, two metallic tumblers, and one fancy quart pitcher."[1] As one generation of Black women joined the ancestors, a new generation, entirely unshaken by the white supremacy that surrounded them, made Brooklyn a city of safety and refuge.

THE GLOUCESTERS OF THE CITY OF BROOKLYN

Brooklyn has long honored its dead. The Lenni-Lenape laid their ancestors to rest in a shallow grave, often lined with bark or dried grass, with vessels of food. Once the dead were departed, families and friends were not to utter their name—with the spirit gone, so was the name.[2] Under distressing conditions, enslaved people created and engaged in rituals of care and community so that their loved ones might finally know peace, a quality that had been robbed from the living. Their sacred stories are well documented at the African Burial Ground in Manhattan and also contained in the earth or empty lots of the Harlem

Elizabeth Gloucester's signature, detail from letter from Elizabeth Gloucester to John Brown, August 1859. (Ferdinand J. Dreer Papers, Collection of the Historical Society of Pennsylvania)

African Burial Ground, Hunts Point and Van Cortlandt Park in the Bronx, and Sankofa Park and the Flatbush African Burial Ground in Brooklyn.[3] Just a mile and a half west from the Flatbush site, remains one of the most decadent resting places for Brooklyn's deceased. In 1838, Brooklynites sought two hundred acres of land in the Gowanus Hills outside of the city's limits to honor Brooklyn's wealthiest in death.[4] In May 1839, the *Long Island Star* celebrated J. H. Colton's map of the city of Brooklyn. Measuring three feet by four feet, the new map included Williamsburg, which would be annexed to the city sixteen years later, and a tiny part of the city of New York. But its main focus was the growing cosmopolitan city of Brooklyn. The map featured churches, lyceums, markets, some noted private residences, and the Brooklyn Navy Yard. A new addition in rural southwestern Kings County showed a cemetery.[5] The result was 478 acres of landscaped hills that make up Green-Wood Cemetery today.

Not far from the Locust Grove Mausoleum in Green-Wood, at lot number 9817, lies a grand stone burial pillar honoring a woman named Elizabeth Gloucester. Her epitaph reads, "The undying love of a mother, is a thing to cherish and keep. We must guard her memory closer now that she has fallen asleep." Buried at the same site are her children Emma (1837–1885), Stephen (1842–1856), Elizabeth (1845–1915), Louisa (1847–1918), James (1851–1930), Charles (1854–1908), and Alfred, who tragically died at age two in 1859. In 1856, Elizabeth and her husband, James, purchased the approximately three-hundred-square-foot plot for $110 (or about $3,000 in today's money). This was a substantial amount for the city's residents and even more so for a Black family living in nineteenth-century Brooklyn. Today, there are no portraits of Elizabeth Gloucester despite her remarkable life. Like so many Black women, her story is buried so deeply in the archives that her contributions to Brooklyn's civic life are nearly erased from mainstream historical narratives. So here follows a retelling of this brilliant Brooklynite's life and that of other women—Sarah Ann Cousins and Mary Wilson—who were her friends and peers, honoring their unwavering commitment to social justice.

In 1823, a six-year-old Elizabeth Amelia Parkhill, born in Richmond, Virginia, had arrived at the home of the Reverend John Gloucester in Philadelphia. It is difficult to piece together the traumatic context that necessitated the young child's move to the North. Very little has been recovered to date on her father's identity, but Elizabeth was frequently listed in census records as "mulatto." Her mother, who was formerly enslaved, might have worked as a cook, but she died when Elizabeth was young. In arriving at the Gloucesters' home in Philadelphia, Elizabeth was at the center of activism, as John was the founder of the Black Presbyterian Church and the city was home to a thriving free Black community. She would have been among the city's Black elite, which included girls and women such as Amy Matilda Cassey, Sarah Louise Forten, and other members of the Philadelphia Female Anti-Slavery Society, and she would have had daily encounters with ordinary working-class Black women too.[6] Her life in Philadelphia, certainly in the immediate years after her arrival, was in marked contrast to her future home of Brooklyn, where slavery was still legal and which was home to a much smaller but active free Black community that lived almost exclusively in Brooklyn's northwestern tip by the Fulton Ferry. In 1836, Elizabeth married John Gloucester's youngest son, James, and the couple moved to the city of New York shortly thereafter. Like Mary Wilson, Elizabeth was a small business owner; Elizabeth initially sold secondhand clothing and later furniture in Manhattan. Her husband, James, "tall and gaunt and dignified," who "stalked through the streets like the personification of knowledge," in 1847 took over pastoral duties at Siloam Presbyterian Church, which met initially at the Hall Buildings at the corner of Fulton and Cranberry Streets until it was formally established two years later at Prince Street between Myrtle and Willoughby Streets.[7] Elizabeth and James settled in Brooklyn sometime in the late 1840s, when the city was an established stop on the Underground Railroad.

THE UNDERGROUND RAILROAD

What will you do with freedom without father, mother, sisters, and brothers?
—James Pennington, *The Fugitive Blacksmith* (1849)

A polite note from Lewis Tappan, last week, informed me that a fugitive slave, nearly as white as himself, would address an audience at Brooklyn; and having curiosity to hear what he would say, I crossed the ferry.
—Lydia Maria Child, *National Anti-Slavery Standard*, October 27, 1842

In 1850, Brooklyn's apparatus for justice—that is, the police department, police court, police officers' room, justices court, and "superintendents of the poor"—were all located in the basement of City Hall in today's Cadman Plaza. Less than half a mile northeast at 201 Jay Street and Concord Street, in a property measuring 19 feet wide by 106 feet long, lived Sarah Ann Cousins and her family. Sarah was born around 1820 in South Carolina, and it is difficult to say if she arrived in the city in 1840 as a free woman or a fugitive.[8] Certainly by 1850, Sarah was living as a free Black woman in Brooklyn with her husband, Robert H. Cousins, some twenty years her senior, together with their children, seven-year-old Emaly, five-year-old Charles, and one-year-old baby Joseph. The $1,500 value of their property made Robert eligible to vote, but for Sarah, as a Black woman, legal frameworks erased her voting rights entirely. It is difficult to say how Robert and Sarah met—whether both were formerly enslaved in the South and looking to build their lives anew in the city or, perhaps, given their age difference and Robert's activist politics, whether he might have harbored Sarah and her Virginia family temporarily when they first arrived in Brooklyn.

Robert was at the center of Brooklyn's activist circle in the 1850s. Born in Virginia around 1800, he is listed in various city directories and census records as a porter, an owner of a clothing store, and a barber.[9] But he was involved in the AME Church and the Brooklyn African Tompkins Society, a mutual aid organization committed to the "improvement of the members in morals and literature, by forming a library and other appropriate means." The society otherwise gained quite the reputation when it had the audacity, according to the Weeksville land investor Henry C. Thompson, to celebrate the opening of the African school in Brooklyn in 1827 by marching and playing music.[10] When the Williamsburg resident James Hamlet was kidnapped in lower Manhattan after the passage of the Fugitive Slave Act in 1850, Robert stood on the platform with other Black abolitionists to raise the money for his release. In 1853, he was a delegate at the Rochester anti-slavery convention along with Joseph Holly, Charles B. Ray, James Pennington, William J. Wilson, Junius Morel, Lewis H. Nelson, James McCune Smith, and Frederick Douglass. And the following year, Robert led a meeting at City Hall in Albany to protest voting discrimination. Finally in 1854, when the Reverend James Morris Williams led his congregation from Brooklyn's AME Church on High Street to a new location on Bridge Street, close to Elizabeth and James Gloucester's home on 290 Bridge Street, Robert marched in the procession.

Sarah and Robert's home in the city's Fourth Ward, or the area we know today as downtown Brooklyn, served as a safe space for fugitives. Unable to rely on formal safety networks such as the police to protect them, Black Brooklynites created their own local and regional networks to assist people from slavery to freedom. Romanticized, mythologized, and often misunderstood in popular culture, the Underground Railroad is predominantly associated with attics, tunnels, and other secretive hiding places. But as historians have often noted, it was neither a railroad nor underground. Instead, the Underground Railroad involved a highly sophisticated and informal network of people, communities, and

organizations working across multiple fundraising campaigns to transport women, men, and children to safety. It was in this radical tradition
that the Cousins family joined a sophisticated network of fundraisers,
activists, and safe houses that formed the Underground Railroad and
were themselves, as one scholar characterized these activists, "guardians
of democracy."[11]

Part of the Underground Railroad's mischaracterization was owed,
in part, to Harriet Beecher Stowe's famous novel *Uncle Tom's Cabin*,
published in 1852, two years after the passage of the Fugitive Slave Act.
Aimed mostly at a white readership, the book became a transatlantic
phenomenon upon publication and inspired theater productions and
ephemera including brooches, children's games, teapots, and wallpaper.
Although the novel's eponymous protagonist dies enslaved, it is the
book's other characters Eliza, George, and Harry Harris and their famous escape that (melo)dramatized the Underground Railroad; Eliza
and her baby, Harry, escape slavery via an icy Ohio river, and George
travels in disguise. The entire family eventually reunites in Canada and
then moves to Liberia. The Brooklynite John N. Still, whose store stood
in close proximity to Mary Wilson's on Atlantic, proposed a traveling
diorama based on the novel, in which scenes from his own family life
under slavery in Maryland would be interweaved. The Still brothers were
well known for their activist work and involvement in the Underground
Railroad. One brother, James, was a self-taught herbalist doctor committed to Black health; another brother, William Still, a Philadelphia
abolitionist, kept meticulous logs detailing the assistance and passage
of fugitives on the Underground Railroad in spite of the danger and
the highly secretive nature of the work.[12] Although the numbers are
imprecise, historians do agree that these fugitives sought freedom in a
variety of locations—not just Canada—and Brooklyn was among the
many destinations that some people eventually called home.[13]

The city was, by no means, a bastion of liberty, and the threat of
kidnapping was an everyday reality. But it did offer pockets of safety
and refuge to its resident free Black communities—anchored by
Weeksville—and to others seeking freedom in the North. Residents

who had originally escaped the horrors of slavery but now called the city of Brooklyn home often spent months, years, or even decades attempting to rescue and reunite with their family members who remained enslaved—often unsuccessfully. James Pennington, one of Brooklyn's more well-known fugitives, hid in plain sight for most of his adult life. In 1851, James finally emancipated himself by paying $150 to the Hooker estate in Maryland, and in spite of assisting countless others in their journey from slavery to freedom, he then spent his subsequent "free" years trying to locate his own family in Maryland.

Black churches were often at the center of this activism, even if the burden on their congregations, often living precariously on the poverty line themselves, were too much to always ensure a successful outcome. In 1849, an opportunity arose to free seventeen-year-old Frances Smith through self-purchase after the death of her enslaver William Gaston, a lawyer, state legislator, and North Carolina Supreme Court judge. Frances's brother William had raised enough money through networks in Washington, DC, and emancipated himself. He then approached communities in Brooklyn to raise the $600 for his sister. In December 1849, the shoemaker Joseph C. Hill, the engineer Jeremiah Powers, William Ray, Charles C. Harrington, the educator and AME minister George Hogarth, and the Weeksville educator Junius C. Morel held a fundraiser in Brooklyn that was "thinly attended." When it failed to raise the necessary money for Frances Smith's release, Frederick Douglass's *North Star* newspaper blamed it on a lack of advertising, coordination, and interest. "Had these meetings been exhibitions of a monkey with a red jacket on," the writer reflected, "the churches which were reluctantly granted for them to be held in, would have been filled to repletion." It is difficult to know if Frances Smith ever found freedom.[14]

In 1849, the same year that activists failed to successfully fundraise for Frances Smith's rescue, Mary Rynar Moore and her children fled Wilmington, North Carolina. They stayed with Sarah and Robert Cousins and their children at Jay Street. Mary's husband, Thomas H. Jones, had been born in 1806 on a plantation near Wilmington, North Carolina, and separated from his parents at the age of nine. Thirteen year later, he found his mother, but his father and five siblings were irretrievably sold. His first wife, Lucilla Smith, and their three children were forcibly separated from Thomas when her enslaver moved to Alabama and took his estate, which included enslaved people, with him. Thomas soon found night work as a stevedore and compensated his enslaver Owen Holmes $150 a year to be able to engage in paid work at night. It was here that he met Mary, and he paid her enslaver $48 a year to be able to see her. The couple soon had one child, who was automatically enslaved by law. After three years and with assistance from a "white friend," Thomas had bought Mary's freedom for $350. However, when North Carolina's General Assembly failed to pass a bill that would have made Mary's emancipation official, Thomas arranged for his wife and children to go to Brooklyn. Three months later, he escaped to join the family.[15]

It was during this separation that Mary and Thomas exchanged a series of letters that he would later incorporate into his published autobiography, *The Experience of Thomas H. Jones*. Their communication reveals the financial and material difficulties that freedom seekers faced when they first arrived in Brooklyn. It is entirely possible that Sarah Cousins had known Mary's family, as they were both from North Carolina, or that anti-slavery networks matched the two women's families on the basis of regional familiarity. Despite the courage and conscience it took to participate in the Underground Railroad, economic pressures still prevailed. Mary was expected to pay rent to Sarah and Robert at three dollars per week. Mary asked Thomas to send money, stating, "You know I don't love to live in this way with my children. It is true that brother Cousins has not said anything to me about it," and she sent another reminder less than two weeks later.[16] Eventually Thomas joined the family, and his point of contact was Robert H. Cousins. But Brooklyn was a temporary stop for Mary and Thomas's family, which eventually relocated to Boston after a short stay in Hartford, Connecticut. Thomas would leave Mary and the children in Boston and escape once more to St. John, New Brunswick, in Canada, insisting that the fear of slave catchers in Massachusetts had triggered previous traumas.[17]

Thomas might have found an audience right here in Brooklyn for his escape narrative, which he would eventually publish; the city had become part a national traveling lecture circuit for former fugitives. On May 27, 1847, Henry Bibb spoke at the Brooklyn Female Academy on Joralemon Street. Less than a week later, on June 3, he recalled to "large audiences" in Brooklyn and New York his "personal observation and experience" of his twenty-five years in enslavement. A fugitive from Kentucky, Henry received accolades for his autobiography, *Narrative of the Life and Adventures of Henry Bibb, an American Slave* (1849), and became a successful touring lecturer. He returned to Brooklyn in 1849, having been invited by the American Missionary Association, an Protestant anti-slavery organization that brought together Black and white men of faith. Henry Bibb spoke at the AME Church, where he raised $2.50 ($73.60 in today's money). During this visit, he also colectured with the New York abolitionist Henry Highland Garnet at the Tabernacle on Pierrepont Street.[18]

Just two blocks from the Cousins' family home, where Mary and Thomas found refuge, and about half a mile away from the Tabernacle, the local white abolitionists Lewis Tappan and William E. Whiting held a "regularly monthly Concert of Prayer for the Slave."[19] Lewis was a long-term resident of Pierrepont Street in Brooklyn Heights. His life was one of privilege compared to the Cousins family, although both were agents on the Underground Railroad. Robert had left Virginia to start a new life in Brooklyn at the relatively older age of forty years old, and in a rarity, he became both a property owner and voter in a short amount of time. But he worked most of his life in low-wage menial labor positions in Brooklyn, as dictated by racial capitalism—in the 1850 and 1855 censuses, he is listed as a porter, and in 1865, he is listed as a laborer. Lewis Tappan, on the other hand, was originally from New England and had earned his money for decades as a merchant based in Manhattan along with his brother Arthur. Following the 1834 anti-Black race riots in the city of New York that saw white mobs attack their Black neighbors and destroy Black institutions and known abolitionist meeting places, Lewis relocated to Brooklyn. Like William Lloyd Garrison,

Lewis also initially believed in colonization—the white-led movement to deport free people of color from the United States to Liberia. Black abolitionists changed his mind, and he soon gained a reputation for his ability to fund Underground Railroad activities, as was the case with the escape of a young girl called Ann(a) Maria Weems.

Born enslaved in Rockville, Maryland, Ann Maria was the daughter of a free father and an enslaved mother. Her parents reached out to the network that made up the Underground Railroad as they attempted to emancipate each family member. Abolitionists set up a Weems Ransom Fund, largely financed by two British Quaker abolitionists, Henry and Anna Richardson, who were based in Newcastle, England. Henry and Anna were good friends with Lewis Tappan, and they gave him and the New York City–based abolitionist and minister Charles B. Ray control of the financial account.[20] The fund had already allowed Ann Maria's sister Stella to escape. In 1855, when Henry and Anna grew concerned that Ann Maria was still enslaved after two failed attempts to rescue her, they wrote to Lewis about the fund. On July 13, 1855, Lewis wrote to Charles B. Ray, "call at my house about a communication from Henry Richardson of England respecting the 'Weems Ransom Fund.'" Charles visited Tappan's Brooklyn Heights home, where he was cross-examined for three hours and reprimanded for removing money from the account. The manner of their exchange laid bare the power dynamic between Black and white abolitionists. According to Lewis, Charles felt that he had spent a considerable amount of uncompensated time on the Weems case. As the opportunity to emancipate the remaining family members did not seem imminent, he used the money to pay for the upkeep of his home and fully intended to return the funds. And yet, Lewis felt comfortable reprimanding his colleague even though the discrepancy in income and opportunity for the two men was stark. Lewis stated that Charles must return the money with interest.[21]

Eventually Ann Maria traveled from Washington, DC, to Philadelphia and onward to Brooklyn. The fourteen-year-old spent two days at Lewis and Sarah Tappan's Brooklyn Heights home and was described by Sarah as having a "fine countenance, intelligent and bright."

Sarah then used $63 from the Weems fund to buy Ann Maria new clothes, as she was still wearing the same boyish clothing with which she had escaped in disguise as "Joe Wright." On November 30, 1855, Ann Maria left for Canada. Charles had originally intended to chaperone her, but when he was unable to leave the city immediately, Amos Freeman, Lewis's colleague at the American Missionary Association, accompanied the young girl instead. Amos was paid $5 per day plus expenses for his work in the Weems case. The pastor of Siloam Presbyterian Church in Brooklyn (he had taken over from James Gloucester) and the young girl traveled by train to the Canadian border and then a further 216 miles to Dresden, where Ann Maria's aunt lived. Amos described the reunion as "very affecting" and observed that Ann Maria had found a "happy home."[22]

"A HOME ON EARTH": EMIGRATION DEBATES

Ever since the annexation of Texas, and the success and triumph of American arms on the plains of Mexico, I have been looking in vain for some home for Afric-Americans. . . . The Canadas, the West Indies, Mexico, British Guiana, and other parts of South America, have all been brought under review. . . . If the colored people of this country ever find a home on earth for the development of their manhood and intellect, it will first be in Liberia or some other part of Africa.
—Augustus Washington, "African Colonization—By a Man of Color," *African Repository*, 1851

No doubt, Ethiop, or William J. Wilson, would have had something to say about the Lewis Tappan–Charles B. Ray episode, as he was always critically aware of the city's racial dynamics, especially among abolitionists. He once called out Brooklyn's and New York's abolitionist organizations for their lack of Black leadership: "W[illia]m. H. Harned, for many years one of the Secretaries in the Anti-Slavery Office, has vacated his place, and another young *white* man has been installed in his stead. What a pity it is that the black cannot occasionally get a sup or two of the anti-slavery pap that is ladled out in this city! Why is this?—Is it incompetency one of the one part—prejudice on the other, or what?"[23] But on July 12, 1855, just one day before the tense conversation between the two abolitionists took place, William published his final column as Ethiop, ending a four-year run as the Brooklyn correspondent for *Frederick Douglass' Paper*. During his tenure, he had long been a proponent of making Brooklyn and New York home and was fiercely opposed to emigration, especially when those debates resurfaced again in the 1850s.

In 1831, at the village's anti-colonization meeting, the resident Henry C. Thompson urged his neighbors to remain in Brooklyn. But if the daily racial violence that surrounded them was too much to bear, then he encouraged residents to explore emigration to Canada rather than Liberia, as a means of securing their safety and freedom. In doing so, he hoped to stymie the work of the white-led American Colonization Society, which asked for a "return" to Africa, and to instead encourage the growth of an anti-slavery network throughout the Americas. Three years later, Henry bought his first parcel of land and, with others, established the intentional, self-sufficient community of Weeksville as an alternative to emigration. During the 1850s, emigration schemes grew to be of interest again to Brooklyn's Black communities. With their cognizance of the hostility that confronted them and being unprotected and attacked by local, state, and federal legislation, together with the seeming lack of racial progress, proposals for a Black-led emigration scheme and settlement beyond the US borders gained fervor.

While Brooklyn's overall population grew, particularly with the influx of German and Irish immigrants and the annexation of Williamsburg in 1855, the actual percentage of Black people decreased significantly— whereas the community had made up 9.7 percent of the population in 1830, it was only 3.7 percent of the population in 1845, with a decrease to 2.9 percent by 1850, 2.1 percent by 1855, and only 1.8 percent by 1860.[24] Part of this decrease was due to emigration to Haiti and Liberia assisted by the African Civilization Society, an organization established by Henry Highland Garnet in Manhattan in 1858. Created partly in response to the Supreme Court's hostile *Dred Scott* decision in 1857, which stated that Black people were not regarded as citizens and, in turn, held no citizenship rights, the organization was intended to promote emigration to West Africa and to encourage a free-labor cotton economy in Yoruba as a serious economic rival to the cotton economy of the South. The organization received support from the cities of Brooklyn, Manhattan, and Philadelphia. But the society also had its critics. Elizabeth Gloucester's husband, James, called it a "miserable blunder" and urged his "downtrodden people not [to look at] colonization and expatriation but justice, reformation, improvement and elevation."[25] His friend and colleague at Siloam Presbyterian William J. Wilson was equally critical: "A distemper long prevalent among the whites, has broken out here among the blacks. It must be speedily cured."[26] But the change in philosophy from anti-colonization—that is, the right to remain on US soil—to a new interest in emigration could be seen in the emotional journey of William's predecessor at Colored School No. 1, Augustus Washington. Born free in Trenton, New Jersey, around 1820, Augustus joined Brooklyn's anti-colonization efforts, in which he also served as educator, temperance advocate, and local agent for the *Colored American* newspaper and directed petition drives and voting rights advocacy on behalf of the town. Augustus left Brooklyn and moved to Hartford, Connecticut, where he lived with his family— wife, Cordelia; and children, Alonzo Seward and Helena Augusta—and worked as a successful daguerreotypist. But as early as 1841, he believed that "the crisis" for African Americans and citizenship had "fully arrived." In November 1853, Augustus and his family sailed to Liberia, which had declared its independence six years earlier. The letters he sent from Liberia reflected the stark realities and difficulties of emigration, in which the themes of sickness, hunger, and despondency are recurrent. In fact, they were so full of misery that the *Provincial Freeman*, a Canadian newspaper, did not hesitate to contrast the tone of Augustus's letter to another communication from Mary Jane Robinson, who resided in Canada. Mary Jane wrote to Sarah Ann Harris, a resident of Weeksville, Brooklyn, about her life in the North, which the newspaper's editor felt depicted a "pleasanter picture than that recently presented to them in Augustus Washington's letters from Liberia."[27]

"YOUR LOVING SISTERS"

The summer of 1854 had been a relatively mild one in Brooklyn. The resident Gabriel Furman noted on July 30 that it had been a "most delightful morning and evening," with "the wind blowing pleasantly from the South." But Gabriel lamented the urban changes he saw. Reminiscing about Clover Hill, "that large and pleasant tract of city" that stretched north and south from Poplar to Joralemon Streets and east to west from Fulton Street to the East River, he recalled there only ever being six houses there when he was seven years old. The lack of development at that time meant that he could see the ocean from the top of the hill. He also recalled how he used to go with friends to the "Old Fort" where Henry Street intersected Pierrepont Street, near Lewis Tappan's home, and could play among the ditches covered in blackberries and catbriers. Still, August 1854 had brought "good, ripe, soft" peaches, fine pears, and apricots for sale in wagons on the streets during days that were cloudy and cool.[28] The same could not be said of the political climate in the United States. That same year, the Kansas-Nebraska Act lifted the restrictions on the expansion of slavery previously established by the Missouri Compromise of 1820, which had banned slavery from proceeding north of the 36°30' latitudinal line. Whether to expand slavery in new territories would now be decided by popular sovereignty, and "Bleeding Kansas" was the violent result.

On May 24, 1856, Willis Hodges's friend John Brown, with whom he had corresponded during his stay in the Adirondacks, led seven men, four of them John's sons, to a proslavery settlement in Pottawatomie Creek, Kansas. Outraged by the proslavery violence he saw around him, the Pottawatomie Massacre saw John Brown drag five men from their cabins and split their heads open.[29] By November of that year, John was in New England raising funds and planning a revolt that would materialize three years later as the raid at Harpers Ferry in West Virginia. Willis and John's friendship ran deep. In 1847, Willis and the Manhattan resident and abolitionist Thomas Van

Rensselaer established the *Ram's Horn*, a New York anti-slavery newspaper. John Brown was a subscriber to the newspaper and submitted a piece for publication titled "Sambo's Mistakes?," in which he insisted violence was necessary to end the institution of slavery. Willis and John's friendship lasted from 1848 until John's death. They exchanged a total of forty-seven letters when they moved to Franklin and Essex Counties, respectively, as part of the Gerrit Smith Timbuctoo experiment in the Adirondacks. John asked his friend Willis to join him at Harpers Ferry, but Willis declined, as would Frederick Douglass and Elizabeth and James Gloucester.

Elizabeth might not have joined the planned raid, but it did not deter her from funding John's radical mission. Her husband, James, had written to John on February 19, 1858, and again on March 9 pledging $25 as John fundraised for Harpers Ferry. The devastating effect of the Fugitive Slave Act, combined with the westward expansion of slavery through the 1854 Kansas-Nebraska Act and the 1857 *Dred Scott* decision, had certainly taken a toll on the family. But there were also profoundly traumatic circumstances in Elizabeth's personal life. On January 23, 1856, their eldest son, Stephen, died at age thirteen. He was the second surviving child after their eldest, Emma (a baby boy born after Emma, called Jeremiah Beman—named for James's late brother—had previously died at ten months old in November 1841).[30] There is little evidence to explain what had happened to the child, who was barely a teenager. But James and Elizabeth expanded their family once more with the arrival in 1857 of Alfred, who joined the six surviving children. Elizabeth would suffer unbearable loss again when Alfred died tragically at age two years and ten months in February 1859. His burial record cited that he had died from "congestion of the brain," possibly caused by infection or a traumatic head injury.[31] Given the long history of poor outcomes in Black maternal and children's health in the United States, it is safe to assume that Alfred more than likely received inferior medical attention, which might have also contributed to his early death. His passing made this the third child the couple was forced to bury while they were residents at 290 Bridge Street. Six months later, Elizabeth wrote to John Brown; on August 18, 1859, she enclosed $10 with her letter in support of John's planned raid on Harpers Ferry, "for the good of the cause." She added that a recent visit by Frederick Douglass to the Gloucesters' home had "somewhat revived [her] rather drooping spirits in the cause."[32]

On the night of October 16, 1859, John Brown and twenty men attempted to seize the federal arsenal at Harpers Ferry, Virginia, in a radical attempt to end slavery. Not a single enslaved person was liberated. By December 2, John Brown and all of the men were executed. While the raid lasted for only thirty-six hours, the repercussions were enormous. The event at Harpers Ferry deeply divided Brooklynites. The *Brooklyn Evening Star* acknowledged the "insanity of Captain Brown" but added, "to us there is something sacred in the madness of this old man and his six sons, one by one shedding their life's blood in the endeavor, however, vain, to remove one great national crime."[33] At Second Unitarian Church, which stood at the corner of Clinton and Congress Streets, John Brown's raid was all too much for parishioner G. Arthur Leavey. After relocating from Brooklyn to Gilmer, Texas, he wrote to the trustees of the church on January 2, 1860, informing them of his intention to withdraw his membership with immediate effect and instructing them to sell his church pew. G. Arthur Leavey took umbrage with both John Brown and Samuel Longfellow, a committed supporter of the abolitionist William Lloyd Garrison and the church's pastor since 1853. The former parishioner acknowledged that his own "views on the 'slavery question' always differed from those of our Pastor Rev. S. Longfellow" but that the pastor's sermon on December 11, 1859, "upholding and eulogizing the lawless and unchristian acts of the late John Brown," was a step too far.[34]

As soon as news reached Brooklyn and New York of John Brown's raid, arrest, and trial, his supporters led prayer meetings. On November 10, 1859, William Hodges held a meeting at his church, and a further meeting led by James Gloucester was held at Siloam Presbyterian. The "Colored Women of Brooklyn" honored John and his work and sent the following letter:

Dear Sir: We, a portion of the American people, would fain offer you our sincere and heartfelt sympathies in the cause you have so nobly espoused, and that you so firmly adhere to. We truly appreciate your most noble and humane effort, and recognize in you a Saviour commissioned to redeem us, the American people, from the great National Sin of Slavery; and though you have apparently failed in the object of your desires, yet the influence that we believe it will eventually exert, will accomplish all your intentions. We consider you a model of true patriotism, and one whom our common country will yet regard as the greatest it has produced, because you have sacrificed all for its sake. . . . And now, in view of the coming crisis which is to terminate all your labors of love for this life, our mortal natures fail to sustain us under the trying affliction.[35]

After John Brown's execution, women in Brooklyn, New York, and Williamsburg wrote to John's wife, Mary, in solidarity and signed the letter, "your loving sisters." On Christmas Eve 1859, a final meeting was called again at William Hodges's church in Williamsburg. Worried about reprisals following John Brown's death, William's sister-in-law Sarah destroyed thirty-five of the letters between her husband, Willis, and John.[36] The raid at Harpers Ferry reflected a more militant Brooklyn, even if its residents were not prepared to join John Brown. James Gloucester, a man of faith, established the *Colored Patriot* newspaper with a motto that reflected the country's crisis: "Truth is Omnipotent. To arms! To arms! Ye loyal scene of patriotic sires! No more union with slaveholder!"[37] The city and country were firmly on the road to the Civil War.

PART IV

BROOKLYN AND
THE NATION

1860s–1870s

Eugene L. Armbruster, black and white photograph of Borough Hall with Montague Hall on right, ca. 1880. (V1974.1.1299, Eugene L. Armbruster Photographs and Scrapbooks, Center for Brooklyn History, Brooklyn Public Library)

"ALL THE *ELITE* AND FASHION OF THIS PORTION OF THE ANGLO-AFRICAN WORLD"

BROOKLYN, 1860

To the Treasurer and Ladies
of the Colored Orphan Asylum,
New York City:

The Managers of the Colored Orphan Asylum Fair, held in the city of Brooklyn on the 26th, 27th, 28th, and 29th of March, beg leave to announce as the result of their efforts, including the exhibition given at Dr. Beecher's Church, and the disbursement of all debts incurred by them for said fair, the realization of the sum of one thousand one hundred dollars, which sum, by the hands of their Secretary and Treasurer, they hereby convey and pay over to the treasurer of said Orphan Asylum $1,100.

MRS C. B. RAY

MRS A. N. FREEMAN } Treasurers

Mrs. J. N. Gloucester, First Directress
Mrs. W. J. Wilson, Secretary
Brooklyn, April 3, 1860
—*Weekly Anglo-African*, April 7, 1860

ELEVEN steam ferries connected the city of Brooklyn to the city of New York by 1860. If you walked uphill from the city's original ferry landing at Fulton, you might have passed Isaac Hunter's shoe business and, just half a mile further still, Brooklyn's City Hall—today's Brooklyn Borough Hall in Cadman Plaza. It had taken one bankruptcy and a nine-year delay, but in 1848, the marble structure built in the Greek Revival style was finally completed. At the very top lay a large cupola with a statue of justice, visible across the city's skyline and a reminder to its East River neighbor that Brooklyn had arrived as a site of urban power—perhaps even competition. It stood on agricultural land that had previously belonged to the Pierrepont and Remsen families, and echoes of their capitalist influence were reflected in the two streets bearing their name that ran up to City Hall. The completion of City Hall heralded a new age for the city of Brooklyn. Here was downtown: a cornucopia of civic, business, cultural, and shopping sites in one commercial and residential district. While a complex municipal network—fire, police, education, gas-light street lighting, and water supplies—extended the city's services throughout an inflated landscape, aided by horse-drawn street railways, introduced in 1854. Brooklyn expanded north when it annexed Williamsburg in 1855, and development continued in what residents then called South Brooklyn, where the neighborhoods of Cobble Hill, Boerum Hill, Carroll Gardens, and Gowanus stand today.

Across the plaza from City Hall, at neighboring Montague Hall, Elizabeth Gloucester, Mary Wilson, and a group of Black women who called Brooklyn home held several institutional fundraisers that were at the center of Black organizational life. The women were the partners, wives, mothers, grandmothers, sisters, and daughters of the Black men who come to life through archival scraps that we have on Black life in nineteenth-century Brooklyn, even as they as women rarely appear in these archives. But these women shaped the discourse and development of Brooklyn from the mid-1850s through the tumultuous Civil War period and into the decades of Reconstruction that followed. Black women as public organizers in Brooklyn and New York had a long, rich history. The abolition movement had offered expanded roles for women from the 1830s onward, which allowed a range of multiracial mutual aid, antislavery, and literary societies to flourish. They included the Ladies' New York Anti-Slavery Society, the African Dorcas Association, Abyssinian Benevolent Daughters of Esther Association, and the New York Ladies Literary Society, run for women by women.[1] These societies could also be riddled with racism, however. In 1836, Julianna Tappan, the daughter of Lewis and his first wife, Susanna, refused to serve alongside Abigail Cox in the Ladies' New York Anti-Slavery Society. One member commented, "Everybody has their own troubles, and the New York brethren have theirs. Mrs. [Abigail] Cox is the life and soul of the New York Society and she is in a very sinful state of wicked prejudice about color; they do not allow any colored women to join their society. The Tappans have none of their prejudice, therefore they and Mrs. Cox are hardly on speaking terms."[2] By 1860, Brooklyn's Black women organized in ways that shut out anti-Black racism from within their organizing, even if they could not avoid it from the outside.

On February 22, 1860, Black women organized an exhibition of the "children belonging to the Colored Orphan Asylum, New York." Held at Cooper Institute (now Cooper Union) in New York just five days before Abraham Lincoln was scheduled to speak there, the benefit consisted of "unusually interesting" singing, lessons, and recitals. Attendees were invited to donate to cover the organization's operating finances, which included a debt of $2,500 (or about $90,000 today), as city and state funds had proven insufficient.[3] The Colored Orphan Asylum, located on Fifth Avenue at Forty-Third Street in Manhattan, had been founded in 1835 by two Quaker women, Anna Shotwell and Mary Murray. Through an act of white benevolence, they created an institution for some of the city's most vulnerable children, and Dr. James McCune Smith became the asylum's in-house physician, creating a much-needed bridge between the organization's white management and the larger Black community from 1843 onward.[4] For Black families living near the poverty line, the use of the Colored Orphan Asylum reflected an agonizing decision—whether their child would receive better care at the institution as a place of temporary refuge, while the caregivers improved their own economic circumstances. This may have been why on March 22, 1854, Matilda Masey admitted her seven-year-old daughter, Emma, to the Colored Orphan Asylum and paid the institution fifty cents a week for her daughter's tuition, board, and clothing. The Masey family had moved from Maryland to Brooklyn, where Joseph Masey worked as a porter until he died of dropsy, or edema. The change to a one-parent household most likely forced Matilda to make this difficult decision, even as she worked and lived at the home of the white abolitionists Lewis and Sarah Tappan on Pierrepont and Henry Streets.[5] It is not clear from the written records why Matilda could not have remained with her young child at the Tappan family home or if and when young Emma was reunited with her mother.

The Cooper Institute exhibition was followed by a four-day fair at Montague Hall. The venue stood across from Brooklyn's City Hall and was regularly used for concerts and dances and as a meeting place for many of the city's reform societies.[6] The multiday event was a lavish fair that "brought together all the elite and fashion of this portion of the Anglo-African world, and much of the Anglo-American in the bargain."[7] The famous oyster merchant Thomas Downing and the caterers Bagwell of Wall Street and Roselle and Barnswell donated fried oysters, pickled oysters, and "chickens celery"—a popular nineteenth-century dish on both sides of the Atlantic in which chicken was boiled with celery juice. The event raised a total of $1,100 (about $40,000 in today's money) for the Colored Orphan Asylum, thereby reducing the institution's debt by about half.[8] Elizabeth Gloucester, Mary Wilson, Christiana Freeman, Mary J. Lyons, Sarah Morel, Sarah Tomkins, Malvania McCune Smith, Cordelia Ray, and Julia Garnett—friends and colleagues—all served on the organizing and fundraising committee for both the exhibition and the multiday fair.[9] If their names seem familiar, it is because they were the wives of Black male activists whose names the written archives have preserved more favorably. The women's erasure from mainstream historical narratives echoes the type of patriarchal and racist abuse they experienced in their own daily lives. While the *Weekly Anglo-African* was all praise for the organizers of the exhibition and fair, who "were all decked in pretty calico gowns, all or, nearly all, of the same stripe, giving thereby a most picturesque effect," the long-running Democrat newspaper the *Brooklyn Daily Eagle* exhibited its usual casual anti-Black racism.[10] Referring to Elizabeth Gloucester, the article stated, "The principal table is presided over by a big old colored lady, as downright in earnest as if she was disposing of clam-soup in Fulton Market."[11] In spite of the unabashed racism faced by Brooklyn's Black elite, they continued organizing.

By this time, in 1860, thirty-seven-year-old Mary Wilson was no longer listed as a business owner in the city directory. This might be partly explained by an influx of wealth into the family. In 1850, the Wilsons were living in the city's Fifth Ward, which we know today as downtown Brooklyn. William was listed in the federal census as owning $600 worth of property, making him a voter. A decade later, the family had moved to Brooklyn's Eleventh Ward, or Fort Greene, and the value of the family's real estate was $5,000, with a personal estate of $1,000. By 1860, blocks of single-family Italianate brick and brownstone row houses were popping up on Fort Greene's streets and whatever open land that remained. It is difficult to know how the family's wealth increased so significantly in such a relatively short time period. A change of neighborhood, even a fast-developing one like Fort Greene, could not have been the sole reason, nor could the family's change in fortunes have come from William's job at Colored School No. 1, which consistently suffered from chronic underfunding. But it is entirely possible that Mary had made her money in business and sold it wholesale to another business owner or continued to bring in a second income to the family. In addition to a change in their financial circumstances, William and Mary together with their teenage daughter, Annie, were now living in a predominantly white neighborhood. Their neighbors were listed as white and either fellow New Yorkers or of English, Irish, and Scottish descent. Only one other Black family—the Bruce family—lived on their block. The head of household, George, was from Virginia and worked in Brooklyn as a steward. The Wilson family was also providing a home to

a twelve-year old, Mary Marshal, for whom we have very little information other than that she was born in New York and attending school. It
is entirely possible that the Wilsons were fostering young Mary because
her family had fallen on hard times.[12]

By 1860, although Mary Wilson had left Brooklyn's Fifth Ward, her
friend forty-two-year-old Elizabeth Gloucester still remained at 290
Bridge Street. But the Gloucesters, like the Wilsons, were similarly improving their material wealth, even while suffering immeasurable personal loss with the death of two-year-old Alfred. Elizabeth owned a
furniture store, according to the 1855 New York State Census, and no
doubt her business acumen was essential to fundraising for the Colored
Orphan Asylum and other organizations. Mary and Elizabeth collabo-
rated again that year on May 26, 1860, when they organized a "grand
social entertainment" for Siloam Presbyterian Church, where James still
served as pastor and William was an elder. This event, held at Grenada
Hall on Myrtle Avenue, was an occasion in which "no pains will be
spared," as "to make it one of the most agreeable festivities of the season. Ice cream extra."[13] In November of that year, Mary, Elizabeth,
Cordelia Ray, Malvina McCune Smith, and Julia Garnett invited the
Philadelphia abolitionist Sarah M. Douglass to lecture on the subject
of physiology in Brooklyn.[14] Black women were creating local, regional,
and national anti-slavery networks even as their work was not as visible
or indeed as theatrical as that of others in Brooklyn.

"AN ACTION OF A MOST EXTRAORDINARY NATURE": HENRY WARD BEECHER'S PLYMOUTH CHURCH

In 2011, my colleague Samantha Gibson and I visited the Manuscripts
and Archives Reading Room at Yale University Library.[15] Tasked with
putting together a narrative so ambitious in its undertaking (my head
still spins slightly when I think about what we as a group of researchers
and an early career historian delivered), Sam and I traveled all over the
US Northeast to research the collections of other repositories holding
documents on the history of Brooklyn and its anti-slavery movement.

We arrived in New Haven as soon as the reading room opened, and the archivist very kindly handed us our preordered materials from the Beecher Family Papers, including box 14, folder 582, "Slaves, Purchase of Freedom." And there in neat penmanship was Pomona Brice's account book detailing all of her struggles to fundraise as a Black woman in the nineteenth-century United States in order to emancipate her family members. The small book was filled with the familiar names of Black and white men whose stories are so often at the center of our historical narratives. It was—as so many people who do research in the archives can attest—an exciting but overwhelming moment. Archivists had processed the collection, a keyword in the finding aid led us to request the materials, and upon delivery, we found a narrative truth so undertold but so clear and utterly obvious: Black women had always been at the center of their own emancipation, defining their freedom.

Although Sam and I were based at the time at Brooklyn Historical Society (BHS; today the Center for Brooklyn History at the Brooklyn Public Library), which has the largest collection of Brooklyn-centered materials in the United States, we were acutely aware that BHS, previously the Long Island Historical Society, also lacked the inclusion of certain voices from the nineteenth century—and more specifically those of Black women. Founded in 1863, BHS was founded by white men resident in Brooklyn, many of them providing leadership to organizations central to the city's infrastructure (banks, libraries, Common Council, churches) but little committed to racial justice. Librarians and archivists since then, many of them peers and colleagues, have worked tirelessly to acquire new collections and revisit the metadata on older ones to redress some of this historical whitewashing. BHS's collection on Plymouth Church of the Pilgrims and Henry Ward Beecher remained a prime example, reflecting the pastor's many achievements that had earned him the title of the "most famous man in America" and also the hate mail he received for his activism, but it included little to nuance the narrative beyond Henry as a white savior.[16] Who were the Black women and girls whom Beecher was "auctioning" at Plymouth Church in the name of abolitionism? What did they have to say about this theatrical voyeurism and patriarchal gift of freedom? What follows is an account in which Black women's undertold stories are honored and centered in the retelling of Henry Ward Beecher's activism.

In 1847, thirty-four-year-old Henry Ward Beecher, son of the prominent Presbyterian minister Lyman Beecher, left Indianapolis and arrived in Brooklyn to lead Plymouth Church, which consisted of twenty-one members. The majority were the church's founders, a like-minded group of New England liberals living in Brooklyn Heights, including Lewis Tappan's son-in-law Henry C. Bowen. By 1850, Plymouth's membership had ballooned to twelve hundred parishioners. Henry Ward Beecher's personality became so intricately intertwined with the city itself that it is said that some people called the Fulton Ferry "Beecher's Boats," because of the number of people who traveled from New York to Brooklyn on a Sunday morning to see him preach.[17] Sally Maria Diggs, or Pinky, was perhaps the most infamous of auctions at Plymouth Church, on Orange and Henry Streets in Brooklyn Heights, where Henry Ward Beecher raised $900 for her emancipation. She was nine years old in 1860 and "nearly white, having only one sixteenth of negro blood, or half an octoroon, a gradation of amalgamation not specifically designated."[18] She would return to Plymouth Church in 1929 as Rose Ward Hunt for the eightieth anniversary of Henry's first sermon, but she lacked enthusiasm: "At the Hunt home the impression was gathered that these Negroes did not enjoy recalling that slave auction of 1860 at Plymouth Church. Hunt himself would discuss his wife's part in it only with the greatest reluctance."[19] The family's reluctance was completely understandable—what might a nine-year-old child have felt other than overwhelming fear at being put in front of Plymouth Church's mostly white congregation and asked to reenact a slave auction for the purpose of fundraising at the behest of its pastor. But it was a problematic performance that Henry had perfected by 1860.

Henry Ward Beecher's first invitation to help fundraise for the emancipation of young Black girls came in 1848 when Paul Edmonson was advised by Washington, DC, abolitionists to approach New York's anti-slavery networks. Paul was trying to purchase his daughters—sixteen-year-old

Mary and thirteen-year-old Emily—at a cost of $2,250 (or about $85,000 today). When James Pennington raised the significant sum of $50 at Shiloh Presbyterian in Manhattan, he organized a larger fundraiser at which Henry Ward Beecher would ask the audience, "Imagine your daughters or sisters in bondage." This was not something that needed to be asked of the average Black family in the cities of Brooklyn and New York, where kidnapping was common. Rather, Henry's audiences were white residents asked to donate through fear and empathy. It became the preacher's trademark style, and he almost exclusively fundraised for light-skinned Black girls and women in a format resembling an auction. By November 4, 1848, the Edmonson sisters, Mary and Emily, were legally emancipated, and although Mary would die from tuberculosis by 1853, after emancipation, the sisters became anti-slavery activists in their own right. In a moving daguerreotype taken in August 1850 at the anti-slavery convention in Cazanovia, New York, they can be seen in plaid flanking Gerrit Smith and standing behind Frederick Douglass.[20]

In June 1856, twenty-two-year-old Sarah, the child of an enslaved woman and a slaveholder in Virginia, was given a "chance to save herself by purchasing her freedom" for $800. Henry placed Sarah on Plymouth Church's platform as a "living slave woman" but made no mention of Sarah's four-year-old son, presumably to avoid scandal and sustain the white audience's sympathy for her. By this stage, Sarah herself had already partly raised the funds needed for her emancipation through abolitionists in DC. Henry was the only abolitionist to replicate a slave sale during the fundraising drive, thereby erasing Sarah's agency as a fundraiser in her own right.[21]

Pomona Brice was a long-term Brooklyn resident living on High Street at Jay Street. She was formerly enslaved in North Carolina, until her manumission on October 22, 1845. In 1857, Pomona learned that she might be able to purchase, and therefore reunite with, her daughter and grandchildren.[22] She approached a number of churches and activists, including Henry Ward Beecher. Robert H. Cousins donated one dollar, Simeon Jocelyn gave another dollar, and a collection at Bethel AME Church in Weeksville and Bridge Street AWME raised seven dollars.

Henry Ward Beecher gave five dollars. Charles B. Ray confirmed Pomona's story and said that he had "no doubt whatsoever of [her] entire truthfulness."[23] At the top of Pomona's subscription book, now in Yale's Manuscripts and Archives, is a cruel but important reminder of the ways in which capitalism underwrote a person's freedom. Pomona is reminded to deposit the money into a bank, until she has raised sufficient funds to emancipate her family: "We the subscribers hereby pay to Pomona Brice, the several sums of money, listed opposite our names, which she is to place in the Savings Bank of Brooklyn (Seamans) until it reaches the amount acquired for the purchase of her Daughter and two children, now in Bondage in Alabama."[24] And in a series of letters, it is clear that raising the money was not enough—Pomona was expected also to pay legal fees for all involved:

Brooklyn, October 22, 1859

Mrs. Price
You have now had sufficient time to come to a conclusion as to whether you intend to do anything through me in regard to your children and as I am in need of money I should like you to pay me $10. Bill rendered.
I am yours & c.
James Packer, near City Hall.

Brooklyn, Nov 11, 1859

Dear Sir & HWB
I write these few lines to inform you that I call on Mr. Johnson in New York and when I was there I learnt that my business could be carried on if they know how they could get the money
    I write this to Mr. Beecher to ask him if he will be kind enough to call on Mr Johnson and give him information about it.
Please excuse
Your servant Pomona Brice

Brooklyn, December 6, 1859

Dr Sir

Last winter I was called upon by Mrs. Brice for professional advice
+ services she then informed me that she had money wherewith to
pay me for my trouble, deposited in your hands.

Upon hearing a statement of the facts from her and others and
a careful and extensive examination of the Laws of N. Carolina
and also of Mississippi, Alabama, & Missouri, in one of which last
named States she supposes her children to be now living and after
giving the subject a careful consideration I came to the conclusion
and so informed Mrs. Brice that all the Laws in regard to the matter were against her and that she stood no chance of success.

I charged her for such services the moderate sum of Ten dollars
she referred me to you for payment.

I have called at your residence several times without being able
to see you.

I am at the present time in great need of money and would feel
obliged if you are in a position to pay the sum if you would forward
to me the amount as soon as possible.

Yours & c

James Packer, No. 9 Court St, Room No. 11

To H W Beecher, Esq.

It is difficult to say whether Pomona was ever reunited with her loved
ones, in spite of Henry Ward Beecher's reputation as an emancipator.

By this time, Henry Ward Beecher was lending his name and likeness
to all sorts of product endorsements, including a lozenge company in 1858
and later Pear's Soap.[25] His fundraising work was different from that of
the respectable exhibitions and fairs of Brooklyn's Black elite. And the
city's approach to protecting its residents could not have been more different with him as a white man. In the aftermath of the Kansas-Nebraska
Act of 1854, which aided the westward expansion of slavery, Henry and

his congregation financed the purchase and transportation of twenty-five Sharpe's Rifles, or "Beecher's Bibles," in order to arm anti-slavery protestors in Kansas. Charged with being an anarchist, Henry Ward Beecher distanced his actions from lawlessness, arguing that "self-defence especially in the case of Freedom, is a sacred duty." He claimed that the rifles were a "truly moral agency" and that "there was more moral power in one of those instruments, so far as the slaveholders of Kansas were concerned than in a hundred Bibles."[26] The chief of police and mayor of Brooklyn dispatched fifty policemen to Henry and Plymouth Church to "check any aggressive or disorderly conduct" when they received warning that the pastor and congregation might be attacked for their radicalism.[27] Henry received a service from the city's police that a Black Brooklynite could never have dreamt of: the promise of safety and protection.

"FEW ORATORICAL GRACES": LINCOLN IN BROOKLYN AND THE REPUBLICAN PARTY

The *Brooklyn Evening Star* was less than impressed with the political newcomer Abraham Lincoln. In the same month that Henry Ward Beecher "auctioned" Sally Maria Diggs, the hopeful Republican presidential nominee spoke at the Cooper Institute in Manhattan, not Henry Ward Beecher's Plymouth Church, as had been hoped. It is not clear why the switch in venue occurred in February 1860, though scholars have suggested that it might have been due to the Cooper Institute having a larger capacity than Plymouth Church, or perhaps the church was too infamous for its radical abolitionist stance, or it was simply too cold for attendees to brave the wintery East River commute. During his speech, Abraham Lincoln denounced John Brown and clarified that the Republican Party was not responsible for sectional tensions. But he also criticized the expansion of slavery and implored Northerners to address the impending crisis. While the editor of the *New York Tribune*, Horace Greeley, gave the presidential candidate his full support, the *Brooklyn Evening Star* was less enthusiastic. The newspaper wrote, "Nature has endowed Mr. Lincoln with few oratorical graces. . . . His voice is harsh and shrill, his action nervous and angular, his address marked by many provincialisms."[28] Although the review was less than favorable, Lincoln's speech established him as the national frontrunner for the party's presidential nomination. The *Brooklyn Evening Star* would ultimately offer Lincoln its support and urged its readers to do the same. By 1860, the paper claimed to have a "larger circulation in families, and among Tax-Payers, in Brooklyn, and on Long-Island, than any other Daily Paper published in the City of New York." Presumably its tagline distinguished its respectable readership from the paper's rival the *Brooklyn Daily Eagle*, the city's Democratic newspaper, which claimed to have the "LARGEST CIRCULATION of any evening paper published in the United States."

Abraham Lincoln was not an abolitionist, but his position on the expansion of slavery in the western territories did represent a political middle ground for abolitionists in Brooklyn and beyond. In Williamsburg, William Hodges and the Colored Political Association of the City of Brooklyn and Kings County actively campaigned for Abraham Lincoln. Established in 1854, the same year as the founding of the Republican Party, the association aimed to consolidate the Black vote. Its officers included William, who acted as president; fellow Williamsburg residents Dr. Peter Ray and Elijah Bundick, who served as vice president and treasurer, respectively; Siloam Presbyterian minister Amos Freeman, who later replaced James Gloucester; and Brooklynite John N. Still, who was assistant secretary.[29] William also recruited his teenage nephew Joseph S. Bowen, the son of his sister, Jacqueline, with whom his brother Willis had stayed in his early years in New York, to participate in the association's activities.

In the summer of 1860, the Colored Political Association organized a tree-planting ceremony to honor the Abraham Lincoln–Hannibal Hamlin ticket. Williamsburg's Black voters turned out "in force." At the event, William Hodges warned, "We are in the midst of a great crisis. This campaign will be one of the most closely contested and exciting, this country has ever witnessed," and he "urged upon his fellow citizens to vote for the republican ticket," arguing, "If the colored voters of this state desire to show themselves men, worthy of the elective franchise without property qualification, now is the time to show it, by using all the efforts in their power."[30] His neighbor Lewis H. Nelson still opposed the emigration schemes of the African Civilization Society, arguing that there was little difference between the activities of the white-led American Colonization Society and the Black-led African Civilization Society— the struggle for political equality needed to remain on US soil.[31]

On Wednesday, July 18, 1860, four days after the Williamsburg ceremony, the James Morris Williams Tabernacle of Love and Charity No. 3 organized "A Grand Union Picnic" at Morris Grove, Jamaica, Long Island, led by Sarah Cousins; her husband, Robert H. Cousins; and their seventeen-year old daughter, Emily. Long Island Railroad cars departed from the corner of Hoyt and Atlantic Streets in Brooklyn at 9 a.m. to Morris Grove so that attendees could hear Henry Highland Garnet speak. The Cousins family celebrated the Union with their neighbors from Brooklyn, Weeksville, and New York.[32] Like members of the Colored Political Association, Robert Cousins and Henry Highland Garnet were property owners, and their support for Abraham Lincoln and the Union was as much a vote for the Republican Party as it was a quest for their own citizenship rights. On November 6, 1860, Abraham Lincoln gained only 43 percent of the vote in Brooklyn but had won the national election.

* * *

By 1861, Brooklyn was the third-largest city in the United States, surpassed only by New York and Philadelphia. It was home to residents who claimed Dutch, British, and New England ancestry, people of African descent, and growing numbers of German and Irish immigrants. And it was precisely these racial and economic tensions between its Black residents and Irish communities—two of the city's most marginalized groups—that would dominate the violent history of the cities of Brooklyn and New York in the early 1860s. Historians call it a riot—that is, a violent public disturbance—but, more precisely, the Tobacco Factory Riots in Brooklyn in 1862 and the Draft Riots of New York in 1863 were violent, racist attacks on Black men, women, and children, and they had huge repercussions on the two cities in the decades that followed.

"THE HALF HAS NEVER BEEN TOLD"

We always feel proud of our city as we walk through the streets on Sunday morning and notice the air of quiet happiness which pervades everything around us, giving the city more of the appearance of some New England village, than a city containing a population of 250,000 people, while in New York, every means have been tried in vain, to make the city assume a decent appearance on Sunday. In Brooklyn, the superior morality and intelligence of our people, renders coercive measures for the attainment of that object unnecessary—Whatever changes the future may bring to us, we hope that no change will ever come which will alter the character of our cherished Sabbath.
—*Brooklyn Evening Star*, January 23, 1860

We desire not war. All our tendencies are to peace. Our active workers and thinkers are desirous to be at ease in their homes and various fields of effort, but if a war is unjustly and unreasonably forced upon us, as a collateral aid to slavery and rebellion, it will be accepted with the ringing of the bells of all the churches, as God's mode for a full deliverance of the Nation.
—*Brooklyn Evening Star*, January 2, 1862

Despite our national troubles, we all managed yesterday, to conform generally to the customs of the day. Now that snow has gone out of fashion—and who don't recollect the old New Years sleigh parties twelve or fourteen years ago—tumbledowns of all kinds—even unto "home-settlers," were in order yesterday. Gay were the people, even though sad the hour and the hopes of the nation. But every cloud has got "a silver lining"—something that illuminates its sombre density, and we all realized yesterday the common sense of the operatic suggestion that "it's better to laugh than to cry." The New Year upon us and the old year past!
—*Brooklyn Daily Eagle*, January 2, 1862

My sketches of the riots of '63; the Underground Railroad; of
episodes of southern plantations; of freedmen and incidents of
the Civil War, never failed to illicit comment. Sometimes the
teacher would question me privately: "Is what you wrote really
true, or have you been letting loose your imagination?" My re-
ply was invariably: "The half has never been told."
—Maritcha Lyons, "Memories of Yesterdays,"
unpublished memoir, 1928

"THE COMING CRISIS"

One week hence, Abraham Lincoln will be inaugurated as
President of the United States. He will find six States in open
revolt against his rule, and nine others demanding explicit
guarantees for the permanence of Slavery in their limits, as the
sole condition on which they can be withheld from joining in
the revolution.
—*Brooklyn Daily Times*, February 25, 1861

O N December 9, 1860, just five weeks after Abraham Lincoln won
the presidential election, Henry Van Dyke, a resident of Brooklyn
Heights, declared that "abolitionism is evil, and only evil." His reflections on the "character and influence of abolitionism" were delivered
as a sermon as part of his duties as the pastor of First Presbyterian
Church, located on the corner of Remsen and Clinton Streets. A proslavery Northern Democrat, Henry Van Dyke blamed the abolitionists
and their radical politics as the sole reason for the fragility of the Union.
He concluded with a biblical justification for slavery's existence and
why it must continue.[1] Eleven days later, South Carolina seceded from
the Union. Eager to show support for the president-elect, the city's
Common Council invited Lincoln to visit Brooklyn. The *Brooklyn
Evening Star* described the "great deal of disappointment" that was
felt after it was "generally expected that the invitation of the Common

M. Dripps, *Map of Brooklyn and Vicinity*, 1862. (B A-1862.Fl, Map Collection, Brooklyn Public Library, Center for Brooklyn History)

Council would have been accepted [by Lincoln] and some preparations were being made to give the President elect a good reception."[2] Instead, Lincoln prepared to address a divided nation.

On March 4, 1861, just five days after Lincoln was sworn in as the nation's sixteenth president, seven states seceded from the Union—South Carolina, Mississippi, Florida, Alabama, Georgia, Louisiana, and Texas—forming the Confederate States of America.[3] According to the *Brooklyn Daily Times*, the city's Republican newspaper founded in 1855, everybody in the city was talking "war, war, war," businesses were virtually suspended, and American flags hung from people's homes and the city's public buildings. Brooklyn's thirteenth mayor, Samuel S. Powell, a city resident since 1838, was a Democrat and had not voted for Lincoln during the election. But on April 22, 1861, ten days after the Civil War had officially begun, he placed a notice in the *Brooklyn Daily Times* urging Brooklynites to meet at Fort Greene and show their "devotion to the Union in the hour of peril."[4] For the Brooklyn Heights resident Lewis Tappan, who had remained an advocate of nonviolence for most of his life, the Civil War was different "from any recorded in history."[5] His journal entry reflected the hopes of his anti-slavery colleagues in Brooklyn for the war's outcome—it was for the Civil War to finally decide if the nation was slave or free, even as racial violence brewed closer to home.

"THE BROOKLYN RIOT," 1862

We regret most profoundly that, a city, so justly celebrated for its law and order as Brooklyn, should have been so disgraced.
—*Brooklyn Daily Eagle*, August 5, 1862

Brooklyn, the city of Churches and noble charities, is usually so well behaved, we could scarcely credit the report that a riot had actually taken place, but a careful and impartial investigation of facts shows that the fair fame of our city has been sullied by a riotous mob of half drunken, ignorant white men and women.
—*Brooklyn Evening Star*, August 6, 1862

Irishmen! The day will come that you will find out that you
are making a sad mistake in assisting to crush out our liberties.
Learn! O learn, that the protection of the feeblest of your fellow beings, is the only guarantee you have of the protection for
your own liberty.
—*The Anglo-African*, August 1862

The recent attack on the negro women and children employed
in a tobacco manufactory in Brooklyn is most disgraceful to
our sister city, and—if it be true that they were fore warned
of it—to our Metropolitan Police, or at least to the Brooklyn
branch of it. That a ruffian mob should be enabled to hold
women and children in mortal terror for hours, gratifying
meantimes their groundless malice by earnest and all but successful attempts to roast them alive in their workshop is a stain
which Brooklyn will not efface.

The Black population of this country have been here for generations. They were brought here by force, and it is now gravely
proposed that they be expelled by force.
—*Douglass' Monthly*, September 1862

In 1858, US Senator William Seward of New York characterized the "irrepressible conflict" as an economic and political tension between the US
North and South.[6] But the senator's neat distinction between the free
and slave states was not so accurate. Cotton, sugar, and tobacco gener-
ated vast amounts of wealth for the white elite in the cities of Brooklyn
and New York in the nineteenth century. And the products of enslaved
labor had created an abundance of exploitative, low-wage jobs in the two
cities, attracting two of its most marginalized groups: its Irish and Black
communities.

Irish immigrants had begun arriving during gradual emancipation,
prior to the potato famine, and lived in the village of Brooklyn's Fifth
Ward, nearest to the Navy Yard. Between 1845 and 1860, Brooklyn
experienced a dramatic increase in its immigrant numbers. In 1845,
Kings County's population was 78,691, and 26,405 were foreign born.
A decade later, Brooklyn's population was 205,250, and 95,874 were
immigrants—meaning just under half of the city was born abroad.

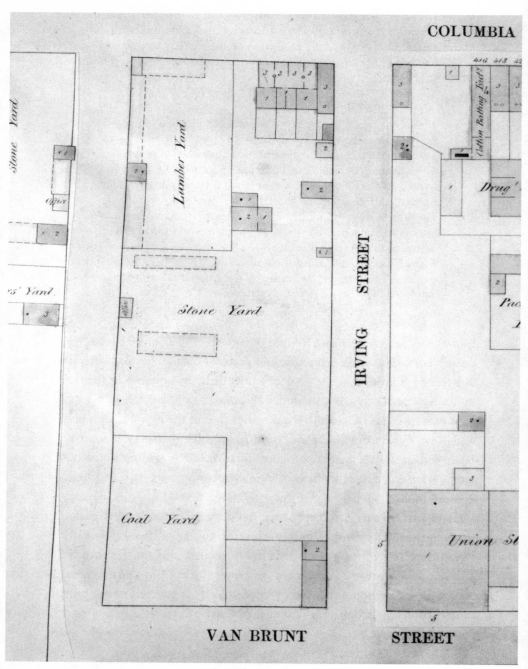

William Perris, detail from *Maps of the City of Brooklyn*, 2nd ed., vol. 1 (1860), plate 6. (Atlas 4, Atlas Collection, Center for Brooklyn History, Brooklyn Public Library)

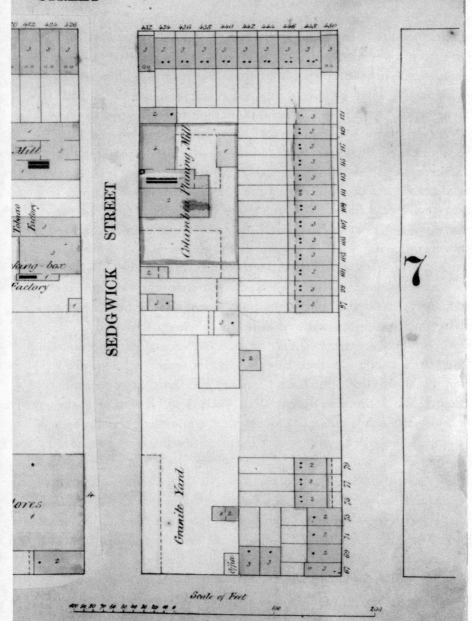

STREET

420 422 424 426

432 434 436 438 440 442 444 446 448 450

SEDGWICK STREET

Mill

Tobacco Factory

hing-box

Factory

Columbian Planing Mill

Granite Yard

tores

Office

Scale of Feet

100   200

7

In 1860, those numbers increased yet again. The city's population was 266,861, and 104,589 (or 37 percent) were born outside the United States. Of that 37 percent, the Irish constituted the largest single ethnicity born abroad (50 percent), followed by the Germans (20 percent). The numbers of the Irish overshadowed the city's Black population—in 1860, for example, there were 56,710 Irish residents living in Brooklyn, compared to 4,900 Black residents.[7] With little money, Brooklyn's Irish immigrant community had hoped to take advantage of the economic opportunities that Brooklyn and New York promised. They were greeted instead with nativist xenophobia and access to a limited labor market. As a result, Brooklyn's Irish residents worked in many of the same occupational fields as the city's long-established Black community—as dockworkers, laborers, servants, waiters, and washerwomen—and they were instrumental in transforming Red Hook from marshland to industrial warehouses during the construction of the Atlantic Docks. During the Civil War, the growing competition for jobs and a fear that scores of fugitives and newly emancipated Black men and women from the South might arrive in Brooklyn exacerbated hostilities between Irish and Black workers. The Democrats actively courted Irish constituents, encouraging them to consider their Black neighbors as an obstacle to their own social progress. This fallacy ignored the fact that generations of native Black Brooklynites and New Yorkers still had to meet the $250 property qualification in order to vote, while the Irish automatically qualified as long as they met the state constitution's residence requirements.[8]

On August 5, 1862, readers of the *Brooklyn Daily Times* might have been struck by two adjacent articles on the newspaper's second page: the first with the headline "Emancipation Jubilee at Myrtle Avenue Park: Five Thousand Colored People in the Woods, a Day of Jollity, Rejoicing, Fun and Frolic," and the second, "Disgraceful Riot in South Brooklyn: Colored Laborers Attacked by a Mob of Irishmen."[9] Emancipation Jubilee detailed that year's West India Emancipation Day celebrations in Myrtle Avenue Park, Brooklyn. The celebration was a long-standing tradition in the city, and residents had organized it even as the war was under way. The year before, celebrants had met in Williamsburg, where Samuel S. Rankins, the principal at Colored School No. 3, delivered the keynote on behalf of William P. Powell, who was a regular speaker at the celebrations but had since relocated to Liverpool, England. William had been born free in Manhattan and managed the Colored Sailors' Home before handing it over to Albro Lyons. Angered by the developments of the 1850s in the US, William moved his family to Liverpool seeking refuge, but he returned during the Civil War. Following Samuel's keynote, Willis Hodges addressed the gathering, and the 1861 event ended with this moving visual: "After but short preparation and the sending off of a small balloon as a small pilot, the mammoth one, on which it appeared in very large letters, "EMANCIPATION," made its way to the heavens, where its movements were watched by thousands of persons until it was lost from sight." The balloon's poetic movement was brought to an abrupt halt, the *Weekly Anglo-African* concluded, as "it probably landed somewhere on Staten Island."[10]

The West India Day Emancipation Celebration was a joyful reminder of long-rooted community building in Brooklyn's Black communities, and the *Brooklyn Daily Times'* decision to print it next to the report of a riot at the tobacco factory confirmed that joy coexisted alongside the daily racial violence the community faced. According to the *New York Times*, the disturbances began at the factory on the Saturday before, when a group of working-class Black women and children were "hooted and stoned by a party of Irishmen."[11] By Monday, August 4, a mob of Irishmen descended on two adjacent tobacco factories. When the first factory, owned by Jacob Lorillard, was closed, they moved toward the Watson factory—a large, three-story building on Sedgwick Street in South Brooklyn. Thomas Watson employed about seventy-five people to work at the factory, of which fifty were Black people and twenty-five were white—but the work was segregated: white employees were responsible for the pressing and general manufacture of tobacco and paid more (men received around $10 per week and women \$4–\$9 per week), while Black women and children rolled the actual tobacco (paid the lowest at \$2–\$6 per week).[12] On the night of the anti-Black race riot, there were twenty Black employees at Watson's factory, five of them men, the rest women and children. The Black press and city press noted that most of the men had been at the West India Emancipation Day celebrations in Myrtle Avenue Park that day. It was reported that Charles Baker, the foreman at the Watson tobacco factory, had stood at top of the stairs ready to protect the employees by wielding an axe. A police captain recalled some of the violence: "I got as far as the door and saw an officer have a Black man by the arm, and some of the crowd had hold of one of his legs; I got him clear and got him back into the factory." The mob attacked Thomas Watson's factory, which had stood there for a little less than a decade, "bombarding [it] with stones and brickbats, and almost every pane of glass in the building [was] broken."[13]

The *Brooklyn Evening Star* complained "that there was not a shadow of pretext for [the attack]."[14] But the riot made clear that anti-Black racism was prevalent among one of the city's most exploited groups. Irish and Irish American residents lived around the tobacco factories, and owner Thomas Watson was accused of regularly employing Black men, women, and children who lived in Manhattan or the "outskirts" of Brooklyn, causing resentment among the local Irish residents. When an Irishman attacked a Black worker at the factory, screaming, "Here is one of the race who brought this war on the country," the *Brooklyn Evening Star* felt that the racial conflict had gone too far. "The idea that a harmless inoffensive colored man should be held responsible for this mighty struggle, is so preposterous," the article stated, "yet there are a class of men in the city, who are so ignorant (or willfully devilish)."[15] On the other hand, the *Brooklyn Daily Times* felt optimistic for the city's future, as it was "not probable that any more disturbances would take place."[16]

But the Tobacco Factory Riots in Brooklyn did not signal an end but rather acted as a prologue to a new chapter of anti-Black violence. In the summer of 1863, on the streets of neighboring New York, it would be on a scale so horrifying that it still remains the largest and bloodiest urban insurrection in US history.

THE NEW YORK CITY DRAFT RIOTS, 1863

During the absence of the police from Brooklyn last night, there was a mob raised in the 2d ward which sacked nearly every house occupied by colored people in that locality, and beat the inmates in a terrible manner. A large number escaped and sought protection at the 1st and 42d Precinct Station Houses, while the crowd demolished their furniture and threw everything moveable into the street. Several houses in Green Lane, near Prospect street, were ransacked by the crowd, and two colored women were badly injured by being struck with stones. They took refuge at the 42d Precinct Station House. Two colored women, residing in Daugherty street, were set upon by the mob and had to take refuge at the station house. They stated that their furniture had all been destroyed. A house occupied by a colored family at No. 56 Tallman street; was visited by the crowd who after driving the people out with stones destroyed their furniture. A house on the corner of Stewart's Alley and Prospect street occupied by a colored family was sacked by a crowd of half-grown boys.

A colored man named Emmanuel McConkey was brought to the 42d Precinct Station-House so badly beaten that his recovery is considered doubtful. He was attacked by a mob in Roosevelt Street, New York but managed to get on the Catharine Ferry-Boat and escaped to Brooklyn. Nearly every colored person seen on the streets last night was attacked and beaten in the brutal manner. The police of the 42d Precinct after being relieved from their duties in New York returned and in a short time dispersed the crowd in the 2d ward.

—*Brooklyn Daily Times*, July 14, 1863

It is a gratifying circumstance that, while, to an unparalleled extent in this country, the spirit of lawlessness has manifested itself in the city of New York, Brooklyn, so nearly allied, socially, politically, and in every other respect with the metropolis, has manifested no organized sympathy, or been materially disturbed.

When a population is composed of property holders, and is generally intelligent, as is the case with us, there is little reason to fear riotous manifestations.
—*Brooklyn Daily Times*, July 15, 1863

A resident of the Eastern part of Brooklyn, who yesterday and the day previous visited the settlement of the colored people in the Ninth Ward of that city, have given us some interesting details of the condition of things in that quarter. There are now known to be about two hundred persons who have sought shelter from their demonic persecutors in New York, in the wild briars, bushes, and low woods which cover the ridge bordering the city. There may be, and probably are others who have not yet made themselves known. There were men, women, and children found among them, some of them in utter destitution. Husbands driven away without the means of knowing what has become of their wives and children, and families burned out and compelled to flee, ignorant if their natural protector is alive or not.

In some instances separated families have accidentally been united. The permanent residents of the district, though themselves cut off from their ordinary employments and threatened with outrage, are active in succoring the refugees, mostly strangers to them, and liberally share their shelter with them so far as able. Many have, however, slept outdoors ever since the riots began, suffering not only from exposure but the effects of terror, such as can hardly be realized.
—*The Anglo-African*, July 25, 1863

On Friday, May 15, 1863, Frederick Douglass spoke at the Brooklyn Academy of Music on Montague Street. The Academy, one block from City Hall, intended for the "purpose of encouraging and cultivating a taste for music, literature, and the arts," had opened just two years earlier, three months before the outbreak of the Civil War, with a twenty-two-hundred-seat theater and a smaller concert hall. Brooklynites were no longer dependent on Manhattan's theaters and concert halls; instead, this area of their city was now a bustling mix of commercial, cultural, and residential activity, so different from the quaint, quiet scene that Francis Guy had captured of the village of Brooklyn in the dead of winter four decades earlier. Frederick Douglass was by now a sought-after lecturer who had built a formidable reputation as an abolitionist on both sides of the Atlantic. His lecture "What Shall Be Done with the Negro?" focused on the ongoing injustice that Black people still had to fight for citizenship rights and examined the racial tensions between Black and Irish communities. He stated, "The only way to secure peace to the nation was to do justice to the negro. He must not only be given freedom, but must be admitted to all the privileges of a citizen of the United States." He then expanded, "There was no more generous, warm-hearted, hospitable people at home than the Irish; none who treated oppression and tyranny with a deeper hatred. [He] had been treated more kindly in Ireland . . . and he could never understand how it was that when the Irish get to this country they become the most cruel, the meanest, and most vindictive of all of the oppressors of his race." His lecture was met with great enthusiasm and was "repeatedly interrupted by laughter and applause."[17]

Anti-Black violence was at the center of William J. Wilson's concerns too. On July 8, 1863, having served as an educator for over ten years at Colored School No. 1, William was forced to write to the city's Board of Education to address the drop in enrollment at the school. William confirmed that there had indeed been a drop in enrollment but went on to clarify why this had occurred. To some extent, parents of color were choosing integrated schools, citing a lack of resources at the Colored School system and also requesting the employment of white teachers, fearing that the schools' long-standing Black teachers lacked qualifications. But the main reason for low enrollment numbers at the Colored School was racial violence. William wrote of sickening scenes in which rocks were thrown through the school's windows, while students were "chas[ed], beat[en], and otherwise maltreated . . . in the streets, and ston[ed] . . . even in their yards while at play." He qualified that children had been not only beaten in the streets but also mugged and their books and other property stolen from them. It began, William confirmed, in the summer of 1862, just before the city's Tobacco Factory Riots, and "kept up till the present date."[18] Unchecked white-supremacist violence was a harbinger of colossal trauma that would visit New York just five days later.

Fifteen-year-old Maritcha Lyons watched the city she called home burn for three nights. From Monday, July 13, to Thursday, July 16, 1863, during some of the hottest days of summer, mobs of white people, mostly working-class Irishmen, tore through Manhattan's streets as a mass protest turned into a full-blown riot.[19] The troubles began as a response to the unpopular National Conscription Act. In March 1863, Congress passed the law, which required all men aged between twenty and thirty-five to serve in the Union Army. But the law also contained a provision allowing the affluent to avoid military service by paying $300. It therefore fell on the Irish working class to fight in a war that they felt they had no stake in, especially when slavery and emancipation was the Civil War's focus. In the violence that followed, rioters attacked every part of the city of New York, including homes along Grand and Division Streets, businesses, and government and public buildings. They destroyed the Colored Sailors' Home, St. Philip's Church, and the Colored Orphan Asylum, so that all 233 children had to be evacuated across the East River. And when they were done destroying public and private buildings, they committed some of the worst atrocities against their neighbors—Black New Yorkers, whose ancestors had once built the city.

Scholars have painstakingly recovered the nonstop violence that permeated through New York's streets on the hot summer days of 1863, and it is not my intention to perpetuate some of that traumatic violence through this book's writing or to suggest that Brooklyn was a bastion of healthy race relations and devoid of violence itself. But in those nightmarish summer days, New York's neighbor emerged as a place of safety and refuge in the most obvious and sometimes surprising of neighborhoods. Among the many New Yorkers seeking safety in Brooklyn were the Lyons family, friends of Elizabeth and James Gloucester. During the riots, the mob destroyed the home of Mary and Albro Lyons. Maritcha's parents sought police protection to get their young family to "steamboats [that] were kept in readiness to either transport fugitives or to outwit rioters by pulling out into mid-stream." Albro Lyons initially remained behind in Manhattan, but Mary and her children, Maritcha, Therese, Pauline, and Albro Jr., es-caped via the Roosevelt Ferry and reached Broadway in Williamsburg. From there, they traveled along the Long Island Sound up to New England and stayed with Charles Remond, a fellow anti-slavery activ-ist, and his family.[20]

The Lyons family was considered a part of New York City's Black elite. For an ordinary working-class Black woman like Nancy Robinson, escaping Manhattan would result in incalculable and traumatic personal loss. A resident of New York's Fourth Ward, the center of the violence by the second day, Nancy and her husband, Jeremiah, together with Nancy's friend, also sought refuge in Brooklyn. Hoping the mob would allow three Black women to pass, Jeremiah dressed in Nancy's cloth-ing, and the group made their way to the Brooklyn ferries. When the disguise failed to completely conceal Jeremiah's beard, a mob murdered him and threw his body into the East River as Nancy escaped via the Grand Street Ferry. The press hinted at the horror of the attack, but the "atrocities [the mob] perpetuated [on him were] so revolting" that it refused to print them in full.[21]

Brooklynites braced themselves for violence. At the Brooklyn Navy Yard, 150 mariners and sailors were dispatched to Manhattan, ordered to protect residents targeted by the rioters; two "32's," or thirty-two-pound artillery, usually attached to warships, "gaped in threatening silence" and stood at the main gate on York Street, while canons loaded with canister and shrapnel lined the yard's various entrances. In Brooklyn's Eastern District, comprising Williamsburg, Bushwick, and Greenpoint, market men who usually carried fresh produce daily from Brooklyn to New York refused to travel after sunset, as they feared for their lives. At the Williamsburg Peck Slip Ferry, which had transported William and Willis between Manhattan and Williamsburg numerous times in the decades prior, not a single person of color could be seen.[22] In adjacent Greenpoint, the majority of residents fled their homes, necessitating the formation of a night patrol designed to protect those who chose to stay.

The neighborhood police placed a canon in front of the station house in case any trouble arrived via the Tenth and Twenty-Third Street Ferries.[23]

As Brooklyn armed itself, in turn, it also offered refuge. In Bushwick and Williamsburg, the German community offered protection at the Turn Verein Hall on Meserole Street near Union Avenue. By 1860, more than two hundred thousand German-speaking immigrants had settled in New York and Brooklyn as furniture and clothing manufacturers and beer brewers, having fled their own homeland due to political turmoil created by the March Revolution in 1848. These largely working-class communities deliberately sought areas of the city that were not overly settled, in which they could build cultural institutions and meeting places. As a result, the Eastern District became heavily German, and the Turn Verein—a community sports hall—was the center of German American civic life. During the Draft Riots, the German communities "assembled in great force," and a "heavy guard was kept all night," while they promised "stern measures" against rioters and a "speedy justice, . . . not because they love the order of the draft, but because they love good order and value life." Their response to the riots aligned with their general political leanings. While the Irish had been heavily courted by the Democrats, Brooklyn and New York's German communities usually backed anti-slavery Republicans.[24] To the East, Weeksville was located much farther away from the East River than was Greenpoint, the Navy Yard, or Williamsburg, but its reputation as a successful intentional free Black community for almost three decades meant that it was an obvious place for Black New Yorkers to flee to. But Manhattan's residents, traumatized into a fight-or-flight response, could not stop running, so that they stopped "not only in Weeksville, Carsville," but also in "new Brooklyn and the whole vicinity extending to Flatbush and Flatlands," where they ran into surrounding woods to find "safety and shelter."[25]

Manhattan was ablaze. After four days of looting, rioting, and murder, the city lay in ruins. The Draft Riots had resulted in almost $1.5 million worth of damage. In a city that valued capitalism over community, this was a catastrophe. But the harm it unleashed on New Yorkers was irreparable. By September 11, 1863, New York's businessmen formed a

Committee of Merchants for the Relief of Colored People Suffering from the Late Riots in the City of New York. Their report offered an assessment of the financial loss suffered by the city's Black businessmen and also tracked the displacement of the city's Black community, while acknowledging that many victims of the racial atrocities had mostly returned to work. The exception was the two hundred workers employed at Brooklyn's tobacco factories. The Merchants Committee reported that "their employers, are afraid, as yet, to set them to work."[26] In spite of this, Black New Yorkers struggling to recover emotionally moved to cities such as Brooklyn and beyond seeking sanctuary. In the aftermath of the riots, the population of Black Brooklynites remained steady at around 5,000 people, but in the city of New York, that number plummeted from 16,350 people in 1840 to just under 10,000 in 1865.

"COLORED CITIZENS, TO ARMS!"

On October 10, 1861, twenty-two-year-old Joseph S. Bowen, a painter by trade, enlisted for general service for three years as a landsman—a sailor ranked with the least experience—in the US Navy.[27] On January 11, 1862, twenty-three-year-old Isaac H. Hunter Jr., a druggist by trade, enlisted as a private in the artillery division of the US Marines. He deserted his military position just under two months later but mustered in again on September 28, 1864, to serve as a sailor.[28] On March 20, 1862, a now fifty-one-year-old Lewis H. Nelson, the famed barber and healer of Williamsburg, signed up as landsman for a three-year term in the US Navy, like Joseph Bowen.[29] On June 12, 1863, twenty-nine-year-old Sylvanus Smith Jr., a waiter by profession, joined the US Navy initially for a one-year term. On May 13, 1863, Peter Vogelsang Sr., a porter by profession, mustered in as a sergeant to the now-famous Fifty-Fourth Massachusetts Infantry Regiment, the first Black regiment raised in the North. At forty-six years old, he was one of the oldest to fight in the Union Army, and in spite of being injured during service on July 16, 1863, in James Island, South Carolina, he served until the end of the Civil War, mustering out on August 20, 1865.[30] On August 21, 1863, twenty-four-year-old Henry Hogarth, a laborer by trade, joined eighteen hundred other men in the Eleventh US Colored Heavy Artillery of the United States Colored Troops.[31] The unit suffered three hundred losses, and another one hundred medical discharges, but Henry served most of the Civil War stationed in Louisiana. On October 2, 1865, he mustered out of New Orleans.[32] Joseph, Isaac, Lewis, Sylvanus, Peter, and Henry were among thirty thousand men from Kings County to enlist in the Union Army and represented scores of ordinary Black men who demonstrated extraordinary courage and commitment to freedom and citizenship, even as they were subject to ongoing discrimination within the military, which included segregated ranks, lesser wages than their white counterparts, and the lack of opportunity for promotion.[33]

If Sylvanus's and Henry's last names sound familiar, it was because they were the children of Sylvanus and Ann Smith and of George and Ellen Hogarth, respectively. Their parents had shaped the city of Brooklyn in the early to mid-nineteenth century—the Smith family as early land investors in Weeksville and the Hogarth family as educators and leaders at the city's AME Church. These parents and elders had a profound effect on the next generation. Although George Hogarth had passed away when Henry was only twelve years old, his son continued his activist legacy and participated in August 1 celebrations at George's former church, where he sang "Liberty and Equality."[34] Joseph S. Bowen was the son of Jacqueline and Benjamin Bowen and the nephew of William and Willis Hodges. There is no written evidence that Willis served in the Union Army in 1863, but he and Sarah moved frequently between Virginia and Brooklyn at this time with their young family, seventeen-year-old Augustus, fifteen-year-old Catherine, and thirteen-year-old Victoria. William had offered to create a militia with other Black men in Williamsburg one year into the war: "Parson Hodges talked of getting up a colored company, and offered its services to the government, but the offer was not accepted."[35] William had also already suffered personal loss at the start of the Civil War, when his wife, Mary Ann Tippon, died in 1861. He remained in Williamsburg most likely to take care of his own young family. The Wilsons and Gloucesters would find ways other than military service to be in community.

Sylvanus Smith Jr.'s, Peter Vogelsang Sr.'s, and Henry Hogarth's official enlistments were made possible by the passage of a now-iconic US historical document familiar to many of us but perhaps in a different context.[36] On January 1, 1863, Lincoln's Emancipation Proclamation went into effect. William J. Wilson gave an enthusiastic speech at the Cooper Institute in Manhattan welcoming a provision in the Emancipation Proclamation that allowed Black men, nearly two years into the war, to join Union troops.[37] A further celebration was held at Brooklyn's AME Church.[38] But the Emancipation Proclamation is also regularly misunderstood with these four simple words: "Lincoln freed the slaves." The reality was that emancipation did not arrive with such ease. The proclamation freed any enslaved person under Confederate control, but it did not emancipate any of the eight hundred thousand enslaved people living in the border states—Delaware, Kentucky, Maryland, and Missouri—that had remained loyal to the Union or parts of the Confederacy occupied by Union troops, that is, Tennessee and parts of Louisiana and Virginia.[39] The Emancipation Proclamation may not have freed a single enslaved person immediately, but it did redefine the ultimate goal of the drawn-out war: to dismantle slavery.

RECONSTRUCTING THE NATION

What are American children taught today about Reconstruction? . . . He would in all probability complete his education without any idea of the part which the black race has played in America; of the tremendous moral problem of abolition; of the cause and meaning of the Civil War and the relation which Reconstruction had to democratic government and the labor movement today.

If, on the other hand, we are going to use history for our pleasure and amusement, for inflating our national ego, and giving us a false but pleasurable sense of accomplishment, then we must give up the idea of history as a science or as an art

using the results of science, and admit frankly that we are using
a version of historic fact in order to influence and educate the
new generation along the way we wish.
—W. E. B. Du Bois, "The Propaganda of History,"
in *Black Reconstruction in America* (1935)

On July 16, 1865, just three months after the Civil War ended, seventy-
four-year-old Matilda Culbreth died at her home at 102 Washington
Avenue, at Park Avenue, in Brooklyn's Second Ward (which today
includes DUMBO and part of downtown Brooklyn). Like so many
other Brooklynites, Matilda had been born enslaved in Maryland but
for decades had made the city of Brooklyn her home. She was born
in 1791, and it is difficult to know when she might have moved here—
whether it was as a child during New York's gradual emancipation
period or as an adult in Brooklyn's post-emancipation decades. Did she
know, for example, the Croger family, who did not live very far from her,
or the Wilsons or Gloucesters before they relocated to other parts of the
city in the early and late 1860s, respectively? As an ordinary working-
class woman, she lived a difficult life—her name appears throughout
1861 and 1862 in both the *Brooklyn Daily Eagle* and *Brooklyn Daily Times*
for unpaid sanitation taxes. It was the Black press who delivered the
most touching eulogy of this woman's achievements. The *Weekly Anglo-
African* described her as a "loving, devoted wife and mother and she ever
labored for the welfare of the family," and continued,

It was our pleasure to be long acquainted with Mrs. Culbreth. She
was born in Maryland but at an early age became a victim of the
domestic slave trade. Having been sold away to South Carolina and
thus separated from some members of her family. She made great
efforts to release all the enslaved members of her family. She was a
woman of singular earnestness in the cause of her race. It was the
theme of her constant study and conversation. She had clear views
of the wrongs of slavery and the just claims of the slave to freedom.
She was widely familiar with the views of public persons in regard to
the cause of the race, and was bold and clear in her criticism of their

views and actions. Her house was the welcome home of strangers and friends, whom she always made happy and comfortable.[40]

Although historians may never recover the vast array of names and stories that made Brooklyn a more just city, we should be certain that there were many ordinary working-class women like Matilda, dedicated to racial justice and at the center of the struggle.

From 1865 to 1877, Reconstruction represented one of the most turbulent chapters in US history, with small glimpses of democratic promise. It marked an unprecedented moment in interracial democracy, as Black men represented themselves and broader constituencies in local, state, and national public office. Yet it also saw the rise of white-supremacist and domestic terrorist organizing that would continue to haunt Black communities into the twentieth century.[41] Peter, Elenor, Benjamin, and Elizabeth Croger had long departed the earth, so they could not see any of their community-building and anti-slavery activist work codified as amendments to the federal Constitution. The Reconstruction Amendments included the Thirteenth Amendment, abolishing slavery in the United States (1863); the Fourteenth Amendment, granting citizenship to anyone born on US soil, in theory guaranteeing equal protection under the law, regardless of race (1868); and the Fifteenth Amendment, extending the right to vote to all US citizens (1870). None of these amendments were an indicator that the struggle was over, as a new generation would live through the Black Codes and later Jim Crow laws.

But during Reconstruction, Black Brooklynites committed themselves to rebuilding the nation, as they had done with their own city in the decades prior—assistance, education, and faith became the focus once more. Sometime around August 1863, Mary, William, and their daughter, Annie Wilson, now fourteen years old, relocated to Washington, DC. It is entirely possible that having borne witness to the racial violence directed at Colored School No. 1 and then the Draft Riots and with the devastation being too hard to bear, the Wilsons saw themselves being needed elsewhere, where they could help newly freed people. William's friend and onetime journalistic rival Dr. James

McCune Smith stated that William was forced to retire after teaching almost twenty years in Brooklyn's school system when a member of the Board of Education demanded his dismissal following William's social justice speeches at the Cooper Institute in 1862 and 1863.[42] William had long stopped contributing as Ethiop to *Frederick Douglass' Paper*, which had also stopped production, but he did write a series of five letters on his experiences in DC for the *Anglo-American Magazine* between August and October 1863.[43] In 1864, William became an educator and director of Camp Barker in Washington, DC, established just two years earlier, thereby continuing his educational career during the Civil War. Mary also joined the Intermediate Department of William's school, where she was responsible for the education of forty-one students in the subjects of reading, writing, and math.[44] It is difficult to say what caused the change in career, but a year later, census records list William as a cashier at a branch of the Freedmen's Bank and National Savings Bank in DC. No doubt this is where daughter Annie met Thomas Boston, an assistant cashier at the Freedmen's Bank, whom she would marry on October 12, 1869. That same year, William became a trustee at Howard University.[45] William died a decade later, on November 26, 1879. Mary, now fifty-four years old, remained in Washington, DC, one year after William's death and was still employed as a teacher; she was joined by thirty-two-year-old Annie, who worked as a teacher too. Both women were boarders at Hannah Peck's Boarding House on L Street in what we know today as the southern end of Logan Circle.[46] By 1904, Mary was back in Brooklyn living in the Wilsons' long-standing family home at 23 Greene Avenue in Fort Greene. The astute businesswoman and educator had lived to the remarkable age of eighty-two.

Exactly three days after William Hodges had spoken at the 1862 West India Emancipation Day Celebration in Myrtle Avenue Park, the *Brooklyn Daily Times* reported "Parson Hodges Going South." The article expanded, "He came to Williamsburgh, built several houses and a church, opened a colored School and has labored faithfully to better the condition of the colored population. Now, he says, the colored people of the district know enough to take care of themselves, and he thinks his services are needed among the poor blacks in the South."[47] William left his position as the pastor of the Eleventh Street African Church in Williamsburg, Brooklyn, and moved back to his place of birth, Norfolk, Virginia, which he had been forced to leave almost four decades earlier. He continued his work in educational reform and social justice by opening a school for Black people in southeastern Virginia. By the summer of 1864, his brother Willis was back in Williamsburg and joined his brother Charles in expressing support for freed people heading north.[48] Three years later, Willis; his wife, Sarah; and their young family relocated to Virginia, and at the end of 1867, Willis was in attendance at the Capitol in Richmond, Virginia, as the county representative to discuss the formation of a new constitution for the state.[49] He returned to Brooklyn once more, where his son Augustus M. Hodges was carving a career for himself as a writer and educator, but he returned to Norfolk one last time, where he died of heart failure on September 24, 1890. His wife, Sarah, had died six months earlier in Brooklyn, and his brother William had passed some years earlier, on September 13, 1872. The political organizing that Willis and William imparted to their nephew Joseph S. Bowen shaped his later years. Although he had been born in Manhattan, Joseph had made Williamsburg home for over thirty years. During that time, Williamsburg transformed from the most western point of the town of Bushwick overlooking the East River to New York City's Sixteenth Ward after the consolidation of 1898, which resulted in the creation of the city's five boroughs that we know today. When Joseph died of natural causes associated with old age, the *Brooklyn Daily Eagle* reported that he was "for a score of years the chairman of the Kings County Colored Republican Committee, and long prominent in Republican politics in the Eastern District." Although Willis and William had not lived in Williamsburg for almost half a century when Joseph passed away, the newspaper was sure to identify him as "the senior nephew of the Hodges brothers, prominent as abolitionist orators fifty years ago."[50]

In 1867, Robert H. Cousins, whose family had been active agents of the Underground Railroad, passed away. The *Times Union* newspaper declared that he died a proud mason of the Widow's Son Lodge No. 11 F&AM, which still stands today in East New York some 174 years after its founding.[51] In the same year as Robert's death, Willis stated his intention to open a school in Princess Anne County, Virginia, funded by the Freedmen's Bureau. The Bureau of Freedmen, Refugees, and Abandoned Lands, known informally as the Freedmen's Bureau, was established by Congress on March 3, 1865, and operated in the North and South. The New York and Brooklyn Freedmen's Bureau was located at 16 Court Street, on the corner of Joralemon Street, and its primary function in Brooklyn and other Northern cities was to provide employment for freed people and white Union refugees. This particular branch made clear to potential employers that there were very few men available for hire through the agency but that "women, from eighteen to thirty years of age," and "boys and girls, from ten to fifteen years old," were available in large numbers and willing to work as domestic servants in the homes of wealthy Brooklynites, in exchange for board, clothing, and an education.[52]

The American Freedmen's Friend Society offered aid to new arrivals on far less exploitative terms than did the Freedmen's Bureau and extended a kinder form of humanitarian assistance to Black soldiers and freedmen. The Brooklyn auxiliary was led by Elizabeth and James Gloucester and based at 118 Myrtle Avenue, in today's downtown Brooklyn. Elizabeth Gloucester was joined at the society by her friend Sarah Morel and newer colleagues such as Harriet Wilson. Her old friend Mary Wilson had already relocated to DC to start teaching there. The Freedmen's Friend Society accepted books, clothing, money, and general goods donations in order to support the city's newer arrivals.[53] Their efforts were mirrored by the Weeksville-based African Civilization Society, which had once facilitated emigration and now concentrated its efforts in education and community work in both Weeksville and the US South. The Weeksville organization was led by Elizabeth and James's friends Christiana and Amos Freeman, who had taken over James's pastoral duties at Siloam Presbyterian. The African Civilization Society employed 127 teachers and teaching assistants and instructed nearly 8,000 students in the South.[54] At home, they produced the *Freedmen's Torchlight*, a Weeksville-based newspaper that began in January 1866 and was an instructional tool in the form of a four-page monthly. In 1868, the work of the organization expanded with the founding of the Brooklyn Howard Colored Orphan Asylum. As the Colored Orphan Asylum in New York had burned down during the Draft Riots, Sarah Tillman, a New York resident, assisted by the secretary of the African Civilization Society, Henry M. Wilson, opened the Howard Colored Orphan Asylum on the corner of Dean Street and Troy Avenue. It stood on the same block as Colored School No. 2 and the African Civilization Society. The home offered refuge to children—orphaned or not—especially when their mothers, many of them freedwomen from the South, could not take their children to work in domestic service.[55]

Returning to Brooklyn after military service in the Civil War provided its own challenges to the city's residents. In August 1869, four years after his service ended, Lewis H. Nelson died from heart disease.[56] When he had signed up for service in the US Navy, he had left his wife, Harriet, and their daughter, who bore her mother's name, at home in Williamsburg. According to probate records, Lewis left the family home on South Seventh Street in Williamsburg, an additional property on Broadway, and his own personal property to his "beloved wife," Harriet.[57] The Nelson family was unusual, however, in the financial security they created through real estate ownership. There is, for example, no mention of Lewis's war pension in his will or probate or any known record in the US Civil War Pension Files held at the National Archives and Records Administration.

In contrast, Sarah Hogarth, Henry's wife and Ellen and George's daughter-in-law, had a far more depressing but common story of trying to access Henry's pension. In spite of his standing in the community and leadership roles, George Hogarth had left his family without generational wealth. In 1874, Henry's older brother, George Hogarth Jr., applied to be the principal at Colored School No. 2 in Weeksville. George, a student of William J. Wilson's, was following in his father's footsteps (George Sr. had taught at the school before William).[58] When George's brother Henry died on May 7, 1894, at the age of fifty-five, he left behind wife, Sarah, and three surviving children (Sarah and Henry's firstborn, Annie, would sadly die at the age of seven in 1872). It is not clear from census records what income Sarah relied on while Henry was at war, but historians have pointed out that Black women frequently sought wage-earning employment and children sometimes were sent to work too.[59] In August 25, 1890, Sarah applied for Henry's Civil War pension. It is difficult to say why exactly Sarah would have applied at this time, as her husband did not die until 1894, but one can infer that Henry might have been in ill health. The application was considered invalid. She applied again on June 1, 1894, as a widow, and this time her application for Henry's pension was successful.[60] Sarah was one of the "lucky" ones. Archives show that working-class Black women were often at the mercy of white pension agents, who would often deny their pension applications, so that the process of applying became a "struggle over race, gender, and the Black family" as families struggled to remain together, unable to stay out of poverty.[61]

The city of Brooklyn itself also underwent significant changes with the founding of Prospect Park in 1867 and the opening of the now-iconic Brooklyn Bridge in 1883. Designed by Frederick Law Olmstead and Calvert Vaux, Prospect Park transformed 800 acres of Indigenous Lenape land, which had also once served as Dutch farmland and had seen some of the bloodiest battles during the Battle of Brooklyn, into a 526-acre landscaped oasis. The design team had cemented their reputation as landscape architects with the opening of Central Park in New York City in 1859, which had subsequently displaced and then erased the thriving free Black community of Seneca Village. Meanwhile, in the city's Second Ward, the homes and institutions associated with Brooklyn's early free Black community that had once called the village home were demolished in the name of progress. In 1869, when construction on the Brooklyn Bridge began, all of the streets surrounding its famous entrance were razed, and so disappeared James Street, the site of the village's first private school intended for the education of Black adults and children during gradual emancipation. When the Brooklyn Bridge was completed, it would be dubbed the eighth wonder of the world, and it challenged the ferries' century-plus dominance of the East River. In the same year as the bridge's construction, New York State established the Town Survey Commission to map the towns of Flatbush, Flatlands, New Utrecht, and Gravesend, and in its plan of 1874, it extended the street grid as a far as Jamaica Bay.

When Elizabeth Gloucester died in August 1883 at the age of sixty-six, the *Brooklyn Daily Eagle* named her "the Richest of her Race in America."[62] It was an impressive feat for any woman in nineteenth-century Brooklyn. But Elizabeth was a Black woman who had arrived as a young orphan at the home of John Gloucester in Philadelphia and was systemically denied the ability to amass, inherit, and distribute wealth, and the newspaper obituary commemorated an exceptional life. Listed as the head of the family on the 1880 census, even as her husband, James, was still alive, Elizabeth had made her money in the way that quintessential New Yorkers do—through real estate. Her biggest purchase was Remsen House, which had previously housed the exclusive white men's club Hamilton House and was now an opulent boarding house on the corner of Remsen and Clinton Streets in Brooklyn Heights and also served as home to the Gloucester family. It was reported that Elizabeth had paid nearly $3 million in today's money for the establishment. Yet, in some ways, while Elizabeth's wealth might not have been typical of an ordinary Black woman living in Brooklyn, her spirit was—she defied all of the racist assumptions made about her race and gender. At her funeral, even though James had served as the pastor at Siloam, it was her friend Amos Freeman who delivered the lengthy address. She also brought together the pastors of the Brooklyn AME Church, the Fleet Street Methodist Episcopal Church, and the Zion Methodist Episcopal Church in death, as she had brought folks together at her home, like Frederick Douglass and John Brown, during her life.[63] When she died, the local press gleefully reported on the fallout between James and his children over Elizabeth's estate. In her will, Elizabeth had left the majority of her substantial property portfolio to her children and very little to James. He took the children to court to contest the will. Detailed accounts of the family animosity were regularly and frequently reported in the *Brooklyn Daily Eagle*.[64] Today, Elizabeth Gloucester is peacefully buried in Green-Wood Cemetery alongside her children and husband, with no indication of the drama that followed her death. The ornate memorial pillar at their burial plot reads, "The undying love of a mother, is a thing to cherish and keep. We must guard her memory closer now that she has fallen asleep."

On August 12, 1883, the *Brooklyn Daily Eagle* ran a long piece on Elizabeth, having published her formal obituary a day earlier. The article lists the late Elizabeth's achievements once more but then abruptly breaks off with a few misogynistic lines at the end:

> When such eminence is won as that occupied by Mrs. Gloucester it is clearly an evidence of ability and penetration of character on the part of the woman who achieves it. It is unnecessary, in connection with this subject, to discuss the relations of a career like that of Mrs. Gloucester to the agitation for a more exalted place for woman in the activities of life. Opinions differ in regard to the advisability of woman suffrage and the decisive weight of public sentiment is still arrayed against it despite the useless endeavors of many well meaning advocates. Experience has not produced any adequate reason for a reversal of the well established view that woman in the broader sense is better fitted for the emotional rather than the practical side of existence.[65]

According to the *Eagle*, Elizabeth was exceptional on her own personal merit, but that did not mean she, or indeed any other woman, deserved the right to vote. It was a backhanded compliment that diminished Elizabeth's activism and the generations of women that followed. These parents had a profound effect on Brooklyn's future generations, and their descendants grappled with an ever-evolving definition of freedom. In October 1869, Maritcha Lyons returned home. Having escaped the city of New York with her family during the terrifying days of the Draft

Riots in 1863, she came back but relocated to the city of Brooklyn, where she began working at what we know today as P.S. 67, the Charles A. Dorsey School in Fort Greene. Inspired by her parents' own sense of activism, and her mother Mary's close involvement in fundraising for Black institutions such as the Colored Orphan Asylum, Maritcha knew how to organize and be in community. She worked together with sisters Sarah Smith Tompkins Garnet and Susan Smith McKinney Steward, the daughters of Ann and Sylvanus Smith, with whom she found companionship. Together, they advocated for universal suffrage and ensured that Black women were included in these debates, through their work in the Equal Suffrage League and the Women's Loyal Union of New York and Brooklyn. They were reminded that there was still tremendous work to be done when they hosted the lecturer and journalist Ida B. Wells at the Brooklyn Literary Union in 1892. Freedom remained out of reach as long as racial violence, lynchings, and disenfranchisement continued in the US South. Ida B. Wells would dedicate the newspaper *The Memphis Free Speech* to "the Afro-American women of New York and Brooklyn."[66] The scholar P. Gabrielle Foreman invites us to be attentive to the "children as their elders organized, hosted, and traveled to such multiday political meetings [at the Colored Conventions] in various states and towns, where they gathered in the churches these children called their own and ate and slept in bedrooms even closer to home."[67] The parents of this new generation of Brooklynites birthed the idea of a modern, culturally pluralistic democracy in the United States—in many ways, we are the lucky ones who bask in their legacy and must continue their struggle.

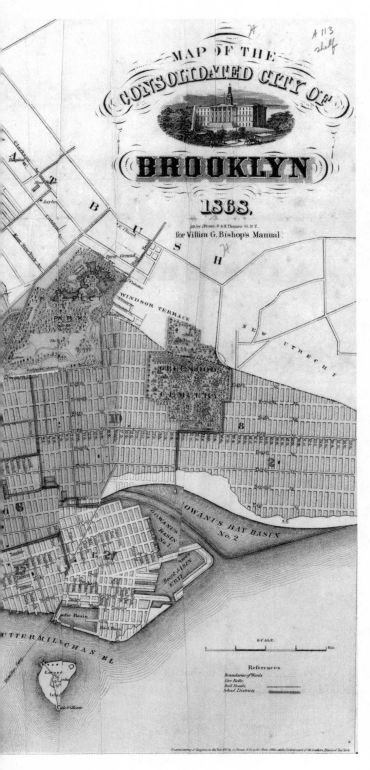

William G. Bishop,
A. Brown & Co., *Map
of the Consolidated
City of Brooklyn*, ca.
1868. (B A-1868b.Fl,
Map Collection, Center
for Brooklyn History,
Brooklyn Public
Library)

EPILOGUE

In spring 2019, I was honored to be invited by my brilliant colleague Zenzelé Cooper, then program manager at Weeksville Heritage Center (WHC), to speak at an event that the organization was hosting in collaboration with the New School's Vera List Center for Art and Politics as part of a yearlong seminar series, *Freedom of Speech: Curriculum for Studies into Darkness.*[1] The event was titled "A Time for Seditious Speech," and WHC staff, stewards of the legacy of its groundbreaking historic community, collectively put together a rich daylong program that reflected Weeksville's long historical connection with activism, art, education, free speech, and self-determination. My talk—which was in dialogue with the work that folks at WHC have been doing for decades, from the inspiring late Dr. Joan Maynard onward—reflected on space, the power of place, being beneficiaries of stolen land, and the right to the city, many of the ideas that had originally germinated this book and its decade-plus-long research. In particular, I wanted to explore how Black people created spaces of freedom in nineteenth-century Brooklyn that would allow for seditious speech to become a possibility and more specifically how Black women made this a reality.[2] It was my entire privilege that Ellen Holly and her granddaughter were in the packed room with us that day. The late Ellen Holly was an actor and the great-great-granddaughter of Susan Smith McKinney Steward—the child of Ann and Sylvanus Smith—who is often celebrated for being the third Black woman to earn a medical degree in the United States and the first in New York State.

The history lovingly restored in this book is not dead. It is living and breathing through the descendants of the Brooklyn families honored in this book, and it is living and breathing in the social justice issues we witness and experience today. We can be witness to Maritcha Lyons's rich life because her nephew Harry Albro Williamson, son of her sister Pauline (formally Mary Elizabeth Pauline), lovingly preserved his family papers and then donated them to the Schomburg Center for Research in Black Culture at New York Public Library, and the brilliant scholar Dr. Carla L. Peterson, Maritcha's great-grandniece, a living descendant, composed her beautiful family history for us to read.[3] We can follow the beautiful story of Willis and Sarah Hodges because their descendant Alexander A. Moore carefully preserved his family memories and ephemera. Some of Alexander Moore's family photos can be found today in the archival collections at Weeksville Heritage Center. Other family archives like the Nelson-Hodges Papers, 1773–1936, often cited as being at the Long Island Historical Society (renamed Brooklyn Historical Society, now Center for Brooklyn History at Brooklyn Public Library), have never been recovered at that repository.[4] The commemoration of these families and their memories of Brooklyn also live on in private family collections—in albums, attics, garages, book shelves, trunks, and closets—which, as the historian Paula C. Austin notes, "[honors] the ways in which Black life defies the confines, but also the historical narratives, of racial segregation and its violence. And the ways that Black families, in some cases, can serve as the conduit for this refusal." The scholar Amaka Okechukwu reminds us too that "Black Archival Practice could be considered a subset of memory work, a broad range of practices that preserve, resurrect, frame, and contest the past.[5]

Families can also take up the activist legacy of their elders and ancestors in continuing to demand their right to the city. On February 2, 2021, the home of the late "Mama" Joy Chatel at 227 Duffield Street was designated a New York City landmark by the Landmarks Preservation Commission. It represented one ending to a two-decade struggle to save her home from demolition, which the city had originally demanded through eminent domain. Her daughter, Shawné Lee, has been part of a grassroots, borough-wide coalition of fellow activists. Together they resisted displacement, rezoning, gentrification, eminent domain, and historical erasure in the name of progress. They continue the struggle to respectfully commemorate and remember our complex past and desire for it not to be erased by a multimillion-dollar, transnationally financed urban development in the present. Now the street is renamed Abolitionist Place, after the Truesdell family that lived there. When I walked past the home in the spring of 2023, I was struck by the enormity—in depth, height, and space—of the luxury condo and commercial buildings that surrounded 227 Duffield and the huge gaping hole to the west of the house that will one day become a park, containing an underground parking lot.[6] Perhaps as you read this, construction on the park is now complete, and the sounds of Brooklyn and its peoples past and present echo through the space.

Historical research had a part to play in resisting the demolition of 227 Duffield Street, as historians, archeologists, and community researchers pointed to the archives to show why this home mattered in the past and therefore in the present. History can play a powerful role in reminding us of what we have lost but also of New Yorkers past, on whose shoulders we stand today. We see the power that history has when we hear our students in our classrooms and audiences during our talks ask collectively, "Why wasn't I taught this history?"; "Why don't we talk more about this history?"; and other variations of the same refrain. There is a wealth of undertold stories waiting to be amplified, but this particular one offers a nuanced history of Brooklyn's past: it invites us to think about how communities shaped their own city, to honor the collective and focus less on the exceptional ("the first to . . ."). As the scholar Keeanga-Yamahata Taylor reminds us, "American exceptionalism disguises structural racism—that the failure is a personal, not structural one, system by design."[7] Brooklyn's nineteenth-century free Black communities bequeathed a legacy of radical possibility, even as the problems they faced—structural racism, police brutality, and racial capitalism—delivered profound challenges to their daily existence. As the scholar Lorgia García-Peña writes, "Black life is rebellion. It is the ultimate contradiction to the isms destroying humanity: colonialism, racism, capitalism. It is the affirmation of possibility through collective, ancestral, radical joy."[8] These Black Brooklynites established an intellectual, political, and activist framework within which notions of freedom and US democracy remain at the center of who we are today and, with hope, tomorrow. To Brooklyn.

ACKNOWLEDGMENTS

THIS book has taken a very long time to write. But at its heart, it is about creating community, and it was community that made this book and project possible. It has taken over a decade to write this book, and I owe an immense debt to a range of educators all rooted in community knowledge, public history, and the academy here in New York City.

This research and writing began with a collaborative, multifaceted public history project called "In Pursuit of Freedom." My public history village included Alex Tronolone, Andrea Del Valle, Chela Scott Weber, Deborah Schwartz, Emily Potter-Ndiaye, Julie Golia, Julie May, Kate Fermoile, Marcia Ely, Sady Sullivan, and Shirley Brown Alleyne, who were then at the Brooklyn Historical Society (now the Center for Brooklyn History at Brooklyn Public Library); Elissa Blount Moorhead, Jennifer Scott, Kadrena Cunningham, Kaitlyn Greenidge, and Pamela Green, then at Weeksville Heritage Center; and Amanda Hinkle, Damen Scranton, Jim Neisen, and Terry Greiss, at Irondale Ensemble Project; a team of wonderful research collaborators, Christine Griffiths, Christopher Babits, Debbie-Ann Paige, Emy Pagano, Heather Wilson, Maggie Schreiner, Michael Chui, Paula Austin, Sarah Moazeni, and Teresa Iacobelli, and my brilliant colleague Samantha Gibson; a network of immensely talented educators and design collaborators, Carol Enseki, Paul Carlos, Tracee Worley, and Urshula Barbour; and Manisha Sinha, Clarence Taylor, Craig Wilder, Cynthia Copeland, Graham Hodges, Gunja Sen Gupta, the late James O. Horton and Lois E. Horton, Judith Wellman, and Shane White, who all served in various capacities as members of the scholarly advisory board. Together, they formed a network of mentors, colleagues, and friends, and I was entirely the lucky one to be surrounded by such brilliant and generous souls. Since then, that village continues to grow, and I am grateful to Brian Purnell,

Dominique Jean-Louis, Eric K. Washington, Gabrielle Bendiner-Viani, Kamau Ware, Katie Uva, Kemi Ilesanmi, Kendra Sullivan, Lauraberth Lima, Maeve Montalvo, Maggie Schreiner, Natiba Guy-Clement, Obden Mondésir, Raymond Codrington, Rebecca Amato, Rob Fields, Sady Sullivan, Shervone Neckles, Ujju Aggarwal, Walis Johnson, and Yvette Ramírez. A small coalition of archivists also sustained this project, and I am forever grateful to Larry Weimer, who worked on the initial "In Pursuit of Freedom" project; Mike Satalof, who digitized a great deal of the visual material you see here; the librarians and archivists at the Center for Brooklyn History at Brooklyn Public Library, who provided the material for publication; and colleagues at New York Public Library, Brooklyn Public Library, Schomburg Center for Research in Black Culture, New-York Historical Society, and the National Archives whose preservation, cataloguing, and descriptions made this narrative never a clichéd "untold" story or one of discovery but rather an undertold one.

At CUNY, friends and colleagues have greeted me with open arms and honed a lot of the themes and ideas of my research and writing over the years. At the Graduate Center (GC), I am grateful to a number of colleagues for their intellectual generosity: Tarry Hum; members of the CPCP seminar, especially Ruth Wilson Gilmore; faculty and staff in the MALS program; and staff at the Center for Humanities, American Social History Project, Futures Initiative, and at the Teaching and Learning Center. At Bronx Community College (BCC), my home campus, I am forever grateful for the collegiality and camaraderie of my colleagues across campus but especially in the History Department and for the friendship of Ahmed Reid, Jordi Getman-Eraso, Kate Culkin, Liz Hardman, Mara Lazda, Paulette Randall, Raquel Otheguy, Seth Offenbach, Stephen Duncan, and Tamar Rothenberg. Within CUNY, Caroline Hong, Linta Varghese, and Soniya Munshi remain beloved sistren. And I cannot overstate how much I owe to BCC and GC students over the years, who have made me a better educator and historian. We have engaged in some of the most moving and meaningful discussions about what it means to create community when liberation is the end goal, and I hope to have done their contributions some justice here.

Various writing groups and partners have given this project the boost of energy and accountability it needed, and their presence is throughout the work: in the summer 2021, my fellow CUNY community college faculty colleagues Judith Anderson, Kersha Smith, Lissette Acosta Corniel, and RaShelle Peck; in the spring and fall of 2022, the Queens College Sit n Write colloquium, led by the brilliant and generous Natanya Duncan; and in the spring of 2023, my brilliant and inspiring friend and colleague Gabrielle Bendiner-Viani, who has helped me navigate both the writing and publishing of this book. I am forever grateful to you all for your friendship and collegiality. The research and completion of this book was made possible by a research sabbatical and funding from a Mellon ACLS Community College Faculty Fellowship and a PSC-CUNY Award, jointly funded by the Professional Staff Congress and the City University of New York. Thank you for supporting scholarly work and providing the resources we all needed, especially during the bleak days of the pandemic. I am also indebted to my fellow NYU Press authors Brian Jones, Kabria Baumgartner, and Paula Austin and the wisdom they shared with this first-time author. And to senior editor Clara Platter, and the entire team at NYU Press, thank you for championing this work.

It is a privilege to put one's name on the front of this book when the research belongs to a village. To all of the community researchers, historians, and educators who were long at the center of knowledge production about Brooklyn when I was still a young person growing up in Liverpool, their presence and wisdom are embedded in this text. I am thinking here especially of the late Dr. Joan Maynard and the profound legacy she has left for generations of educators and of museum educators both past and present, who are often at the center of radical education.

Finally, to my family, the best support and hype crew a person could ask for.

This book is dedicated to the City of New York, in all its maddening beauty and its glorious people. The project began when I was a newly minted PhD graduate and a newer immigrant to New York and the

United States. More than two decades on, I cannot show enough gratitude to networks of New Yorkers who have made this desi scouser entirely at home.

It is my honor to be able to write about the lives of people who graced Brooklyn's streets long before us, especially right now. If we listen to the past, nineteenth-century Black Brooklynites show us how to strategize against white supremacy, state-sanctioned violence, and structural racism. If we listen to the past, we may pay our respect to those who made certain freedoms a possibility. If we listen to the past, we can be a conduit for the knowledge they created and pass it onto the next generation. Black Lives Matter—yesterday, today, tomorrow—always.

NOTES

Prologue

1 Alexander, *African or American?*; Blight, *Passages to Freedom*; Foner, *Gateway to Freedom*; L. Harris, *In the Shadow of Slavery*; G. Hodges, *Root and Branch*; Horton and Horton, *In Hope of Liberty*; Litwack, *North of Slavery*; Nash, *Forging Freedom*; Newman, Rael, and Lapsansky, *Pamphlets of Protest*; Peterson, *Black Gotham*; Quarles, *Black Abolitionists*; Sinha, *Slave's Cause*; Sterling, *We Are Your Sisters*; Wellman, *Brooklyn's Promised Land*; Wilder, *Covenant with Color*; Yee, *Black Women Abolitionists*.

2 Kushner, "Is Prison Necessary?"

3 Hartman, *Wayward Lives, Beautiful Experiments*, xiv.

4 This book models itself on the scholar Martha S. Jones brilliant reflection on historical narratives, that far from being "untold" or "rediscovered," these stories are simply undertold and are waiting to be heard once again. Dunbar, *Fragile Freedom*; Foreman, *Activist Sentiments*; Fuentes, *Dispossessed Lives*; Hartman, *Wayward Lives, Beautiful Experiments*; Hunter, *Bound in Wedlock*; M. Jones, *Vanguard*; Lightfoot, *Troubling Freedom*; J. Morgan, *Laboring Women*; Trouillot, *Silencing the Past*; White, *Ar'n't I a Woman?*

5 Harvey, *Rebel Cities*, 4.

6 A note on naming conventions: I have tried throughout this book to use first names wherever possible. Enslaved people of African descent did not possess the luxury of bearing their last name, even as their enslavers did. My intention is to elevate each person to their own narrative importance rather than the one the archives have privileged, so I use first names for all. Moreover, as this book focuses on families in New York's post-emancipation period, who often shared the same last name, I also use first names to distinguish between various family

members. For more on the Ratzer map, see Del Valle, Golia, and Potter-Ndiaye, *Exploring Pre-Revolutionary New York.*

7 Bill of sale for Jin, 1777, folder 11, box 1, Hubbard Family Papers, 1974.044, Center for Brooklyn History, Brooklyn Public Library.

8 Benardo and Weiss, *Brooklyn by Name,* 165; Tronolone and Alleyne, *Mapping Freedom and Slavery.*

9 S. Browne, "Everybody's Got a Little Light."

10 Nell, *Colored Patriots of the American Revolution;* Quarles, *Negro in the American Revolution;* Davis, *Problem of Slavery in the Age of Revolution;* Berlin and Hoffman, *Slavery and Freedom in the Age of the American Revolution;* Nash, *Forgotten Fifth.*

11 Isabella (Item 1120) and Isabella (Item 1117), "Carleton Papers—Book of Negroes, 1783," Library and Archives Canada, www.bac-lac.gc.ca.

12 Slipper, *Descendants in the Vanderpoel Branch.*

13 S. Browne, "Everybody's Got a Little Light," 548.

14 *Brooklyn Daily Eagle,* November 19, 1892.

15 Alexiou, *Gowanus,* 89; Campanella, *Brooklyn,* 32.

16 For discussion of the paradox, see the groundbreaking work of E. Morgan, *American Slavery, American Freedom.*

17 Miscellanies, 1854, folder 2, box 6, Gabriel Furman Papers, ARC.190, Center for Brooklyn History, Brooklyn Public Library.

18 Worley and Kanakamedala, *In Pursuit of Freedom Teacher's Manual,* 9–12.

19 Connolly, *Ghetto Grows in Brooklyn,* chap. 1.

20 Najack = Nayak lived where the southern neighborhoods of Bay Ridge and Fort Hamilton exist today. Excerpt from Jasper Danckaerts's journal, September 30, 1679, Jasper Danckaerts and Peter Sluyter Journals, 1679–1683, 1974.024, Center for Brooklyn History, Brooklyn Public Library.

21 Tchen, *New York before Chinatown,* chap. 3.

22 Moreau de Saint-Méry, *Moreau de St. Mery's American Journey,* 169.

23 Jea, *Life, History, and Unparalleled Sufferings,* 3, 4. On the identification of John Jea's enslavers being Albert and Anetje Terhune of Flatbush, see G. Hodges, *Black Itinerants of the Gospel,* 44. I have intentionally chosen to highlight the journeys of Isabella and Jin, two Black women, in this book. While John Jea's story is vital to the ways we understand slavery in Brooklyn, his narrative is also exceptional, as a young person who learns to read and write in Dutch and English and whose spiritual awakening leads to his manumission, followed by his life as a free itinerant preacher traveling the world. It is important to note that this story is remarkable but was not the norm for countless enslaved people in Kings County. But for more on his story and the history of slavery in Brooklyn, see Kanakamedala, "Gradual Emancipation."

1. An Emerging City

1 Dwight, *Travels in New England and New York*, 315.
2 Notes and Memoranda, vol. 7, 36–37 (1824), folder 3, box 2, Gabriel Furman Papers, ARC.190, Center for Brooklyn History, Brooklyn Public Library.
3 Moreau de Saint-Méry, *American Journey*, 168–169.
4 *Spooner's Brooklyn Directory for the Year 1822*, Center for Brooklyn History, Brooklyn Public Library.
5 Ibid.
6 Francis Guy would go onto reimagine this same scene with people, without people, in the winter, and in the summer. Today the Center for Brooklyn History at Brooklyn Public Library, Brooklyn Museum, Crystal Bridges Museum of American Art, and the Dallas Museum of Art all own versions of Francis Guy's "scene."
7 *Key to Winter Scene in Brooklyn by Francis Guy*, photograph, 8 5/8 × 13 1/4 in. (21.9 × 33.7 cm), gift of Dr. John Moffatt, 00.63, Brooklyn Museum.
8 Stiles, "Key to Guy's Brooklyn Snow Scene," in *History of the City of Brooklyn*, 2:88.
9 Dwight, *Travels*, 315.
10 "Village of Brooklyn," in *Spooner's Brooklyn Directory for the Year 1822*, 34.
11 Curry, *Free Black in Urban America*, 73–74; Snyder-Grenier, *Brooklyn*, 27.
12 Hartman, *Wayward Lives*, xv.
13 Regarding Samuel Anderson, presumably this was not the same Samuel Anderson whom the *Brooklyn Daily Eagle* would feature decades later and who would be discussed by the historian Judith Wellman as one of Weeksville's early land investors. That Samuel Anderson was born enslaved in Flatbush and continued to live nearby for most of his life. "Born a Slave in Flatbush," *Brooklyn Daily Eagle*, September 18, 1898; Wellman, *Brooklyn's Promised Land*, 14–15.
14 From 1829, the city directory would eliminate the word "black" and add an asterisk next to the names of Black Brooklynites.
15 *Spooner's Brooklyn Directory for the Year 1822*.
16 Berlin, *Many Thousands Gone*, chap. 1; Gellman, *Emancipating New York*, chap. 3; Litwack, *North of Slavery*, chap. 1.
17 John Baxter Journal, 1790, 1791, 1804, 1807, 1812, 1815, 1824, folders 1 and 2, box 1, and folder 1, box 2, John and Garret S. Baxter Journals, ARC.257, Center for Brooklyn History, Brooklyn Public Library.
18 *Long Island Star*, June 9, 1812.
19 *Long Island Star*, May 31, 1820.
20 *Long Island Star*, January 10, 1822.
21 Bill of sale for transfer of young girl Sine, from John Ditmars of the town of Flatlands, Kings County, to Jacob Duryee of the town of Flatbush, 1825, John Ditmars and Jacob Duryee enslaved woman bill of sale, 1977.583, Center for Brooklyn History, Brooklyn Public Library.
22 *Long Island Star*, July 25, 1822.

23 Miscellanies, 85 (1854), folder 2, box 6, Gabriel Furman Papers, ARC.190, Center for Brooklyn History, Brooklyn Public Library.

24 Parts of this section appear in Kanakamedala, "Black Entrepreneurship."

25 Brooklyn African Woolman Benevolent Society, *Constitution*, 20; *Long Island Star*, February 18, 1818; *Long Island Star*, November 22, 1821; Kanakamedala, "Black Entrepreneurship"; Perlman, "Organizations of the Free Negro in New York City"; Roff, "Brooklyn African Woolman Benevolent Society Rediscovered"; Wilder, *In the Company of Black Men*, 1, 84, 245n26; Zuille, *Historical Sketch of the New York African Society for Mutual Relief*; New York African Society for Mutual Relief, *Constitution*.

26 SenGupta, *From Slavery to Poverty*, 9.

27 Wilder, *In the Company of Black Men*, 104; see also table 4.1, "Select African Voluntary Associations, 1784–1865," 74–76.

28 Stiles, *History of the City of Brooklyn*, 2:65.

29 For more on New York's Quakers, see Barbour et al., *Quaker Crosscurrents*.

30 L. Harris, *In the Shadow of Slavery*, 61–65; G. Hodges, *Root and Branch*, 166–193; S. White, *Somewhat More Independent*, 81–84.

31 Minutes, vol. 10 (1807–1817), New-York Manumission Society Records, MS 1465, New-York Historical Society.

32 Report of the Standing Committee of the New York Manumission Society, March 18, 1814, April 19, 1814, New-York Manumission Society Records, New-York Historical Society, cited in S. White, *Stories of Freedom in Black New York*, 14–15.

33 *Long Island Star*, January 18, 1815; Swan, "Did Brooklyn Blacks Have Unusual Control over Their Schools?," 25–26.

34 *Long Island Star*, May 8, 1816, quoted in Swan, "Synoptic History of Black Public Schools," 63.

35 Cobb, "Black Organizational Life," 15–18.

36 Newman, *Freedom's Prophet*; Allen, *Collection of Hymns and Spiritual Songs*.

37 Stiles, *History of the City of Brooklyn*, 2:65.

38 *Spooner's Brooklyn Directory for the Year 1822*.

39 Bridge Street African Wesleyan Methodist Episcopal Church, *History of the African Wesleyan Methodist Episcopal Church*; Swan, "Black Church in Brooklyn"; Morrone, *Architectural Guidebook to Brooklyn*, 36.

40 *Long Island Star*, February 18, 1818.

41 Latimer, "Brooklyn," 169.

42 *Long Island Star*, September 16, 1839.

43 Stiles, *History of the City of Brooklyn*, 2:65; Brooklyn Common Council, "Slavery on Long Island."

44 C. Taylor, *Black Churches of Brooklyn*.

45 *Frederick Douglass' Paper*, January 26, 1855.

46 Sinha, *Slave's Cause*.

47 Alexander, *African or American?*, chaps. 2, 3, and 4; L. Harris, *In the Shadow of Slavery*, chaps. 3 and 4; Horton and Horton, *In Hope of Liberty*, chap. 6; Horton and Horton, *Black Bostonians*.

2. "The Time Has Now Arrived"

1 J. Smith, introduction to *Memorial Discourse*, 24.
2 Rosenwaike, *Population History of New York City*, 31; S. White, *Somewhat More Independent*, 39.
3 *Long Island Star*, July 19, 1827.
4 *Freedom's Journal*, March 16, 1827.
5 Bacon, *Freedom's Journal*.
6 Kanakamedala, "Considered a Citizen of the United States"; Peterson, *Black Gotham*, 37–38; Wilder, *In the Company of Black Men*, 249n8.
7 "To the Public," *Long Island Star*, October 4, 1827.
8 "Brooklyn Boblashun! Hurore for Jackson." For more on "bobalition," a deliberate corruption of the word "abolition," see S. White, *Stories of Freedom*, 200–203; and Wood, *Horrible Gift of Freedom*, 66–67.
9 Finley, *Thoughts on the Colonization of Free Blacks*, 1.
10 *Long Island Star*, June 3, 1831, reprinted in *The Liberator*, June 25 and July 2, 1831; Wilder, *Covenant with Color*, 71.
11 *The Liberator*, July 2, 1831.
12 Walker, *Walker's Appeal*.
13 Garrison, *Thoughts on Colonization*, 23–24, 27.
14 *Frederick Douglass' Paper*, April 6, 1855.
15 Stiles, *History of the City of Brooklyn*, 2:210.
16 Brooklyn Common Council, *Manual of the Common Council of the City of Brooklyn for 1863*, 167.
17 L. Harris, *In the Shadow of Slavery*, 77–78.
18 William Lloyd Garrison to Ebenezer Dole, April 15, 1834, Rare Books Department, Boston Public Library.
19 *The Liberator*, May 25, 1833.
20 Notes and Memoranda, 20 and 390 (1832), vol. 10, folder 1, box 4, Gabriel Furman Papers, ARC.190, Center for Brooklyn History, Brooklyn Public Library.
21 *Frederick Douglass' Paper*, April 6, 1855.
22 Foreman, "Black Organizing, Print Advocacy, and Collective Authorship," 36–39.

3. Village to City

1 Sturm-Lind, *Actors of Globalization*, chap. 2; Moffat, *Pierrepont Genealogies*, 161.
2 Jackson, *Crabgrass Frontier*, 25–32.
3 Miscellanies, 67 (1854), folder 2, box 6, Gabriel Furman Papers, ARC.190, Center for Brooklyn History, Brooklyn Public Library.
4 *Long Island Star*, July 10, 1834.

5 *Long Island Star*, January 7, 1836.

6 Jackson, *Crabgrass Frontier*, 25–30; Pessen, "Social and Economic Portrait of Jacksonian Brooklyn"; Snyder-Grenier, *Brooklyn!*, 86–88.

7 Merlis, *Brooklyn's Williamsburgh*; Swan, "Some Historic Notes on Black Williamsburgh and Brooklyn"; Stiles, *History of the Town of Bushwick*, 25–29.

8 Stiles, *History of the Town of Bushwick*, 25–29.

9 US Census Bureau, 1850 United States Federal Census, ancestry.com.

10 W. Hodges, *Free Man of Color*, 9.

11 Gibson, "Patriotic Brothers," 5.

12 W. Hodges, *Free Man of Color*, 8–20, 36.

13 Although Crow Hill's nomenclature is unconfirmed, historians such as Robert Swan and Judith Wellman believe that it may have earned its name from the large number of crows that made their way overhead to Jamaica Bay. Wellman, *Brooklyn's Promised Land*, 18, 30–34.

14 *Colored American*, June 8, 1839.

15 Gibson, "Patriotic Brothers," 43.

16 W. Hodges, *Free Man of Color*, 39.

17 Ibid.

18 Ibid., 45.

19 Ibid., 18.

20 Ibid., 49.

21 Judd, "History of Brooklyn," 160.

22 Second Constitution of New York, 1821.

23 *New York Daily Times*, September 7, 1857.

24 Institute for the Exploration of Seneca Village, *Seneca Village Project*; Wall, Rothschild, and Copeland, "Seneca Village and Little Africa"; Manevitz, "Great Injustice."

25 Wellman, *Brooklyn's Promised Land*, 27.

26 Ibid.; Swan, "Origin of Black Bedford-Stuyvesant."

27 W. Hodges, *Free Man of Color*, 50.

28 *Colored American*, August 22, 1840.

29 456 Inhabitants of the City of New York for the Prohibition of the International Slave Trade, February 14, 1838, HR25A-H1.8, box 6, 25th Congress, National Archives and Records Administration, Washington, DC.

30 Williamsburgh Voters in the County of Kings, 1841, H27A-H1.6, 27th Congress, National Archives and Records Administration, Washington, DC.

31 Johnson, *Liberty Party*; McPherson, "Fight against the Gag Rule"; Sewell, *Ballots for Freedom*.

32 *Colored American*, December 5, 1840.

33 "Brooklyn Mass Meeting at the M.E.W Church," *Colored American*, January 23, 1841.

34 *New York Daily Tribune*, January 23, 1846.

35 *Williamsburg Gazette*, April 15, 1846.

36 *Brooklyn Evening Star*, April 9, 1846.

37 *Williamsburg Gazette*, April 22, 1846.
38 W. Hodges, *Freeman of Color*, 76, quoted in Gibson, "Patriotic Brothers," 34.
39 Penn, *Afro-American Press and Its Editors*, 61–65.
40 John Brown to Willis Hodges, October 28, 1848, reprinted in W. Hodges, *Free Man of Color*, 81.

4. An Anti-Slavery Picnic

1 *Colored American*, August 14, 1841.
2 Ibid.
3 *Frederick Douglass' Paper*, September 4, 1851; *National Anti-Slavery Standard*, August 11, 1855; *Brooklyn Daily Eagle*, August 3, 1858; *Weekly Anglo-African*, August 10, 1861; *Brooklyn Daily Times*, July 30, 1862; *Brooklyn Evening Star*, August 2, 1862; *Brooklyn Daily Eagle*, August 2, 1862; *The Liberator*, August 15, 1862. For context, see Kerr-Ritchie, *Rites of August*.
4 *National Anti-Slavery Standard*, August 11, 1858.
5 Pennington, *Fugitive Blacksmith*, 51.
6 Blaakman, Brown Alleyne, and Potter-Ndiaye, *Dutch Breukelen*, 48–49.
7 *Long Island Star*, May 8, 1816.
8 *Long Island Star*, June 2, 1830.
9 *Colored American*, August 7, 1841.
10 *Colored American*, October 30, 1841; US Census Bureau, 1850 United States Federal Census, ancestry.com.
11 William J. Wilson to Henry R. Stiles, ca. 1863, folder 4, box 1, Henry Reed Stiles Correspondence, ARC.218, Center for Brooklyn History, Brooklyn Public Library.
12 *Colored American*, April 24, 1841; *Long Island Star*, April 26, 1841. For a beautiful account of Rosetta's life, see Baumgartner, *In Pursuit of Knowledge*, 86–102.
13 *Colored American*, November 13, 1841.
14 *Colored American*, July 7 and July 21, 1838; *Colored American*, April 11, July 11, July 18, and December 5, 1840; *Colored American*, January 2, April 24, and August 28, 1841, October 2 and December 25, 1841.
15 *Brooklyn Daily Eagle*, February 8, 1842.
16 *Brooklyn Daily Eagle*, February 9 and June 29, 1843; Baumgartner, *In Pursuit of Knowledge*, 79.
17 Field, *Historical Sketch of the Public Schools*, 74–77.
18 Wellman, *Brooklyn's Promised Land*, 67–70.
19 W. Hodges, *Free Man of Color*, 50–51.
20 Ibid., 8–9.
21 *Colored American*, July 3, 1841.
22 *Williamsburg Gazette*, July 21, 1841; *Long Island Star*, July 23, 1841.
23 *Williamsburg Gazette*, March 9, 1842.
24 Gibson, "Patriotic Brothers," 27–28.
25 *Brooklyn Daily Eagle*, September 4, 1847.

26 "John Zuille on Education at the Convention of Citizens of Color," *North Star*, April 17, 1851. For more on Maria Stewart's remarkable life, see Waters, *Maria W. Stewart*.

27 Brooklyn Common Council, *Manual of the Common Council of the City of Brooklyn for 1859–60*.

28 *Brooklyn Daily Eagle*, August 7, 1845, and November 23, 1846.

29 *Long Island Star*, May 2, 1831; "Colored Man Who Pays Taxes," *Long Island Star*, April 3, 1833.

30 *Long Island Star*, March 30, 1831; *The Liberator*, April 21, 1831; *Brooklyn Evening Star*, reprinted in *Colored American*, September 4, 1841.

31 *Williamsburg Gazette*, June 4, 1842; *Brooklyn Daily Eagle*, August 4, 1845; *Brooklyn Daily Eagle*, January 26, 1850; *Brooklyn Daily Eagle*; November 15, 1851.

32 Duane, "Like a Motherless Child," 475.

33 Wills and Indexes, 1787–1923, Author: New York, Surrogate's Court (Kings County), Probate Place: Kings, New York Description Notes: Wills, Vol. 0010–0011, 1846–1850, ancestry.com.

34 *Long Island Star*, September 21, 1837.

5. City of Commerce

1 Stiles, *History of the City of Brooklyn*, 2:146, 154.

2 Atlantic Street description from *Brooklyn Daily Advertiser*, October 1, 1846.

3 "Wilson, Mrs. William J.," in *Hearnes' Brooklyn City Directory 1853–1854*, 575, Center for Brooklyn History, Brooklyn Public Library.

4 Cantwell and Wall, *Unearthing Gotham*.

5 *Frederick Douglass' Paper*, June 9, 1854.

6 "Communications from Our Brooklyn Correspondent," *Frederick Douglass' Paper*, May 27, 1852. It is difficult to say with certainty why William lists Mary's business at 58 Atlantic in 1852, as the city directory lists it as 66 Atlantic one year later. However, it is entirely possible that the crockery store moved locations within the year.

7 *Colored American*, September 16, 1837.

8 *Frederick Douglass' Paper*, December 8, 1845; *Brooklyn Evening Star*, January 17, 1863.

9 L. Harris, *In the Shadow of Slavery*, 219, 241. From the evidence recovered to date, Black workers in the city of Brooklyn joined the American League of Colored Laborers given its national reach and nearby Manhattan-based headquarters but did not form a local auxiliary and organize in other more formal ways within Brooklyn itself.

10 Berek, "Fort Greene," 471.

11 William J. Wilson to Henry R. Stiles, ca. 1863, folder 4, box 1, Henry Reed Stiles Correspondence, ARC.218, Center for Brooklyn History, Brooklyn Public Library.

12 *Frederick Douglass' Paper*, November 17, 1854.

13 *Brooklyn Daily Eagle*, February 12, 1847.

14 *North Star*, April 17, 1851.

15 "Common School Review—No. III," *Colored American*, August 22, 1840.

16 *Brooklyn Daily Eagle*, February 4, 1843.

17 *Frederick Douglass' Paper*, April 1, 1852.

18 *Frederick Douglass' Paper*, September 22, 1854.

19 *Frederick Douglass' Paper*, October 13, 1854.

20 *Long Island Star*, October 20, 1830; see also Mabee, *Black Education in New York State*, chap. 3.

21 *Brooklyn Daily Eagle*, May 25, 1855; *Annual Report of the Board of Managers of the Brooklyn Sabbath School Union*, 1857, Brooklyn Sabbath School Union Collection, 1985.111, Center for Brooklyn History, Brooklyn Public Library.

22 *Brooklyn Daily Eagle*, May 25, 1859.

23 Heller "Poor Man's Carriage," iv.

24 Bobo, *Glimpses of New York City*, 78.

25 *New York Times*, August 11, 1853.

26 *Friends' Intelligencer*, September 15, 1860; J. Harris, *Last Slave Ships*, 1–12.

27 Golia, "Brooklyn Waterfront History."

28 Alexiou, *Gowanus*, 9.

29 Miscellanies, pp. 84–85 (1854), folder 2, box 6, Gabriel Furman Papers, ARC.190, Center for Brooklyn History, Brooklyn Public Library.

30 *Prospectus of the Atlantic Dock Company* (New York: Printed for George F. Nesbitt, 1840), 4, Atlantic Dock Company Collection, 1978.151, Center for Brooklyn History, Brooklyn Public Library. See also D. Browne, *Increase of Commerce of New York*.

31 *Prospectus of the Atlantic Dock Company*, 5.

32 Mintz, *Sweetness and Power*; Muhammad, "Barbaric History of Sugar in America"; Parker, *Sugar Barons*; Walvin, *Sugar*.

33 Wilder, *Covenant with Color*, 56.

34 Ibid., 55–58; Havemeyer, *Merchants of Williamsburgh*.

35 Dunn, *Sugar and Slaves*, 188–223; Follett, *Sugar Masters*, 3–13.

36 Ryan, *When Brooklyn Was Queer*, 18.

37 *Non-Slaveholder*, January 1, 1848; *The Age*, October 12, 1848; Free Produce Association of Friends of New York, *Report of the Board of Managers*; *North Star*, September 7, 1849; Faulkner, "Root of Evil."

38 *Long Island Star*, June 15, 1831.

39 *Frederick Douglass' Paper*, May 27, 1852.

40 *Brooklyn Evening Star*, November 29, 1842.

41 Ibid.

42 US Census Bureau, 1850 United States Federal Census, ancestry.com; *Hearne's Brooklyn City Directory 1849–1850*, Center for Brooklyn History, Brooklyn Public Library; *Hearne's Brooklyn City Directory 1850–1851*, Center for Brooklyn History, Brooklyn Public Library.

43 Mills, *Cutting along the Color Line*, 119–125.

44 *Weekly Advocate*, January 14, 1837.

45 *Colored American*, October 20, 1838.

46 Samuel and T. F. Reynolds, *Reynolds' Williamsburgh City Directory and Business Advertiser, for 1852,* Center for Brooklyn History, Brooklyn Public Library.

47 Wellman, *Brooklyn's Promised Land,* 91–92.

48 *The Liberator,* April 9, 1834.

49 *Williamsburg Gazette,* March 23, 1842.

50 *Frederick Douglass' Paper,* July 29, 1853; *Frederick Douglass' Paper,* March 24, 1854; *Smith's Brooklyn Directory for 1857,* Center for Brooklyn History, Brooklyn Public Library.

51 *Provincial Freeman,* December 23, 1854.

52 New York State Legislature Assembly, *Documents, 1854,* 532; *New York Times,* October 27, 1853.

53 Articles of Incorporation, 1848, Brooklyn Brush Manufacturing Company Articles of Incorporation, 1978.191, Center for Brooklyn History, Brooklyn Public Library.

6. Brooklyn, 1850

1 *North Star,* October 3, 1850; *The Liberator,* October 4, 1850; *National Era,* October 10, 1850; see also Alexander, *African or American?,* 123–124; Peterson, *Black Gotham,* 194–196; Wilder, *Covenant with Color,* 74–75.

2 *Brooklyn Evening Star,* October 1, 1850.

3 *Brooklyn Daily Eagle,* September 28, 1850.

4 *Williamsburgh Daily Gazette,* October 1, 1850.

5 *The Liberator,* October 18, 1850, and October 25, 1850.

6 *Impartial Citizen,* October 26, 1850.

7 *Williamsburgh Daily Gazette,* October 5, 1850.

8 American and Foreign Anti-Slavery Society, *Fugitive Slave Bill.*

9 *The Liberator,* May 24, 1850.

10 Ichabod Spencer, *The Religious Duty of Obedience to Law* (1850).

11 *Williamsburgh Daily Gazette,* October 7, 1850.

12 *Long Island Star,* September 16, 1839; Fales, *Brooklyn's Guardians,* 34–35.

13 *The Liberator,* November 25, 1842.

14 *New York Daily Tribune,* December 25, 1848; *The Liberator,* December 29, 1848; *Christian Advocate,* January 3, 1849; *The Liberator,* January 5, 1849; *National Era,* January 11, 1849; *North Star,* January 12, 1849; *The Independent,* January 18, 1849; Edmonds, *Reports of Select Cases,* 93–110. Special thanks to Samantha Gibson for researching this case.

15 *Impartial Citizen,* October 5, 1850; *The Liberator,* May 9, 1851; L. Horton, "Kidnapping and Resistance"; and J. Horton, "Crusade for Freedom."

16 *Frederick Douglass' Paper,* December 25, 1851, and January 8 and February 5, 1852.

17 US Census Bureau, 1850 United States Federal Census, ancestry.com; New York County, District and Probate Courts, Wills and Indexes, 1787–1923, New York. Surrogate's Court (Kings County), Probate Place, Kings, New York, ancestry.com.

7. City of Refuge

1 Will and Probate of Elenor Croger, June 14, 1853, Wills and Indexes, 1787–1923, New York. Surrogate's Court (Kings County), Probate Place: Kings, New York.

2 Krombie, *Death in New York*, 19–22.

3 The violent erasure of these sacred grounds through development and displacement continues to be addressed by activists, community researchers, educators, students, and historians doing significant work so that we may continue honor the dead. See Diouf, "Harlem Burial Ground"; NYC Parks, "Sankofa Park"; Flatbush African Burial Ground Coalition, www.flatbushafricanburialground. org; Hunts Point Slave Burial Ground, https://hpsbg.weebly.com; Van Cortlandt Park Alliance, "African Burial Ground."

4 *Long Island Star*, October 22, 1838.

5 *Long Island Star*, May23, 1839.

6 Dunbar, *Fragile Freedom*, 1–7, 48–69.

7 Douglas, *History of Siloam Presbyterian Church*.

8 New York State Census, 1855, https://FamilySearch.org.

9 US Census Bureau, 1850 United States Federal Census, ancestry.com; New York State Census, 1855, https://FamilySearch.org; *Hearnes' Brooklyn City Directory 1853–1854*, Center for Brooklyn History, Brooklyn Public Library; *Hearnes' Brooklyn City Directory 1854–1855*, Center for Brooklyn History, Brooklyn Public Library; *Hearnes' Brooklyn City Directory 1857*, Center for Brooklyn History, Brooklyn Public Library; *Christian Recorder*, April 27, 1867; Bridge Street African Wesleyan Methodist Episcopal Church, *History of the African Wesleyan Methodist Episcopal Church*.

10 *Long Island Star*, October 4, 1827; New York State, *Laws of the State of New York*, 242–243; *Christian Recorder*, April 27, 1867; Wilder, "Rise and Influence of the New York African Society for Mutual Relief."

11 Sorin, *Driving While Black*, 10.

12 *Frederick Douglass' Paper*, February 1, 1856; Ripley, *Black Abolitionist Papers*, 108–112n3.

13 For more on the Underground Railroad, see Blight, *Passages to Freedom*; Foner, *Gateway to Freedom*, where pages 256 and 258 reference my research here; Sinha, *Slave's Cause*, 381–420.

14 *North Star*, December 14, 1849.

15 There are multiple editions of Thomas Jones's narrative. For this analysis, I have consulted the 1862 edition: T. Jones, *Experience of Thomas H. Jones*. See also Davies et al., *North Carolina Slave Narratives*.

16 T. Jones, *Experience of Thomas H. Jones*, 43.

17 Massachusetts Anti-Slavery Society, *Eighteenth Annual Report*.

18 Ripley, *Black Abolitionist Papers*, 461nn1–2; American and Foreign Anti-Slavery Society, *Annual Report*; *Brooklyn Daily Eagle*, May 17 and May 27, 1847; *Brooklyn Evening Star*, May 27, 1847; Henry Bibb to Lewis Tappan, March 16, 1849, American Missionary Association Archives, Amistad Research Center, Tulane University. On lecture circuit, see Blackett, *Building an Anti-Slavery Wall*; Brooks, *Bodies in Dissent*, chap. 2.

19 *Brooklyn Daily Eagle*, March 30, 1846.

20 Still, *Underground Railroad*, 177–188; Prince, *Shadow on the Household*; William Still's journal entries in which he discusses the Weems family are digitized at https://hsp.org.

21 Journals and Notebooks, July 19, 1855, Lewis Tappan Papers, Manuscript Division, Library of Congress, Washington, DC.

22 Still, *Underground Railroad*, 685–687.

23 *Frederick Douglass' Paper*, April 15, 1853.

24 Rosenwaike, *Population History in New York City*, 32 (table 5, "Population of Kings County and Richmond County by Race, 1790–1860"); Wilder, *Covenant with Color*, 61.

25 *Weekly Anglo-African*, March 31 and April 14, 1860.

26 *Frederick Douglass' Paper*, December 25, 1851.

27 Washington continued his work as an educator and daguerreotypist, completing a series of images of Liberia's leaders including Philip Coker, an AME missionary, and President Edward James Roye. He died in Liberia on June 7, 1875. *Colored American*, January 12 and January 19, 1839, January 30, July 31, and August 2, 1841; *The Liberator*, January 10, 1851; *Frederick Douglass' Paper*, September 4, 1851, April 15, 1852, and November 25, 1853; *Anti-Slavery Standard*, January 1, 3, 1855; Shumard, *Durable Memento*; Willis, *Reflections in Black*.

28 "Weather," Miscellaneous (1854), folder 2, box 6, Gabriel Furman Papers, ARC.190, Center for Brooklyn History, Brooklyn Public Library.

29 SenGupta, *For God and Mammon*.

30 *Colored American*, November 13, 1841.

31 "Alfred P. Gloucester," February 24, 1859, Burial and Vital Records: 1840–1937, Green-Wood Cemetery, www.green-wood.com.

32 Elizabeth Gloucester to John Brown, August 1859, Ferdinand J. Dreer Papers, Historical Society of Pennsylvania.

33 *Brooklyn Evening Star*, October 22, 1859.

34 G. Arthur Leavey to the trustees of the Second Unitarian Society, 1860, folder 4, box 101, First Unitarian Congregational Society of Brooklyn Records, ARC.109, Center for Brooklyn History, Brooklyn Public Library.

35 Redpath, *Echoes of Harpers Ferry*, 419.

36 Gibson, "Patriotic Brothers," 43.

37 Douglas, *History of Siloam Presbyterian Church*.

8. "All the *Elite* and Fashion of This Portion of the Anglo-African World"

1 Peterson, "And We Claim Our Rights." It is worth noting that during one of the archeological digs following Weeksville's "rediscovery" in 1968, a copy of the constitution of the Abyssinian Benevolent Daughters of Esther Association was recovered, suggesting a strong New York and Weeksville connection.

2 Anna Warren Weston to Deborah Weston, Weston Papers, Boston Public Library, quoted in Swerdlow, "Abolition's Conservative Sisters," 40.

3   *Weekly Anglo-African*, March 24, 1860.

4   L. Harris, *In the Shadow of Slavery*, chap. 5.

5   Vol. 24, Series III: Admission Records, 1837–1942, Association for the Benefit of Colored Orphans Records, New-York Historical Society.

6   It was also a rival to the Brooklyn Atheneum, then located on the corner of Atlantic and Clinton Streets. Brazee, *Borough Hall Skyscraper Historic District Designation Report*, 9.

7   *Weekly Anglo-African*, March 24, 1860.

8   *Weekly Anglo-African*, April 7, 1860.

9   Thank you to Debbie-Ann Paige for identifying the first names of these brilliant women.

10 *Weekly Anglo-African*, April 7, 1860.

11 *Brooklyn Daily Eagle*, March 29, 1860.

12 US Census Bureau, 1860 United States Federal Census.

13 *Weekly Anglo-African*, May 26, 1860.

14 *Weekly Anglo-African*, November 24, 1860.

15 This section's title is from *Friends' Intelligencer*, June 21, 1856.

16 Applegate, *Most Famous Man in America*; Plymouth Church of the Pilgrims and Henry Ward Beecher Collection, ARC.212, Center for Brooklyn History, Brooklyn Public Library.

17 Burrows and Wallace, *Gotham*, 729–730.

18 "Purchase of a Slave in Plymouth Church," *Brooklyn Daily Eagle*, February 6, 1860.

19 *Brooklyn Daily Eagle*, May 11, 1927; Guy-Clement, "Story of Pinky."

20 Pennington, *Fugitive Blacksmith*, viii–ix; *North Star*, November 17, 1848; Pacheco, *Pearl*; Weld, *Frederick Douglass with the Edmonson Sisters*.

21 Beecher and Plymouth Church, *Manual of Plymouth Church*, 117; *Friends' Intelligencer*, June 21, 1856; *New York Times*, June 3 and August 9, 1856.

22 Leslie and Leslie, *Brooklyn Alphabetical and Street Directory*.

23 William Lloyd Garrison "To a Friend in New Bedford," November 1, 1857, in *Letters of William Lloyd Garrison*, 498–499.

24 "Slaves, Purchase of Freedom, 1859," folder 582, box 14, Beecher Family Papers (MS 71), Manuscripts and Archives, Yale University Library. It can now be viewed at https://archives.yale.edu.

25 Henry Ward Beecher to lozenge company endorsing product, October 15, 1858, folder 9, box 1, Plymouth Church of the Pilgrims and Henry Ward Beecher Collection, ARC.212, Center for Brooklyn History, Brooklyn Public Library.

26 *New York Daily Tribune*, February 8, 1856.

27 *The Liberator*, June 13, 1856.

28 *Brooklyn Evening Star*, February 28, 1860.

29 *New York Daily Tribune*, October 18, 1854; *Brooklyn Daily Eagle*, October 18 and 21, 1854; W. Smith, *Brooklyn and Kings County Record*, 200–201.

30 *Weekly Anglo-African*, July 7, 1860.

31 *The Liberator*, May 4, 1860.
32 *Weekly Anglo-African*, July 14, 1860.

9. "The Half Has Never Been Told"

1 Van Dyke, *Character and Influence of Abolitionism*.
2 *Brooklyn Evening Star*, February 20, 1861; see also *Brooklyn Times Extra*, March 4, 1861.
3 For broader context, see Sinha, *Counterrevolution of Slavery*; Sewell, *House Divided*; McPherson, *Ordeal by Fire*.
4 *Brooklyn Daily Times*, April 18 and April 25, 1861.
5 Journals and Notebooks, September 12, 1861, Lewis Tappan Papers, Manuscript Division, Library of Congress, Washington, DC.
6 Seward, *Irrepressible Conflict*.
7 Rosenwaike, *Population History of New York City*, 63.
8 Ignatiev, *How the Irish Became White*.
9 *Brooklyn Daily Times*, August 5, 1862.
10 *Weekly Anglo-African*, August 10, 1861.
11 *New York Times*, August 6 and 12, 1862.
12 *Brooklyn Daily Eagle*, August 5, 1862; *Brooklyn Evening Star*, August 5, 6, and 9, 1862.
13 *New York Times*, August 12, 1862; *Brooklyn Daily Times*, August 5, 1862.
14 *Brooklyn Evening Star*, August 5, 1862; see also Quarles, *Negro in the Civil War*, 237; Peterson, *Black Gotham*, 292–295; Wilder, *Covenant with Color*, 97.
15 *Brooklyn Evening Star*, August 5, 1862.
16 *Brooklyn Daily Times*, August 5, 1862.
17 *New York Times*, May 16, 1863.
18 "Mr. Wilson's Explanation," *Brooklyn Daily Eagle*, July 8, 1863.
19 *Brooklyn Daily Times*, July 14, 15, 16, 17, 1863. For further discussion of the Draft Riots, see Bernstein, *New York City Draft Riots*; Schecter, *Devil's Own Work*; Alexander, *African or American?*, 175–177; L. Harris, *In the Shadow of Slavery*, 280–286; Peterson, *Black Gotham*, 223–258; Wilder, *Covenant with Color*, 99–103.
20 Maritcha Lyons, "Memories of Yesterdays: All of Which I Saw and Part of Which I Was, An Autobiography," 20, Harry Albro Williamson Papers, Schomburg Center for Research in Black Culture, New York Public Library.
21 Committee of Merchants for the Relief of Colored People Suffering from the Late Riots in the City of New York, *Report*, 15; *New York Commercial Advertiser*, July 16, 1863.
22 *Brooklyn City News*, July 14, 1863.
23 *Brooklyn Daily Times*, July 20, 1863.
24 Honeck, *We Are the Revolutionists*; Nadel, *Little Germany*; Snyder-Grenier, *Brooklyn!*, 39–40.
25 Committee of Merchants for the Relief of Colored People Suffering from the Late Riots in the City of New York, "Brooklyn," in *Report*, 30.
26 Ibid.

27 US Navy, *Naval Enlistment Rendezvous.* The title of this section comes from "Colored Citizens to Arms!," a Civil War–era recruitment poster seeking army recruits, ca. 1863, M1975.387.1, Francis & Loutrel, Center for Brooklyn History, Brooklyn Public Library.

28 New York, US, Civil War Muster Roll Abstracts, 1861–1900, New York State Archives, Albany, New York, Civil War Muster Roll Abstracts of New York State Volunteers, United States Sharpshooters, and United States Colored Troops [ca. 1861–1900], box 835, Soldiers and Sailors Database, Sailors, National Park Service, www.nps.gov, ancestry.com.

29 US Navy, *Naval Enlistment Rendezvous.*

30 Historical Data Systems, comp. US, Civil War Soldier Records and Profiles, 1861–1865, Provo, UT, ancestry.com; Peterson, *Black Gotham*, 265–272; Wilder, *Covenant with Color*, 103; Blatt, Brown, and Yacovone, *Hope and Glory.*

31 Compiled Military Service Records of Volunteer Union Soldiers who served in the United States Colored Troops: Artillery Organizations, NARA, Washington, DC, ancestry.com.

32 Annual Report of the Adjutant General, 1865, ancestry.com; US, Adjutant General Military Records, 1631–1976. Provo, UT, ancestry.com.

33 Cornish, *Sable Arm*; Emilio, *History of the Fifty-Fourth Regiment*; Berlin, Reidy, and Rowland, *Freedom's Soldiers.*

34 *Brooklyn Daily Eagle*, August 2 and 3, 1858.

35 *Brooklyn Daily Times*, July 29, 1862.

36 Joseph, Isaac, and Lewis signed up before 1863 and therefore would have been unofficial recruits until the passage of the Emancipation Proclamation made their service in the Union Army legal and entitled to all the benefits of an active recruit.

37 *National Anti-Slavery Standard*, January 10, 1863.

38 *Douglass' Monthly*, February 1863.

39 Manning, *What This Cruel War Was Over*; Sinha, "Allies for Emancipation."

40 *Weekly Anglo-African*, August 12, 1865.

41 Foner, *Reconstruction*; Foner, *Nothing but Liberty*; Anderson and Moss, *Facts of Reconstruction*; Berlin, Fields, and Glymph, *Freedom*; Litwack, *Been in the Storm Too Long*; Richardson, *Death of Reconstruction.*

42 James McCune Smith to Secretary-AMA, June 21, 1864, American Missionary Association Archives, Amistad Research Center, Tulane University.

43 Weir, "Where All Eyes Are Turned." William would also write a beautiful survey of African American history titled "The Afric-American Picture Gallery" for the *Anglo-African Magazine* in 1859. See Eckstrom and Rusert, "Afric-American Picture Gallery."

44 [Mary A. Wilson Teacher's Monthly Report], January 1866, American Missionary Association Archives, 1828–1969, Amistad Research Center, Tulane University; Wilder, *Covenant with Color*, 110.

45 Logan, *Howard University*, 64.

46 US Census Bureau, 1870 United States Federal Census, ancestry.com.

47 *Brooklyn Daily Times*, August 7, 1862.

48 Gibson, "Patriotic Brothers," 44.

49 Lowe, "Willis Augustus Hodges"; Foner, *Freedom's Lawmakers*.

50 *Brooklyn Daily Eagle*, August 26, 1910.

51 *Times Union*, July 29, 1867.

52 *Friends' Intelligencer*, November 24, 1866.

53 American Freedmen's Friend Society (Brooklyn), ca. 1864, folder 7, box 5, Collection of Brooklyn, N.Y., Civil War Relief Associations Records, Ephemera and Other Material, ARC.245, Center for Brooklyn History, Brooklyn Public Library.

54 *New York Times*, May 8, 1868; *Christian Recorder*, February 20, 1865; Faulkner, "Proper Recognition of Our Manhood"; Wellman, *Brooklyn's Promised Land*, 125–127.

55 Young, "Roads to Travel"; SenGupta, *From Slavery to Poverty*, chap. 6.

56 New York State Education Department, Office of Cultural Education, Albany, New York, US Census Mortality Schedules, New York, 1850–1880, Archive Roll Number: M6, Census Year: 1869, Census Place: Brooklyn, Kings, New York.

57 Wills, Vol. 0038–0039, 1869–1870, New York County, District and Probate Courts, ancestry.com; *New York, U.S., Wills and Probate Records, 1659–1999* (database online), Lehi, UT, ancestry.com

58 *Brooklyn Daily Eagle*, April 8, 1874.

59 Pinheiro, "Black Soldiers and Their Families' Activism"; Mendez, *Great Sacrifice*.

60 National Archives and Records Administration, US, *Civil War Pension Index: General Index to Pension Files, 1861–1934* (database online), Lehi, UT, ancestry.com. Original data: General Index to Pension Files, 1861–1934, T288, 546 rolls, National Archives and Records Administration, Washington, DC.

61 Green, "Black Widows and the Struggle for Pensions"; Pinheiro, "Black Women and Civil War Pensions"; Pinheiro, *Families' Civil War*.

62 *Brooklyn Daily Eagle*, August 11, 1883.

63 Ibid.

64 *Brooklyn Daily Eagle*, September 13, 14, and 16, and October 6 and 8, 1883.

65 *Brooklyn Daily Eagle*, August, 12, 1883.

66 Brown, *Homespun Heroines and Other Women of Distinction*; Sterling, *We Are Your Sisters*; Peterson, *Black Gotham*, 350–358.

67 Foreman, "Black Organizing, Print Advocacy, and Collective Authorship," 27.

Epilogue

1 Weeksville Heritage Center and Vera List Center for Art and Politics, "Time for Seditious Speech."

2 Kanakamedala with Mondésir, "Time for Seditious Speech."

3 Peterson, *Black Gotham*.

4 W. Hodges, "Bibliography," in *Free Man of Color*, 87.

5 Austin, "Narratives of Interiority"; Austin with Nelson and Wilson, "How Family History Opens New Archives"; Okechukwu, "Notes on Black Archival Practice," 27.

6 On the same walk, it was jarring to see the site of Peter and Elenor Croger's former home in DUMBO, now a colossal metal and concrete tower so tall that even my smartphone could not capture the landscape's misshapen skyline.

7 K.-Y. Taylor, *From #BlackLivesMatter to Black Liberation*, 21–32.

8 García-Peña, "Note 189: Life," 268.

BIBLIOGRAPHY

THE book's research came out of a public history project, and public engagement is at the center of this book.

For quick historical context, lesson plans that you can use inside and outside of the traditional classroom, see the following:

Tracee Worley and Prithi Kanakamedala, *In Pursuit of Freedom Teacher's Manual* (New York: Brooklyn Historical Society / Brooklyn Public Library, Center for Brooklyn History, 2012), http://pursuitoffreedom.org.

For walking tours of the sites and neighborhoods explored in this book, see the following:

Kate Fermoile, Samantha Gibson, Prithi Kanakamedala, Suzanne Spellen, and Larry Weimer, *In Pursuit of Freedom: Brooklyn Walking Tours* (New York: Brooklyn Historical Society / Brooklyn Public Library, Center for Brooklyn History, 2014), http://pursuitoffreedom.org.

Select Archival Sources

Brooklyn Public Library, Center for Brooklyn History
    Atlantic Dock Company Collection
    Brooklyn Brush Manufacturing Company Articles of Incorporation
    Brooklyn Photograph and Illustration Collection
    Brooklyn Sabbath School Union Collection
    City directories (various years)
    Civil War Relief Associations Records

First Unitarian Congregational Society of Brooklyn Records
Gabriel Furman Papers
Henry Reed Stiles Correspondence
Hubbard Family Papers
Jasper Danckaerts and Peter Sluyter Journals
Plymouth Church of the Pilgrims and Henry Ward Beecher Collection
Library of Congress, Manuscript Division, Washington, DC
Lewis Tappan Papers
National Archives and Records Administration, Washington, DC
New-York Historical Society
Association for the Benefit of Colored Orphans Records
New-York Manumission Society Records
New York Public Library, Schomburg Center for Research in Black Culture
Harry Albro Williamson Papers

Select Newspapers

The Anglo-African
Brooklyn Daily Eagle
Brooklyn Daily Times
Brooklyn Evening Star
Colored American
Frederick Douglass' Paper
Freedom's Journal
The Liberator
Long Island Star
New York Daily Tribune
New York Times
North Star
Williamsburg Gazette

Primary and Secondary Sources

Alexander, Leslie M. *African or American? Black Identity and Political Activism in New York City, 1784–1861.* Urbana: University of Illinois Press, 2011.

Alexiou, Joseph. *Gowanus: Brooklyn's Curious Canal.* New York: New York University Press, 2020.

Allen, Richard. *A Collection of Hymns and Spiritual Songs.* Philadelphia, John Ormond, 1801.

American and Foreign Anti-Slavery Society. *Annual Report of the American and Foreign Anti-Slavery Society.* 1847.

———. *The Fugitive Slave Bill: Its History and Unconstitutionality with an account of the seizure and enslavement of James Hamlet, and his subsequent restoration to liberty.* 1st and 3rd eds. New York: W. Harned, 1850.

Anderson, Eric, and Alfred A. Moss Jr., eds. *The Facts of Reconstruction: Essays in Honor of John Hope Franklin*. Baton Rouge: Louisiana State University Press, 1991.

Applegate, Debbie. *The Most Famous Man in America: The Biography of Henry Ward Beecher*. New York: Doubleday, 2006.

Austin, Paula C. "Narratives of Interiority: Archival Practices of Care and Affection (and its Limits)." *Black Scholar* 52, no. 2 (2022): 63–73.

Austin, Paula C., with Catherine Nelson and Donna Payne Wilson. "How Family History Opens New Archives." *Black Perspectives* (African American Intellectual History Society), November 18, 2022. www.aaihs.org.

Bacon, Jacqueline. *Freedom's Journal: The First African-American Newspaper*. Lanham, MD: Lexington Books, 2007.

Barbour, Hugh, Christopher Densmore, Elizabeth H. Moger, Nancy C. Sorel, Alson D. Van Wagner, and Arthur J. Worrall, eds. *Quaker Crosscurrents: Three Hundred Years of Friends in the New York Yearly Meetings*. Syracuse, NY: Syracuse University Press, 1995.

Baumgartner, Kabria. *In Pursuit of Knowledge: Black Women and Educational Activism in Antebellum America*. New York: New York University Press, 2019.

Beecher, Henry Ward, and Plymouth Church. *Manual of Plymouth Church*. 5th ed. Brooklyn, NY, 1874.

Benardo, Leonard, and Jennifer Weiss. *Brooklyn by Name: How the Neighborhoods, Streets, Parks, Bridges, and More Got Their Names*. New York: New York University Press, 2006.

Berek, Judith. "Fort Greene." In *Encyclopedia of New York City*, 2nd ed., edited by Kenneth T. Jackson, Lisa Keller, and Nancy Flood, 471. New Haven, CT: Yale University Press, 2010.

Berlin, Ira. *Many Thousands Gone: The First Two Centuries of Slavery in North America*. Cambridge, MA: Harvard University Press, 2000.

Berlin, Ira, Barbara Fields, and Thavolia Glymph, eds. *Freedom: A Documentary History of Emancipation, 1861–1867*. 2 vols. New York: Cambridge University Press, 1982–1993.

Berlin, Ira, and Ronald Hoffman, eds. *Slavery and Freedom in the Age of the American Revolution*. Charlottesville: University of Virginia Press, 1983.

Berlin, Ira, Joseph R. Reidy, and Leslie S. Rowland. *Freedom's Soldiers: The Black Military Experience in the Civil War*. New York: Cambridge University Press, 1985.

Bernstein, Iver. *The New York City Draft Riots: Their Significance for American Society and Politics in the Age of Civil War*. Oxford: Oxford University Press, 1990.

Blaakman, Michael, Shirley Brown Alleyne, and Emily Potter-Ndiaye. *Dutch Breukelen: Where Brooklyn Began*. Curriculum guide. Brooklyn, NY: Brooklyn Historical Society, Center for Brooklyn History, Brooklyn Public Library, 2015. www.bklynlibrary.org.

Blackett, R. J. M. *Building an Anti-Slavery Wall: Black Americans in the Atlantic Abolitionist Movement*. Baton Rouge: Louisiana State University Press, 1983.

Blatt, Martin H., Thomas J. Brown, Donald Yacovone. *Hope and Glory: Essays on the Legacy of the Fifty-Fourth Massachusetts Regiment*. Amherst: University of Massachusetts in association with the Massachusetts Historical Society, 2001.

Blight, David W., ed. *Passages to Freedom: The Underground Railroad in History and Memory*. Washington, DC: Smithsonian Books, 2004.

Bobo, William M. *Glimpses of New York City*. Charleston, SC: J. J. McCarter, 1852.

Brazee, Christopher D. *Borough Hall Skyscraper Historic District Designation Report*. New York: New York City Landmarks Preservation Commission, 2011.

Bridge Street African Wesleyan Methodist Episcopal Church. *History of the African Wesleyan Methodist Episcopal Church: Known as Bridge Street AWME Church, Org. 1766–Inc. 1818*. Brooklyn, NY: The Church, 2001.

Brooklyn African Woolman Benevolent Society. *Constitution of Brooklyn African Woolman Benevolent Society, Adopted March 16, 1810*. Brooklyn, NY: Printed by E. Worthington, 1820.

"Brooklyn Boblashun! Hurore for Jackson." Brooklyn, NY: Christian Brown, 1829.

Brooklyn Common Council. *Manual of the Common Council of the City of Brooklyn for 1859–60*. Brooklyn, NY: George C. Bennett, 1859.

———. *Manual of the Common Council of the City of Brooklyn for 1863*. Brooklyn, NY: Isaac Van Anden, 1863.

———. "Slavery on Long Island." In *Manual of the Common Council of the City of Brooklyn for 1864*, 153–165. Brooklyn, NY: A. Brown, 1864.

Brooks, Daphne A. *Bodies in Dissent: Spectacular Performances of Race and Freedom, 1850–1910*. Durham, NC: Duke University Press, 2006.

Brown, Hallie Q. *Homespun Heroines and Other Women of Distinction*. 1926. Reprint, New York: Oxford University Press, 1988.

Browne, D. J. *Increase of Commerce of New York: Atlantic Dock, Docks on the Thames, Liverpool Docks, Bute Dock, Humber and Hull Docks, Basins at Haver, Marseilles, Antwerp and Albany*. New York: George F. Nesbitt, 1841.

Browne, Simone. "Everybody's Got a Little Light under the Sun: Black Luminosity and the Visual Culture of Surveillance." *Cultural Studies* 26, no. 4 (July 2012): 542–564.

Burrows, Edwin G., and Mike Wallace. *Gotham: A History of New York City to 1898*. New York: Oxford University Press, 1998.

Campanella, Thomas. *Brooklyn: The Once and Future City*. Princeton, NJ: Princeton University Press, 2019.

Cantwell, Anne-Marie E., and Diana diZerega Wall. *Unearthing Gotham: The Archaeology of New York City*. New Haven, CT: Yale University Press, 2013.

Cobb, Jasmine Nichole. "Black Organizational Life before 1830." In *African American Literature in Transition, 1800–1830*, vol. 2, ed. Jasmine Nichole Cobb, 15–18. New York: Cambridge University Press, 2021.

Committee of Merchants for the Relief of Colored People Suffering from the Late Riots in the City of New York. *Report of the Committee of Merchants for the Relief of Colored People Suffering from the Late Riots in the City of New York*. New York: George A. Whitehorne, 1863.

Connolly, Harold X. *A Ghetto Grows in Brooklyn*. New York: New York University Press, 1977.

Cornish, Dudley Taylor. *The Sable Arm: Negro Troops in the Union Army, 1861–1865*. New York, 1956.

Curry, Leonard. *Free Black in Urban America, 1800–1850: The Shadow of the Dream.* Chicago: University of Chicago Press, 1981.

Davies, David A., Tampathia Evans, Ian Frederick Finseth, and Andrea N. Williams, eds. *North Carolina Slave Narratives: The Lives of Moses Roper, Lunsford Lane, Moses Grandy, and Thomas H. Jones.* Chapel Hill: University of North Carolina Press, 2003.

Davis, David Brion. *The Problem of Slavery in the Age of Revolution.* Ithaca, NY: Cornell University Press, 1975.

Del Valle, Andrea, Julie Golia, and Emily Potter-Ndiaye. *Exploring Pre-Revolutionary New York: The Ratzer Map.* Curriculum guide. Brooklyn, NY: Brooklyn Historical Society, Center for Brooklyn History, Brooklyn Public Library, 2012.

Diouf, Sylviane A. "The Harlem Burial Ground." *New York Public Library Blog,* January 25, 2016. www.nypl.org.

Douglas, Stanley M. *The History of Siloam Presbyterian Church.* Brooklyn, NY: Dodd Bros., 1949.

Duane, Anna Mae. "'Like a Motherless Child': Radical Education at the New York African Free School and in *My Bondage and My Freedom.*" *American Literature* 82, no. 3 (September 2010): 461–488.

Dunbar, Erica Armstrong. *A Fragile Freedom: African American Women and Emancipation in the Antebellum City.* New Haven, CT: Yale University Press, 2008.

Dunn, Richard S. *Sugar and Slaves: The Rise of the Planter Class in the English West Indies, 1624–1713.* Chapel Hill: University of North Carolina Press, 2000.

Dwight, Timothy. *Travels in New England and New York.* London: Baynes, 1823.

Eckstrom, Leif, and Britt Rusert. "Afric-American Picture Gallery, 1859." *Common Place: The Journal of Early American Life,* Fall 2015. http://jtoaa.common-place.org.

Edmonds, John Worth. *Reports of Select Cases Decided in the Courts of New York: Not Heretofore Reported, or Reported Only Partially.* New York: Peloubet, 1883.

Emilio, Luis F. *History of the Fifty-Fourth Regiment of Massachusetts Volunteer Infantry, 1863–1865.* Boston: Boston Book Company, 1894.

Fales, William E. S. *Brooklyn's Guardians: A Record of the Faith and Heroic Men Who Preserve the Peace in the City of Homes.* Brooklyn, NY, 1887.

Faulkner, Carol. "A Proper Recognition of Our Manhood': The African Civilization Society and the Freedmen's Aid Movement." *African Americans in New York Life and History* 24, no. 1 (2000): 41–62.

———. "Root of Evil: Free Produce and Radical Antislavery, 1830–1860." *Journal of the Early Republic* 27, no. 3 (2007): 377–405.

Field, Thomas W. *Historical Sketch of the Public Schools and Board of. Education of the City of Brooklyn.* Brooklyn, NY: R. M. Whiting, 1873.

Finley, Robert. *Thoughts on the Colonization of Free Blacks.* 1816.

Follett, Richard. *The Sugar Masters: Planters and Slaves in Louisiana's Cane World, 1820–1860.* Baton Rouge: Louisiana State University Press, 2005.

Foner, Eric. *Freedom's Lawmakers: A Directory of Black Officeholders during Reconstruction.* New York: Oxford University Press, 1993.

————. *Gateway to Freedom: The Hidden History of the Underground Railroad*. New York: Norton, 2015.

————. *Nothing but Liberty: Emancipation and Its Legacy*. Baton Rouge: Louisiana State University Press, 2007.

————. *Reconstruction: America's Unfinished Revolution, 1863–1877*. New York: Harper and Row, 1988.

Foreman, P. Gabrielle. *Activist Sentiments: Reading Black Women in the Nineteenth Century*. Urbana: University of Illinois Press, 2009.

————. "Black Organizing, Print Advocacy, and Collective Authorship: The Long History of the Colored Conventions Movement." In *The Colored Conventions Movement: Black Organizing in the Nineteenth Century*, ed. Jim Casey, P. Gabrielle Foreman, and Sarah Lynn Patterson, 21–71. Chapel Hill: University of North Carolina Press, 2021.

Free Produce Association of Friends of New York. *Report of the Board of Managers of the Free Produce Association of Friends of New York*. New York: Collins, Browne, 1853.

Fuentes, Marisa J. *Dispossessed Lives: Enslaved Women, Violence, and the Archive*. Philadelphia: University of Pennsylvania Press, 2016.

García-Peña, Lorgia. "Note 189: Life." In *Ordinary Notes*, by Christina Sharpe, 268. New York: Farrar, Straus and Giroux, 2023.

Garrison, William Lloyd. *The Letters of William Lloyd Garrison: From Disunionism to the Brink of War, 1850–1860*. Cambridge, MA: Harvard University Press, 1975.

————. *Thoughts on Colonization; or, An Impartial Exhibition of the Doctrines, Principles and Purposes of the American Colonization Society*. Boston, 1832.

Gellman, David. *Emancipating New York: The Politics of Slavery and Freedom, 1777–1827*. Baton Rouge: Louisiana State University Press, 2006.

Gibson, Samantha. "'The Patriotic Brothers': William and Willis Hodges and Black Activism in Antebellum New York." Unpublished manuscript, 2010.

Golia, Julie. "Brooklyn Waterfront History." Accessed July 7, 2022. www.bkwaterfronthistory.org.

Green, Hilary. "Black Widows and the Struggle for Pensions after the Civil War." *Black Perspectives* (African American Intellectual History Society), January 12, 2023. www.aaihs.org.

Guy-Clement, Natiba. "The Story of Pinky." *Brooklyn Public Library Blog*, March 28, 2017. www.bklynlibrary.org.

Harris, John. *The Last Slave Ships: New York and the end of the Middle Passage*. New Haven, CT: Yale University Press, 2020.

Harris, Leslie M. *In the Shadow of Slavery*. Chicago: University of Chicago Press, 2003.

Hartman, Saidiya V. *Wayward Lives, Beautiful Experiments: Intimate Histories of Riotous Black Girls, Troublesome Women, and Queer Radicals*. New York: Norton, 2019.

Harvey, David. *Rebel Cities: From the Right to the City to the Urban Revolution*. Brooklyn, NY: Verso Books, 2012.

Havemeyer, Harry W. *Merchants of Williamsburgh*. Brooklyn, NY: Privately printed, 1989.

Heller, Darryl M. "The Poor Man's Carriage: Street Railways and Their Publics in Brooklyn and New York, 1850–1896." PhD diss., University of Chicago, 2012.

Hodges, Graham Russell. *Black Itinerants of the Gospel: The Narratives of John Jea and George White*. New York: Palgrave, 2002.

———. *Root and Branch: African Americans in New York and East Jersey, 1613–1863*. Chapel Hill: University of North Carolina Press, 1999.

Hodges, Willis Augustus. *Free Man of Color: The Autobiography of Willis Augustus Hodges*. Knoxville: University of Tennessee Press, 1982.

Honeck, Moscha. *We Are the Revolutionists: German-Speaking Immigrants and American Abolitionists after 1848*. Athens: University of Georgia Press, 2011.

Horton, James O. "A Crusade for Freedom: William Still and the Underground Railroad." In *Passages to Freedom: The Underground Railroad in History and Memory*, ed. David W. Blight, 175–194.

Horton, James O., and Lois E. Horton. *Black Bostonians: Family Life and Community Struggle in the Antebellum North*. New York: Holmes and Meier, 1979.

———. *In Hope of Liberty: Culture, Community, and Protest among Northern Free Blacks*. New York: Oxford University Press, 1997.

Horton, Lois E. "Kidnapping and Resistance: Antislavery Direct Action in the 1850s." In *Passages to Freedom: The Underground Railroad in History and Memory*, ed. David W. Blight, 149–174. Washington, DC: Smithsonian Books, 2004.

Hunter, Tera W. *Bound in Wedlock: Slave and Free Black Marriage in the Nineteenth Century*. Cambridge, MA: Harvard University Press, 2019.

Ignatiev, Noel. *How the Irish Became White*. New York: Routledge, 1995.

Institute for the Exploration of Seneca Village. *Seneca Village Project: The History and Archaeology of African Americans and Irish Immigrants in Nineteenth Century New York City*. Accessed April 12, 2022. https://projects.mcah.columbia.edu.

Jackson, Kenneth T. *Crabgrass Frontier: The Suburbanization of the United States*. New York: Oxford University Press, 1987.

Jea, John. *The Life, History, and Unparalleled Sufferings of John Jea, the African Preacher*. 1800.

Johnson, Rhinehard O. *The Liberty Party, 1840–1848: Anti-Slavery Third Party Politics in the United States*. Baton Rouge: Louisiana State University Press, 2009.

Jones, Martha S. *Vanguard: How Black Women Broke Barriers, Won the Vote, and Insisted on Equality for All*. New York: Basic Books, 2020.

Jones, Thomas H. *Experience of Thomas H. Jones, Who Was a Slave for Forty-Three Years, written by a Friend, as Related to Him by Brother Jones*. Boston: Bazin and Chandler, 1862.

Judd, Jacob. "The History of Brooklyn, 1834–1855: Political and Administrative Aspects." PhD diss., New York University, 1959.

Kanakamedala, Prithi. "Black Entrepreneurship, Economic Self-Determination and Early Print in Antebellum Brooklyn." In *African American Literature in Transition, 1800–1830*, vol. 2, ed. Jasmine Nichole Cobb, 71–90. New York: Cambridge University Press, 2021.

————. "'Considered a Citizen of the United States': George DeGrasse, a South Asian in Early (African) America." In *India in the American Imaginary, 1780s–1880s*, ed. Anupama Arora, Rajender Kaur, 229–243. New York: Palgrave, 2017.

————. "Gradual Emancipation." *In Pursuit of Freedom*, 2013. https://pursuitoffreedom. org.

Kanakamedala, Prithi, with Obden Mondésir. "A Time for Seditious Speech: Reflections on Weeksville." In *Studies into Darkness: The Perils and Promise of Freedom of Speech*, edited by Carin Kuoni and Laura Raicovich, 211–222. Amherst, MA: Amherst College Press, 2022.

Kerr-Ritchie, Jeffrey R. *Rites of August: Emancipation Day in the Black Atlantic World.* Baton Rouge: Louisiana State University Press, 2007.

Krombie, K. *Death in New York: History and Culture of Burials, Undertakers and Executions.* Charleston, SC: Arcadia, 2021.

Kushner, Rachel. "Is Prison Necessary? Ruth Wilson Gilmore Might Change Your Mind." *New York Times*, April 17, 2019. www.nytimes.com.

Latimer, Margaret. "Brooklyn." In *Encyclopedia of New York City*, 2nd ed., edited by Kenneth T. Jackson, Lisa Keller, and Nancy Flood, 168–173. New Haven, CT: Yale University Press, 2010.

Lightfoot, Natasha. *Troubling Freedom: Antigua and the Aftermath of British Emancipation.* Durham, NC: Duke University Press, 2015.

Litwack, Leon F. *Been in the Storm Too Long: The Aftermath of Slavery.* New York: Knopf, 1979.

————. *North of Slavery: The Negro in the Free States.* Chicago: University of Chicago Press, 1961.

Logan, Rayford W. *Howard University: The First Hundred Years, 1867–1967.* New York: New York University Press, 1969.

Lowe, Richard. "Willis Augustus Hodges: 'We Are Now Coming to New Things.'" In *Human Tradition in the Civil War and Reconstruction*, edited by Steven E. Woodworth, 213–223. Wilmington, DE: Scholarly Resources Books, 2000.

Mabee, Carleton. *Black Education in New York State.* Syracuse, NY: Syracuse University Press, 1979.

Manevitz, Alexander. "'A Great Injustice': Urban Capitalism and the Limits of Freedom in Nineteenth-Century New York City." *Journal of Urban History* 48, no. 6 (2022): 1365–1382. https://doi.org/10.1177/0096144220976119.

Manning, Chandra. *What This Cruel War Was Over: Soldiers, Slavery and the Civil War.* New York: Knopf, 2007.

Massachusetts Anti-Slavery Society. *Eighteenth Annual Report*, January 25, 1850.

McPherson, James M. "The Fight against the Gag Rule." *Journal of Negro History* 48, no. 3 (July 1963): 177–195.

————. *Ordeal by Fire: The Civil War and Reconstruction.* New York: Random House, 1982.

Mendez, James G. *A Great Sacrifice: Northern Black Soldiers, Their Families, and the Experience of Civil War.* New York: Fordham University Press, 2019.

Merlis, Brian. *Brooklyn's Williamsburgh, City within a City*. Brooklyn, NY: Israelowitz, 2005.

Mills, Quincy T. *Cutting along the Color Line: Black Barbers and Barber Shops in America*. Philadelphia: University of Pennsylvania Press, 2013.

Mintz, Sidney. *Sweetness and Power: The Place of Sugar in Modern History*. New York: Viking, 1985.

Moffat, R. Burnham. *Pierrepont Genealogies from Norman Times to 1913*. New York: L. Middleditch, 1913.

Moreau de Saint-Méry. *Moreau de St. Mery's American Journey, 1793–1798*. Translated and edited by Kenneth Roberts and Anna M. Roberts. Garden City, NY: Doubleday, 1947.

Morgan, Edmund. *American Slavery, American Freedom: The Ordeal of Colonial Virginia*. New York: Norton, 1975.

Morgan, Jennifer L. *Laboring Women: Reproduction and Gender in New World Slavery*. Philadelphia: University of Pennsylvania Press, 2011.

Morrone, Francis. *An Architectural Guidebook to Brooklyn*. Layton, UT: Gibbs Smith, 2001.

Muhammad, Khalil Gibran. "The Barbaric History of Sugar in America." 1619 Project. *New York Times*, August 14, 2019. www.nytimes.com.

Nadel, Stanley. *Little Germany: Ethnicity, Religion, and Class in New York City, 1845–80*. Urbana: University of Illinois Press, 1990.

Nash, Gary B. *Forging Freedom: The Formation of Philadelphia's Black Community, 1720–1840*. Cambridge, MA: Harvard University Press, 1988.

———. *The Forgotten Fifth: African Americans in the Age of the Revolution*. Cambridge, MA: Harvard University Press, 2006.

Nell, William C. *The Colored Patriots of the American Revolution*. Boston: Robert F. Wallcut, 1855.

Newman, Richard S. *Freedom's Prophet: Richard Allen, the AME Church, and the Black Founding Fathers*. New York: New York University Press, 2008.

Newman, Richard S., Patrick Rael, and Phil Lapsansky, eds. *Pamphlets of Protest: An Anthology of Early African American Protest Literature, 1790–1860*. New York: Routledge, 2001.

New York African Society for Mutual Relief. *Constitution of the New York African Society for Mutual Relief*. New York: R. Sears, 1838.

New York State. *Laws of the State of New York, Passed at the 68th Session of the Legislature*. Albany, NY, 1845.

New York State Legislature Assembly. *Documents of the Assembly of the State of New York, 1854*. Vol. 5. Albany, NY, 1854.

NYC Parks. "Sankofa Park." Accessed January 14, 2022. www.nycgovparks.org.

Okechukwu, Amaka. "Notes on Black Archival Practice: A Relationship to Evidence of Black Life." *Black Scholar* 52, no. 4 (2022): 27–42.

Pacheco, Josephine F. *The Pearl: A Failed Slave Escape on the Potomac*. Chapel Hill: University of North Carolina Press, 2005.

Parker, Matthew. *The Sugar Barons*. New York: Random House, 2011.

Penn, Irvine Garland. *The Afro-American Press and Its Editors*. Springfield, MA: Wiley, 1981.

Pennington, James W. C. *The Fugitive Blacksmith; or, Events in the History of James W. C. Pennington, Pastor of a Presbyterian Church, New York, Formerly a Slave in the State of Maryland, United States*. 3rd ed. London: Charles Gilpin, 1850.

Perlman, Daniel. "Organizations of the Free Negro in New York City, 1800–1860." *Journal of Negro History* 56, no. 3 (July 1971): 181–197.

Pessen, Edward. "A Social and Economic Portrait of Jacksonian Brooklyn." *New York Historical Society Quarterly* 55 (October 1971): 316–353.

Peterson, Carla L. "'And We Claim Our Rights': The Rights Rhetoric of Black and White Women Activists before the Civil War." In *Sister Circle: Black Women and Work*, ed. Sharon Harley, 128–145. New Brunswick, NJ: Rutgers University Press, 2002.

———. *Black Gotham: A Family History of African Americans in Nineteenth-Century New York City*. New Haven, CT: Yale University Press, 2012.

Pinheiro, Holly A., Jr. "Black Soldiers and Their Families' Activism during the Antebellum Era." *Black Perspectives* (African American Intellectual History Society), April 24, 2023. www.aaihs.org.

———. "Black Women and Civil War Pensions." *Black Perspectives* (African American Intellectual History Society), September 1, 2021. www.aaihs.org.

———. *The Families' Civil War: Black Soldiers and the Fight for Racial Justice*. Athens: University of Georgia Press, 2022.

Prince, Bryan. *A Shadow on the Household: One Enslaved Family's Incredible Struggle for Freedom*. Toronto: Emblem Editions, 2010.

Quarles, Benjamin. *Black Abolitionists*. New York: Hachette Books, 1969.

———. *The Negro in the American Revolution*. Chapel Hill: University of North Carolina Press, 1961.

———. *The Negro in the Civil War*. 1953. Reprint, New York: Da Capo, 1989.

Redpath, James. *Echoes of Harpers Ferry*. Boston: Thayer and Eldridge, 1860.

Richardson, Heather Cox. *The Death of Reconstruction: Race, Labor, and Politics in the Post–Civil War North, 1865–1901*. Cambridge, MA: Harvard University Press, 2001.

Ripley, C. Peter, ed. *Black Abolitionist Papers*. Vol. 4. Chapel Hill: University of North Carolina Press, 1992.

Roff, Sandra Shoiock. "The Brooklyn African Woolman Benevolent Society Rediscovered." *Afro-Americans in New York Life and History* 10 (1986): 55–63.

Rosenwaike, Ira. *Population History of New York City*. Syracuse, NY: Syracuse University Press, 1972.

Ryan, Hugh. *When Brooklyn Was Queer*. New York: St. Martin's, 2019.

Schecter, Barnet. *The Devil's Own Work: The Civil War Draft Riots and the Fight to Reconstruct America*. New York: Walker, 2005.

SenGupta, Gunja. *For God and Mammon: Evangelicals and Entrepreneurs, Masters and Slaves in Territorial Kansas, 1854–1860*. Athens: University of Georgia Press, 1996.

———. *From Slavery to Poverty: The Racial Origins of Welfare in New York, 1840–1918*. New York: New York University Press, 2009.

Seward, William H. *The Irrepressible Conflict: A Speech Delivered at Rochester, Monday, October 25, 1858*. New York, 1858.

Sewell, Richard. *Ballots for Freedom: Antislavery Politics in the United States, 1837–1860*. New York: Oxford University Press, 1976.

———. *A House Divided: Sectionalist and the Civil War, 1848–1865*. Baltimore: Johns Hopkins University, 1988.

Shumard, Ann M. *A Durable Memento: Portraits by Augustus Washington, African American Daguerreotypist*. Washington, DC: National Portrait Gallery, 2000.

Sinha, Manisha. "Allies for Emancipation." In *Our Lincoln: New Perspectives on Lincoln and His World*, ed. Eric Foner, 167–198. New York: Norton, 2008.

———. *The Counterrevolution of Slavery: Politics and Ideology in Antebellum South Carolina*. Chapel Hill: University of North Carolina Press, 2000.

———. *The Slave's Cause: A History of Abolition*. New Haven, CT: Yale University Press, 2017.

Slipper, James Henry. *Descendants in the Vanderpoel Branch of Resolved Waldron, Who Came from Holland to New Amsterdam in 1650*. New York: MacGowan and Slipper, 1910.

Smith, James McCune. Introduction to *A Memorial Discourse*, by Rev. Henry Highland Garnet, 17–68. Philadelphia: Joseph M. Wilson, 1865.

Snyder-Grenier, Ellen. *Brooklyn! An Illustrated History*. Philadelphia: Temple University Press, 1996.

Sorin, Gretchen. *Driving While Black: African American Travel and the Road to Civil Rights*. New York: Liveright, 2020.

Spencer, Ichabod. *The Religious Duty of Obedience to Law*. New York, 1850.

Sterling, Dorothy. *We Are Your Sisters: Black Women in the Nineteenth Century*. New York: Norton, 1984.

Stiles, Henry R. *A History of the City of Brooklyn including the Old Town and Village of Brooklyn, the Town of Bushwick, and the Village and City of Williamsburgh*. 2 vols. Brooklyn, NY, 1869.

———. *A History of the Town of Bushwick, Kings County, NY, and of the Town, Village and City of Williamsburgh, Kings County, NY*. Brooklyn NY, 1884.

Still, William. *The Underground Railroad*. Philadelphia: Porter and Coates, 1872.

Sturm-Lind, Lisa. *Actors of Globalization: New York Merchants in Global Trade, 1784–1812*. Leiden: Brill, 2017.

Swan, Robert J. "The Black Church in Brooklyn." In *An Introduction to the Black Contribution to the Development of Brooklyn*, ed. Charlene Claye Van Derzee, Mario Drummonds, et al., 53–62. Brooklyn, NY: New Muse Community Museum of Brooklyn, 1977.

———. "Did Brooklyn Blacks Have Unusual Control over Their Schools? Period I: 1815–1845." *Afro-Americans in New York Life and History* 7, no. 2 (July 31, 1983): 25–46.

———. "The Origin of Black Bedford-Stuyvesant." In *An Introduction to the Black Contribution to the Development of Brooklyn*, ed. Charlene Claye Van Derzee, Mario

Drummonds, et al., 72–84. Brooklyn NY: New Muse Community Museum of Brooklyn, 1977.

———. "Some Historic Notes on Black Williamsburgh and Brooklyn," in *An Introduction to the Black Contribution to the Development of Brooklyn*, eds., Charlene Claye Van Derzee, Mario Drummonds, et al., 117–128. Brooklyn NY: New Muse Community Museum of Brooklyn, 1977.

———. "A Synoptic History of Black Public Schools in Brooklyn." In *An Introduction to the Black Contribution to the Development of Brooklyn*, ed. Charlene Claye Van Derzee, Mario Drummonds, et al., 63–71. Brooklyn, NY: New Muse Community Museum of Brooklyn, 1977.

Swerdlow, Amy. "Abolition's Conservative Sisters: The Ladies' New York Anti-Slavery Societies, 1834–1840." In *The Abolitionist Sisterhood: Women's Political Culture in Antebellum America*, edited by Jean Fagan Yellin and John C. Van Horne, 31–44. Ithaca, NY: Cornell University Press, 1994.

Taylor, Clarence. *The Black Churches of Brooklyn*. New York: Columbia University Press, 1996.

Taylor, Keeanga-Yamahtta. *From #BlackLivesMatter to Black Liberation*. Chicago: Haymarket Books, 2016.

Tchen, John Kuo Wei. *New York before Chinatown: Orientalism and the Shaping of American Culture, 1776–1882*. Baltimore: John Hopkins University Press, 2001.

Tronolone, Alex, and Shirley Brown Alleyne. *Mapping Freedom and Slavery*. Curriculum guide. Brooklyn, NY: Brooklyn Historical Society, Center for Brooklyn History, Brooklyn Public Library, 2019. www.bklynlibrary.org.

Trouillot, Michel-Rolph. *Silencing the Past: Power and the Production of History*. Boston: Beacon, 1995.

US Navy. *Naval Enlistment Rendezvous, 1855–1891*. Salt Lake City, UT: FamilySearch, 2013.

Van Cortlandt Park Alliance. "African Burial Ground." Accessed March 4, 2022. https://vancortlandt.org.

Van Dyke, Henry J. *The Character and Influence of Abolitionism: A Sermon Preached in the First Presbyterian Church Brooklyn on Sabbath Evening*. New York: D. Appleton, 1860.

Walker, David. *Walker's Appeal, in Four Articles: Together with a Preamble, to the Colored Citizens of the World, but in Particular, and Very Expressly to Those of the United States of America. Written in Boston, in the State of Massachusetts, Sept. 28th, 1829*. Boston: David Walker, 1830.

Wall, Diana diZerega, Nan A. Rothschild, and Cynthia Copeland. "Seneca Village and Little Africa: Two African American Communities in Antebellum New York City." *Historical Archaeology* 42, no. 1 (2008): 97–107. https://doi.org/10.1007/BF03377066.

Walvin, James. *Sugar: The World Corrupted from Slavery to Obesity*. Boston: Little, Brown, 2017.

Waters, Kristin. *Maria W. Stewart and the Roots of Black Political Thought*. Jackson: University Press of Mississippi, 2021.

Weeksville Heritage Center and Vera List Center for Art and Politics. "A Time for Seditious Speech." April 26, 2019. www.veralistcenter.org.

Weir, R. J. "Where All Eyes Are Turned: Letters from Washington in *The Anglo-African*, 1863–1864." Civil War Washington. Accessed March 4, 2022. https://civil-wardc.org.

Weld, Ezra Greenleaf. *Frederick Douglass with the Edmonson Sisters at Fugitive Slave Law Convention, Cazenovia, New York*. Half-plate copy daguerreotype. 1850. National Portrait Gallery, Washington, DC.

Wellman, Judith. *Brooklyn's Promised Land: The Free Black Community of Weeksville, New York*. New York: New York University Press, 2017.

White, Deborah Gray. *Ar'n't I a Woman? Female Slaves in the Plantation South*. New York: Norton, 1999.

White, Shane. *Somewhat More Independent: The End of Slavery in New York City 1770–1810*. Athens: University of Georgia Press, 1991.

———. *Stories of Freedom in Black New York*. Cambridge, MA: Harvard University Press, 2002.

Wilder, Craig S. *A Covenant with Color*. New York: Columbia University Press, 2001.

———. *In the Company of Black Men: The African Influence on African American Culture in New York City*. New York: New York University Press, 2001.

———. "The Rise and Influence of the New York African Society for Mutual Relief, 1808–1865." *Afro-Americans in New York Life and History* 22 (1998): 7–18.

Willis, Deborah. *Reflections in Black: A History of Black Photographers, 1840–1999*. New York: Norton, 2000.

Wood, Marcus. *The Horrible Gift of Freedom: Atlantic Slavery and the Representation of Emancipation*. Athens: University of Georgia Press, 2010.

Worley, Tracee, and Prithi Kanakamedala. *In Pursuit of Freedom Teacher's Manual*. Brooklyn, NY: Brooklyn Historical Society, Center for Brooklyn History, Brooklyn Public Library, 2012. http://pursuitoffreedom.org.

Yee, Shirley. *Black Women Abolitionists: A Study in Activism, 1828–1860*. Knoxville: University of Tennessee Press, 1992.

Young, Patricia A. "Roads to Travel: A Historical look at *The Freedman's Torchlight*—An African American Contribution to 19th-Century Instructional Technologies." *Journal of Black Studies* 31, no. 5 (2001): 671–698.

Zuille, John. *Historical Sketch of the New York African Society for Mutual Relief*. New York, 1892.

INDEX

Page numbers in italics indicate Figures

ABOUT THE AUTHOR

PRITHI KANAKAMEDALA is Associate Professor of History at Bronx Community College and at The Graduate Center of the City University of New York. Originally from Liverpool, England, she is an active public historian in New York City and writes about archives, public history, and the history of New York City.